Women in the Two Germanies

Pergamon Titles of Related Interest

Baehr   WOMEN AND MEDIA
Bauer & Ritt   FREE AND ENOBLED
Foster   COMPARATIVE PUBLIC POLICY AND CITIZEN
   PARTICIPATION
Schulz & Adams   POLITICAL PARTICIPATION IN COMMUNIST
      SYSTEMS
Stewart   THE WOMEN'S MOVEMENT IN COMMUNITY POLITICS
   IN THE U.S.
Welsh   SURVEY RESEARCH AND PUBLIC ATTITUDES IN
   EASTERN ERUOPE AND THE SOVIET UNION

Related Journals*

CHILDREN AND YOUTH SERVICES REVIEW
HABITAT INTERNATIONAL
SOCIAL SCIENCE AND MEDICINE: Part C: Medical Economics
WOMEN'S STUDIES INTERNATIONAL QUARTERLY
WORLD DEVELOPMENT

*Free specimen copies available upon request.

PERGAMON POLICY STUDIES ON SOCIAL ISSUES

Women in the Two Germanies
A Comparative Study of A Socialist and a Non-Socialist Society

Harry G. Shaffer

Pergamon Press
NEW YORK • OXFORD • TORONTO • SYDNEY • PARIS • FRANKFURT

Pergamon Press Offices:

U.S.A.	Pergamon Press Inc., Maxwell House, Fairview Park, Elmsford, New York 10523, U.S.A.
U.K.	Pergamon Press Ltd., Headington Hill Hall, Oxford OX3 OBW, England
CANADA	Pergamon of Canada, Ltd., Suite 104, 150 Consumers Road, Willowdale, Ontario M2J 1P9, Canada
AUSTRALIA	Pergamon Press (Aust.) Pty. Ltd., P.O. Box 544, Potts Point, NSW 2011, Australia
FRANCE	Pergamon Press SARL, 24 rue des Ecoles, 75240 Paris, Cedex 05, France
FEDERAL REPUBLIC OF GERMANY	Pergamon Press GmbH, Hammerweg 6, Postfach 1305, 6242 Kronberg/Taunus, Federal Republic of Germany

Copyright © 1981 Pergamon Press Inc.

Library of Congress Cataloging in Publication Data

Shaffer, Harry G
  Women in the two Germanies.

  (Pergamon policy studies on social issues)
  Bibliography: p.
  Includes index.
  1. Women—Germany, East. 2. Women—Employment—Germany, East. 3. Education of women—Germany, East. 4. Women's rights—Germany, East. 5. Women—Germany, West. 6. Women—Employment—Germany, West. 7. Education of Women—Germany, West. 8. Women's rights—Germany, West. I. Title. II. Series.
HQ1630.5.S52 1981   305.4'2'0943   80-22624
ISBN 0-08-023862-9

All Rights reserved. No part of this publication may be reproduced, stored in a retrieval system or transmitted in any form or by any means: electronic, electrostatic, magnetic tape, mechanical, photocopying, recording or otherwise, without permission in writing from the publishers.

Printed in the United States of America

To my children Bernie, Ron, Lennie and Tanya —
and to women everywhere who struggle
for equal rights and opportunities

Contents

List of Tables and Figures ... xi

Preface ... xiii

Chapter

1 INTRODUCTION ... 1

    The Two German States at the Outset: A Brief Comparison ... 1
    European Men and Women in Historical Perspective: A Few Introductory Comments ... 3
    The Status of German Women in the Pre-1945 Era: A Brief Summary ... 5
    The Comparative Status of Women in the Two Post-War Germanies: Some Introductory Observations ... 6

2 GERMAN WOMEN UNDER THE LAW ... 12

    Equal Rights Under the Constitution ... 12
    Labor Law ... 13
        Guaranteed employment ... 14
        Equal remuneration ... 16
        Paid maternity leave ... 16
        Time off to take care of a sick child ... 17
        A day off for household chores ... 17
        Childcare facilities ... 19
        Women's furtherance ... 19
        Part-time employment ... 23
        Protective legislation ... 23
    Family Law and Social Security Legislation ... 28

CONTENTS

Divorce	33
Minimum age for marriage	40
Choice of family name	40
State child support	40
Old age and survivors benefits	43
Laws on the interruption of pregnancies	49

3 GERMAN WOMEN AT WORK — 55

Participation in the Labor Force	55
Ideological differences	56
Differences in attitudes	58
Unemployment vs. labor shortage	61
Why German women work: economic and non-economic reasons	67
Part-Time Employment	68
What Jobs for German Women?	71
The reality of "equal job opportunities"	71
Women in leading positions in the economy	77
German Women in Public Life	83
Women in elected government offices	84
Women in political parties	89
Why fewer German women than men in politics?	91
Women in labor unions	94
Equal Pay for Equal Work	95
And What to do with the Children?	103
Child care facilities: availability and cost	103
Quality of child care facilities	107

4 THE EDUCATION AND TRAINING OF GERMAN WOMEN — 110

Education Starts in the Family	111
Children's Books	114
Preschool and Grade School Education	117
Secondary Education	119
Vocational Training and Education	124
Higher Education	128
Faculty attitudes toward female students	129
Who decides who goes to college and who doesn't?	130
Who pays for a college education?	131
And what do female German college students study?	133

5 GERMAN WOMEN IN THE HOME AND FAMILY — 136

To be or Not to Be a "Mere" Housewife? — and Who Should do the Household Chores Anyway?	136
More Marriages End in Divorce	148

6	WOMEN'S ORGANIZATIONS	153
	Regular FRG Women's Organizations	153
	West German Religious Women's Organizations	154
	Associations of West German Professional Women	155
	Women's Groups in West German Political Parties	156
	West German Feminists	157
	The GDR's "Democratic Women's League of Germany"	158
7	SUMMARY AND CONCLUSIONS	161
Notes		169
Glossary		205
References		211
List of Periodicals		223
Index		227
About the Author		235

List of Tables and Figures

Tables

1.1	Area and Pre- and Post-World War II Population, (FRG and GDR)	3
1.2	Population, 1939-1978 (FRG and GDR)	7
2.1	Current Legal Regulations on Paid Leave to Take Care of Sick Child (FRG and GDR)	18
2.2	Theoretical Retirement Income of Spouses Divorced At Age 65 or Older (FRG)	37
2.3	Monthly State Child Subsidies (FRG and GDR)	41
2.4	Maternal Death Rates (FRG and GDR)	51
2.5	Reasons for Abortions Legally Performed in the FRG (FRG)	54
3.1	Labor Force (FRG and GDR)	56
3.2	Gainfully Employed (FRG and GDR)	57
3.3	Unemployment (FRG)	63
3.4	Part-Time Work (FRG and GDR)	69
3.5	Twenty Major Reasons Why GDR Women Choose Part-Time Employment (GDR)	70
3.6	Participation of German Women in Selected Service Industries (1936)	71
3.7	Female Participation in Selected Branches of the Economy (FRG and GDR)	72
3.8	Female Trainees for Skilled Workers' Positions (FRG and GDR)	73
3.9	Women's Participation Rate in Selected Professions, Other Than Government (FRG and GDR)	76
3.10	Titles of Honor Bestowed on Meritorious Workers (GDR)	79
3.11	Women in Western National Parliaments (1972)	84
3.12	Female Delegates to the National Parliaments (FRG and GDR)	85

3.13	Women in Elected Political Positions (FRG and GDR)	86
3.14	Female Members of the West and East German National Parliaments by Professions and Age Groups (FRG and GDR)	87
3.15	Female Members and Female Candidate Members of the SED Central Committee 1950-1971 (GDR)	90
3.16	Female Participation in SED District Leadership Secretariats 1949-1971 (GDR)	91
3.17	Women in Major West German Political Parties (FRG)	92
3.18	Women in Responsible DGB Positions (FRG)	94
3.19	Average Gross Income of Gainfully Employed (FRG)	97
3.20	Monthly Net Income of Gainfully Employed (FRG)	98
3.21	Places Available in West German Child Care Facilities	104
3.22	Places Available in GDR Child Care Facilities	106
4.1	West German Schools	119
4.2	Girls Enrolled in West German Schools	123
4.3	Enrollment in Vocational Schools (GDR)	126
4.4	Female Students Enrolled in German Institutions of Higher Learning (FRG and GDR)	129
4.5	Enrollment in West German Institutions of Higher Learning, 1978-79	133
4.6	Gainfully Employed Female College Graduates in Selected Disciplines, 1971 (GDR)	135
5.1	Children Born Out of Wedlock (FRG and GDR)	143
5.2	Distribution of Household Chores in Multi-Person Homes, GDR	145
5.3	Marriages and Divorces (FRG and GDR)	149
5.4	Divorces (FRG and GDR)	150
5.5	Divorce Proceedings Initiated by the Wife (FRG)	152

Figure

4.1	GDR School System	124

Preface

The problem of women's rights has become one of the most burning issues of present days. The United Nations has adopted conventions and passed declarations aimed at the elimination of discrimination against women; 1975 was proclaimed International Women's Year; heads of nations East and West have addressed themselves to the problem of equal rights for women; books galore have been published on the subject; and appropriate legislation has been enacted in countries around the globe. In the West in particular, periodicals have appeared and organizations have been formed whose primary if not exclusive goal is the emancipation of women. Western non-socialist countries point to progress achieved, but are aware of prevailing inadequacies and of prejudices and discriminatory treatment yet to be overcome. Socialist countries(1) hold that the true emancipation of women is impossible under capitalism; they proclaim that under their system women have already achieved equality under the law and that in actual practice they are far ahead of non-socialist countries; but they do not deny that they have not yet attained full equality of the sexes in all aspects of life.

For several years now, I have been interested in the status of women in socialist as compared with non-socialist countries, and in the progress women have made under their respective systems. In 1977, I published a study on "How Emancipated is the Soviet Woman as Compared to her Sister in the United States."(2) But due to widely

---

(1) Here and henceforth, unless otherwise stated, "socialist" shall refer to the Marxist-Leninist type of socialism in such countries as the Soviet Union, Poland, or East Germany (the GDR), who assert to be working toward the goal of a perfectly communist society.

(2) Oesterreichische Osthefte, Winter 1977, pp. 245-64; a slightly shortened and less footnoted version of it was published in Kansas Business Review, November 1977, pp. 1-9.

divergent historic, cultural, and social backgrounds, there is a world of difference between Russian and American women. In a sense, the emancipation of Soviet women is the more impressive because the Soviets inherited a social environment in which women had been more deprived, more downtrodden, more at the mercy of their men, and in which they were surely less educated and less aware than women in the United States or, for that matter, anywhere in the West. Yet, I saw great merit in comparing women with essentially the same background, currently living under different social systems. Hence my decision to engage in a comparative study of the position of women in the FRG (Federal Republic of Germany – West Germany) and the GDR (German Democratic Republic – East Germany).

What is to be compared, then, is the status and position of women in the two Germanies: in the West, a pluralistic, basically free-enterprise society, much more welfare-oriented than the United States (tuition-free universities, paid maternity leaves, a nationwide prepaid health insurance program for all workers, etc.), but still with but limited functions reserved for government, its attitudes shaped largely by its Judeo-Christian background, and in the international arena aligned with Western countries; in East Germany, a socialist planned economy, with the Socialist Unity Party (SED) in control, officially committed to Marxist-Leninist ideology, and aligned with the Soviet Union and the socialist countries of Eastern Europe.

In comparing the status and position of women in the two Germanies, a wide variety of legal, economic, political, and social aspects of life in the two countries will be taken into consideration, such as equality or the lack thereof under the law, in education, on the job, and in the home. On the other hand, the fact that, for instance, such basic necessities as milk, bread, and apartment rents are cheaper in East than in West Germany but good clothing or appliances are much more expensive, or that FRG citizens are free to travel to Paris but GDR citizens are not, might also be interesting facets of life in the two Germanies; however since these apply to men and women equally, they would not be directly relevant to this study and have therefore been omitted.

I began my research on the status of women in the two Germanies in 1977, and in 1978, spent eight months there. While there, I made extensive use of excellent library facilities, especially at the East Europe Institute of the Free University in West Berlin. I also succeeded in obtaining much valuable material from such official agencies and organizations as the Federal Ministry for Youth, Family, and Health in Bonn or the GDR Committee for Human Rights in Berlin, GDR.

During my stay in Germany, I also carried out extensive interviews, both East and West. But I soon became aware of my limitations; to obtain a scientifically valid, stratified, random sample, it would have been necessary to interview many hundreds, if not thousands, of individuals in all walks of life and from all parts of the FRG and the GDR. Unable to do this, I decided on a more modest approach. While I did talk to and asked questions of university students, workers, house-

PREFACE xv

wives, and others, I focused my attention primarily on women "in the know," women close to the problem I was investigating. I interviewed such women as Gisela Helwig in Cologne and Jutta Menschik in West Berlin who have published books on women in the FRG and the GDR and who have reached somewhat divergent conclusions; Professor Helge Pross at Siegen, who has published books and engaged in extensive original research projects on the problems of women in the FRG; Inge Gabert in Munich, who is a member of the Bavarian legislative assembly and head of Bavaria's Social-Democratic Women; Beate Hesse, Assistant Expert Adviser on Women at the Federal Ministry for Youth, Family and Health in Bonn; Liselotte Funcke, Delegate from North Rhine-Westphalia and Vice President of the West German Parliament, also in Bonn; and Erika Runge, author of many books and TV scripts on social problems in East and West Germany, director of West German TV films, and member of the Communist Party of West Germany. In the GDR, I interviewed, among others, Professor Traute Schoenrath, who teaches theory of state and law at the Karl Marx University in Leipzig and has been much concerned with legal aspects of women's rights in the GDR; Dr. Herta Kuhrig, Director of the research team "The Woman in Socialist Society" at the GDR Academy of Sciences in Berlin; and Dr. Helga Hoerz, Chairperson of the Department of Ethics at Humboldt University, Berlin, and GDR Representative to the UN Commission on the Status of Women.

Some critics will undoubtedly ask whether this kind of research ought to be carried out by a man. I plead nolo contendere to being a man; but I do not feel that a study on women must necessarily be made by a member of the female sex, any more than a study of the culture of American Indians must necessarily be made by an Indian. I could point out that a masterpiece on the evolution of democratic society in the United States was produced by a Frenchman who spent only one year in this country;(3) that the best known work on the history of Nazi Germany was written by an American;(4) that more than a century and a quarter ago, an early piece advocating women's rights was written and published by a renowned nineteenth century male social scientist;(5) and that the pathbreaking work on American race relations comes from the pen of a Swede.(6) Although I do not mean to compare my humble efforts with those of the authors mentioned above, I do not believe that my sex interfered with my comprehension or in any way prejudiced my analysis of the issues treated in this book.

---

(3) Alexis de Tocqueville, Democracy in America, 4 vols, 1835-40.

(4) William L. Shirer, The Rise and Fall of the Third Reich, 1959.

(5) John Stuart Mill, Enfranchisement of Women, 1851.

(6) Gunner Myrdal, An American Dilemma, 1944.

I want to take this opportunity to express my gratitude to the University of Kansas for granting a sabbatical leave which enabled me to undertake this study, and to the United Stated Department of Health, Education and Welfare (changed in May, 1980 to the Department of Health and Human Resources and an independent department of education) for supplementary grants; to the East Europe Institute of the Free University in West Berlin and especially to the head of its economics section, Professor Erich Klinkmueller, who made the arrangements for my use of its extensive facilities; to the agencies and organizations in the FRG and the GDR who so generously supplied me with material for my research; and to individuals East and West who granted me interviews and subjected themselves to long hours of questioning. I am particularly grateful to Professor Hermann Klenner of Humboldt University; to his wife, Dr. Annelise Klenner, who teaches at the Party vocational school; and to Siegfried Forberger, Secretary of the GDR Committee for Human Rights, for their hospitality and for their invaluable assistance in arranging interviews in the GDR for me. I am deeply indebted to Professor Frank Durgin of the University of Southern Maine, to his assistant and graduate student Mike Edwards, and to Kansas University graduate student Barbara Dooley who went over the entire manuscript page by page and sentence by sentence and who made innumerable valuable suggestions for alterations and improvements. Although I alone bear sole responsibility for the contents and for any remaining errors and shortcomings, the book could not have been what it is without their help. And these acknowledgments would not be complete without expressing my appreciation to the eight or ten secretaries who, over a period of two years, helped so graciously with the typing of what often was a hard to decipher manuscript, among them especially Evalyn Gelhaus, Sara Henderson, Jackie Bryan, and Connie Hellmer.

Last, but certainly not least, I want to thank my daughter Tanya, then 11 years of age, who accompanied me to Berlin and on most of my travels from there, for helping me with xeroxing and even with the preparation of some of the tables, and for being so patient, often reading or otherwise occupying herself for hours while I carried out interviews or was otherwise engaged in my research.

1 Introduction

THE TWO GERMAN STATES AT THE OUTSET:
A BRIEF COMPARISON

When in the summer of 1945, shortly before the end of World War II, Roosevelt, Churchill, and Stalin met at Potsdam, they agreed to treat the defeated Germany as a single economic unit.(1) Shortly thereafter, the United States, Great Britain, France, and the Soviet Union each established its own zone of occupation. By 1948, it had become evident that the Soviet zone would go its own way and that the concept of a unified Germany was shattered, although reunification remained the avowed aim, especially of official West German policy; and the hope for eventual reunification has not been completely abandoned as yet. In May 1949, separate constitutions for the two German states were drawn up; in the West, for a "Federal Republic of Germany" (FRG — West Germany); in the East, for a "German Democratic Republic" (GDR — East Germany). Although still under military occupation, both German states were officially in existence before the end of that year. On March 25, 1954, the USSR declared the GDR an independent, sovereign state; by the Paris agreements of October 23, 1954, the FRG assumed sovereignty on May 5, 1955.(2)

By language, by culture, and by tradition, the two German states are perhaps more similar to each other than the North and the South of the United States; what differences exist are marginal, and they pale in comparison with common features. In the economic sphere, before World War II, the per capita income in the territory that today constitutes the GDR was about two percent below that of the western parts of Germany; in per capita industrial output however, official postwar West German sources show the GDR territory as having been ahead by 16 percent in 1939.(3) But at the end of the war and in the immediate postwar era, the Soviet occupied zone, and subsequently the GDR, found itself for numerous reasons at a great disadvantage:

2   WOMEN IN THE TWO GERMANIES

1. In the prewar era, most raw material production, including 97 percent of the Reich's pig iron output and 91 percent of unfinished steel, had issued from the western parts of Germany,(4) which left the GDR with a less favorable resource base.
2. In the east, the most important sources of energy had been located in Silesia, now incorporated into Poland, so that the GDR was stripped of much of the energy base necessary for the reconstruction and subsequent operation of its war-torn industries.
3. War damage and destruction, although extensive everywhere, were greater in the eastern than in the western parts of Germany. (In the eastern part of Germany, reportedly some 45 percent of its industrial plants, 70 percent of power generating capacity, 50 percent of urban housing, and 30 percent of machinery had been destroyed or rendered unserviceable.)(5)
4. For the incredible destruction inflicted on the Soviet people by the Nazi invaders, the Soviet Union, for almost a decade, exacted reparation payments from East Germany, and moved entire factories to the USSR. It is estimated that demontage plus wartime destruction wiped out half of the GDR's, but only a fourth of the FRG's, 1943 industrial capacity.(6) The Western allies, and especially the United States, on the other hand, exacted no reparations but, instead, began almost immediately to pour billions of dollars into the reconstruction of West Germany.(7)
5. At the outset, the Soviet occupied zone constituted 30 percent of the total area on which the GDR and the FRG were to be established and close to 29 percent of the total German population of the two states-to-be. But by the time of the completion of the Berlin wall in August 1961, the population of the Soviet zone had dropped to under 24 percent (see table 1.1). The "brain drain" contributed greatly to a labor shortage in the GDR, especially in the professional fields, that has not been completely overcome to this very day.

Under their respective economic and social systems, both German states have made extraordinary economic headway. The FRG's economic recovery and progress (although occasionally marred by cyclical fluctuations) was such that the West dubbed it an "economic miracle"; and today the FRG is among the world leaders in per capita output, income, and living standards. The GDR, likewise, has been very successful. In spite of all the handicaps referred to above, she has made rapid economic strides, and some Western analysts consider her economic achievements the "real economic miracle" in Europe. Although still behind the FRG in overall living standards, growth rates during the 1960s and early 1970s were about equal for the two Germanies at 4.6 percent average annual growth of real GNP.(8) Her economic system has enabled the GDR to avoid the unemployment and inflation that have afflicted the FRG (and most of the rest of the Western world) in recent years(9), and she is today among the ten most industrialized nations on earth(10) and can boast of the highest living standard among all the socialist countries, since the mid-1970s, slightly ahead even of Czechoslovakia.(11)

Table 1.1. Area and Pre- and Post-World War II Population, FRG and GDR

	Area (sq. mi.)	Population (in 1000's)		
		1939	1946	1960
FRG[a]	95,993	43,008	46,190	55,433
of which W. Berlin	186	2,751	2,013	2,197
GDR[b]	41,768	16,745	18,488	17,241
of which E. Berlin	156	1,588	1,175	1,055
GDR as % of FRG	43.5	38.9	40.0	31.1[c]
GDR as % of total (FRG + GDR)	30.3	28.0	28.6	23.7[c]

---

[a] Includes West Berlin; also includes the Saar, reunited with West Germany as of January 1, 1957 (area: 991 sq. mi.; 1961 population, 1,072,600).
[b] Includes East Berlin.
[c] In the first seven and a half months of 1961, before East Berlin was sealed off by the Berlin wall, this percentage was further reduced by some 200,000 GDR citizens who swelled the ranks of East German refugees that found their way into the FRG.

Sources: Statistical Yearbook, FRG, 1951, p. 12; 1969, p. 15; 1977, p. 38. Statistical Yearbook, GDR, 1977, p. 1; Encyclopaedia Britannica, 1969, Vol. 10, p. 343.

EUROPEAN MEN AND WOMEN IN HISTORICAL PERSPECTIVE: A FEW INTRODUCTORY COMMENTS

In Europe's middle-and upper-class families, the traditional division of labor had for centuries relegated women primarily to tasks connected with the care of the home and the raising of the children — although the "lady of the house" might have had servants to do her bidding. Since the man was generally the one who earned a living, the exclusion from gainful work made the woman totally dependent on the "breadwinner," gave her subordinate social status, and effectively deprived her of legal rights. The advent of the industrial revolution left this state of affairs at first virtually unchanged in these families.

For working class families, the situation was different. In the preindustrial era, the rural peasant family had been the producing unit, with work divided among the members of the family. The father, for instance, would plow the fields, make simple tools, repair a leaking roof; the mother would weave, spin, cook; the young son might help to erect a fence or bring in the firewood; the young daughter might wash the dishes, feed the chickens, collect the eggs. The urban laborer of the industrial era, on the other hand, earns his living away from home. With most working men's income inadequate to keep the family going, during the early days of industrial capitalism, their wives would also turn to the factory for a job. And factories had an insatiable demand for low-priced labor, to be selected from the oversupply of male and female workers — an oversupply which was one of the immediate side effects of the mechanization of production. Quite naturally, women (and often their children) were willing to work for much less than their male counterparts because their wages were only supplemental to the incomes of the "bread winners." Laboring for long hours and under harsh conditions, these women had little time and strength left to devote to their home and children; and men, brought up in the traditions of yesteryear, showed little inclination to share in domestic chores. Thus, the inclusion of working class women in the productive process tended to disrupt their family life during the early days of industrial capitalism.

As industrial capitalism scored economic progress in the Western world, and as living standards began to rise, "My wife doesn't have to work" became a status symbol for more skilled workers who earned enough to support the family by themselves. The middle class "women-belong-in-the-home" philosophy found its reinforcement in rather permanent, and periodically severe, unemployment. When jobs are hard to come by, male workers are even more reluctant than usual to let women take "their jobs" away from them. Women, therefore, needing work desperately and unable to find it, swelled the ranks of those seeking domestic employ in the homes of the well-to-do, while among the young, many turned to prostitution.

When working women began to raise their voices in a struggle for a better life, their interest focused primarily on more adequate and more equal pay, on improved working conditions, and on protective legislation that would shield them from excessively long, strenuous, harmful, and potentially dangerous job assignments. Forced by economic necessity to work, they were usually qualified only for the most menial tasks; hence, any demands on their part for equal opportunities for advancement and promotion had to await a later date. Middle class women, on the other hand, found themselves with somewhat more time on their hands. With a drastic decline in the number of children per family, and with the gradual increase in such amenities as modern household equipment and precooked foods to ease their chores, many of them began to broaden their interests and horizons. Vying for changes in their social position and status, these middle class women centered their efforts on attempts to win the franchise; to have the doors of institutions of higher learning opened to women; and to gain access to occupations of their own choosing, including the professions and positions in government and public administration.(12)

THE STATUS OF GERMAN WOMEN IN THE PRE-1945 ERA: A BRIEF SUMMARY

In Germany, women began to unite for their common struggle in the mid-nineteenth century. In 1848, the first German women's periodical, left-wing in its orientation, made its appearance, only to be shut down by the authorities four years later. In 1865, the first German women's conference met in Leipzig. There, the struggle for the franchise and for equal political rights with men was abandoned, for the time being anyhow, and all that remained were demands for an equal right to vocational training and education. In 1893, the first college preparatory classes for women were offered in Berlin; and by the turn of the century, female students could pursue university studies. In 1908, German women were, for the first time, admitted to membership in political parties; in 1918, they were given the right to vote; and the 1919 Constitution of the Weimar Republic laid the legal foundation for equal civil rights and responsibilities for men and women.

Middle class women found employment first in such "typically female" positions as low-level teachers and nurses; but soon, they were to succeed also in penetrating white collar jobs in factory offices, commerce, banking, and transportation. A few isolated women were even elected to the German parliament.(13) And some of today's laws, allegedly aimed at protecting women from overexertion and occupational hazards on their jobs, date back to the interwar years.(14) But all this was merely a beginning; women's emancipation in Germany had but taken the first timid steps,(15) and any conclusions to the contrary would be in error.

Throughout all of Germany's written history, masculinity had been regarded as a badge of natural superiority, and femininity as weakness. It had been a man's world throughout; and, in spite of some progress, it was still a man's world in the days of the Weimar Republic. Virtually all the means of education and communication, from textbooks and pictures on school classroom walls to newspapers and magazines, propagated the "noble" traditional values of Germany's military past. Men were always portrayed as the heroes, the leaders in war and in peace, the successful business executives, the breadwinners, the heads of the household; women cared for the kitchen and the children. And in the absence, with but few exceptions, of coeducational curricula at schools and at colleges, the inequality of the sexes tended to be perpetuated. In the home, at school, and on the job if they had one, girls learned that men were superior, that they were to be obeyed. Traditions that had long discriminated between men and women in regard to property rights, to the rights to make decisions in the home, and in many other areas were barely touched; ideas of equal-pay-for-equal work were still in their infancy. The general equality of the sexes decreed by the 1919 Weimar Constitution proved impossible to implement.(16) And worse was yet to come.

Whatever limited advances German women had made came to an end with Hitler's rise to power. The Third Reich promulgated an ideology and implemented policies that made manhood supreme, deprived women of virtually all their newly gained rights, and made it their primary if not exclusive calling to bear "Aryan" children for the perpetuation of the "master race." Here is how <u>The ABC of National Socialism</u> expressed it: "German women want to be wives and mothers. . . . They have no longing for the factory, no longing for the office, no longing for the Parliament. A cozy home, a loving husband, and a flock of happy children is closer to their heart."(17) But when rearmament policies called ever more workers to the factories and ever more young men to arms, official attitudes changed. Gainful employment of women outside the home became not only respectable but a patriotic duty. As the war progressed, the labor shortage became increasingly desperate. In 1944 and early 1945 especially, protective laws that had placed limitations on women's work were one after another repealed, suspended, or simply ignored, and women were made to work.

THE COMPARATIVE STATUS OF WOMEN IN THE TWO POST-WAR GERMANIES: SOME INTRODUCTORY OBSERVATIONS

In May 1945, the war in Europe came to an end. Germany was in shambles. With millions of her men, and especially her young men, killed, injured, or still in prisoner of war camps, much of the burden of rebuilding the war-torn country fell upon German women. Greatly outnumbering men – a numerical superiority that has diminished but has not yet completely disappeared (see table 1.2)(18) – they rose to the task. But as far as interest in their own emancipation and in active participation in government and public administration was concerned, they were torn in different directions by the psychological impact of conflicting experiences. On the one hand, the legacy of years of exposure to the all-pervasive male supremacy of the Nazi era (superimposed on customs and traditions that had kept women subordinated to men since time immemorial) could not fail to leave its imprint; but on the other hand, their total immersion during the war in all areas of economic life and their active participation in the postwar reconstruction of society made them increasingly aware of the role they, as women, might be able to play in the future.

Gradually, as the years went by, memories of yesteryear began to fade into the distance and new generations of girls, born and reared in the two postwar Germanies, grew into womanhood. Age-old legacies cannot be discarded easily. Yet, as new social orders were built on the ashes of the old, the awareness and the aspirations of German women increased, as did their belief that, by right, they ought to have equal rights and opportunities in all spheres of life, and that their own lives and affairs should no longer be superintended by a "stronger sex." And

Table 1.2. Population, 1939-1978, FRG and GDR (in 1000's)

Year[a]	Total		Male		Female		Female as % of total	
	FRG	GDR	FRG	GDR	FRG	GDR	FRG	GDR
1939	43,008	16,745	21,388	8,191	21,620	8,555	49.7	51.1
1946	46,190	18,488	20,725	7,860	25,465	10,629	55.1	57.5
1950	47,522	18,388	22,250	8,161	25,272	10,227	53.2	55.6
1955	52,382	17,944	24,672	8,018	27,710	9,926	52.9	55.3
1960	55,433	17,241	25,974	7,762	29,459	9,479	53.1	54.9
1965	58,619	17,020	27,787	7,762	30,832	9,258	52.6	54.4
1970	60,651	17,058	28,867	7,851	31,784	9,207	52.4	54.0
1975	61,829	16,850	29,500	7,823	32,329	9,027	52.3	53.6
1976	61,531	16,785	29,316	7,808	32,215	8,978	52.4	53.5
1977	61,400	16,765	29,243	7,813	32,157	8,952	52.4	53.4
1978	61,327	16,756	29,210	7,826	32,116	8,930	52.4	53.3

[a]Various dates, usually around mid-year, for the FRG; average for the GDR, except Dec. 31, 1946.

Sources: Compiled and computed from Statistical Yearbook, FRG, 1951, p. 12; 1955, p. 21; 1956, p. 21; 1969, p. 15; 1957, p. 29; and 1979, p. 29. Statistical Yearbook, GDR, 1979, p. 1.

in both the FRG and the GDR, they found post-war political parties and public administrators apparently more sympathetic to their demands than ever before.

Equal rights provisions were incorporated into the 1949 constitutions of the FRG and the GDR. Indeed, the original position, as set forth in relevant paragraphs of their respective constitutions, would seem to have been very similar. But it takes more than words, more even than legal provisions, to bring about meaningful equality of the sexes. However, there were and there remain significant differences between the attitudes of the FRG and the GDR regarding the extent of women's aspirations for a new relationship between the sexes, and society's ideological and spiritual commitment to the cause of the equality of the sexes and the true emancipation of women. Therefore, differences also remain regarding the implementation of the laws and the progress actually achieved.

In the West, a basically capitalist democracy was established. In a sense, it involved a restoration of the economic and political system of pre-Nazi Germany, interspersed with an ever-widening range of welfare measures. There was no revolutionary reconstitution of society at large. Hence, there was nothing per se in the ideology on which the FRG was founded that would provide for the emancipation of women — no social or religious background that would engender a truly new relationship between the sexes. Whatever changes there were to be introduced had to be evolutionary in nature, reflecting not a long-standing commitment but a gradual alteration in the social structure, to a greater or lesser degree typical of Western industrialized societies everywhere in the latter part of the twentieth century.

In the GDR on the other hand, a socialist society was set up, based on Marxist-Leninist thought and patterned after the Soviet model. All the ideological fathers of this new system had been life-long advocates of equal rights of women. To them, the emancipation of women was not an independent social problem; they saw it (and most of their followers today see it) as a part of the proletariat's class struggle for the emancipation of all of mankind. "The first suppression of one class by another is that of the female by the male sex," wrote Marx's lifelong friend, collaborator, and financial supporter, Friedrich Engels.(19) They saw it as an indispensible part of that struggle. "Anyone who has a smattering of history also knows," wrote Marx, "that major social transformations are impossible without female ferment. Social progress can be measured exactly by the social standing of the fairer sex."(20) "The proletariat cannot achieve complete liberty until it has won complete liberty for women," added Lenin.(21) And Marxists have always held that true emancipation of women was impossible under capitalism, but that it could and would be achieved under socialism. "Woman's full equality with man, socially and politically, ... is under the present social and political institutions as impossible as the solution of workers' problems," wrote German socialist author and champion August Bebel, while in prison in the 1870s. But "in the new society of socialism," Bebel affirmed, "woman is socially and economically completely independent, not subject any longer to even the slightest exploitation. She is an equal of man, in free and sole control of her destiny. . . ."(22) And Lenin, likewise, promised that socialism would bring to women "complete equality of rights with men, both legal and in practice, in the family, the state, and in society."(23)

Moreover, the United States has not been a good model for West Germans who are intent on rapid emancipation. Although some progress has certainly been made in the United States, especially during the past decade or two, as this book goes to press, an equal rights amendment to the U.S. Constitution still does not have the necessary approval of two-thirds of the states. The fight of American women for true equality of the sexes is still an uphill struggle. The GDR, on the other hand, has a Soviet model in which the very first Constitution, adopted in 1918, provided that "Women in the U.S.S.R. are accorded equal rights with men in all spheres of economic, government, cultural, political and other public activity. . . ." and that "women have the right to elect and be elected on equal terms with men." At that time, the United States, then close to 150 years old, had not yet given her women the franchise.(24)

Surely in part because of these models, but even more directly because of their different social systems, the approach to the problem of equality of the sexes, as also to other social problems, is different in the two German states. In the FRG, the individual stands in the foreground; and whether it be women aspiring to equal rights or workers bent on higher wages and job security, individuals, alone or in groups, are thought of as the initiators of public change, and the government as but the agency to legislate and implement it, always with an eye on compromise between conflicting class and group interests. The GDR, on the other hand, gives priority to society. There, individuals are conceived of not as nonentities (as anti-Marxists so often describe them) but as members of society with common aims, working together toward the construction of a perfect world order in which the happiness of each is to find its fulfillment in the happiness of all. Hence, in the GDR it is not the individual but society itself, through its leading party and government agencies, whose duty it is to unearth and to find solutions to social problems. Little wonder, then, that even apart from economic influences (for instance, unemployment in the West and a labor shortage in the East), sex equality tends to progress more slowly in a decentralized system such as that of the FRG than under the consciously planned social system of the GDR. And even where practical measures look similar, behind them often stand very different motivations, intentions, and priorities.

When the Friedrich-Ebert Foundation, one of West Germany's most prestigious foundations, attempted recently to document the FRG's progress in sex equality, it found occasional setbacks and bitter opposition that had to be overcome. The authors of the study would grant that in the mid-1970s the GDR was still "a nose length ahead" in sex equality; but concluded that the FRG had "reached a position it need not be ashamed of," and expressed conviction that "the forces that push for reforms cannot be stopped."(25)

Progress has undoubtedly been made. But official West German authorities are the first to admit that much work still needs to be done.

10 WOMEN IN THE TWO GERMANIES

On November 8, 1973, the West German Parliament set up an "Investigative Commission on Woman and Society" for the "preparation for decisions intended to lead to the complete legal and social equality of women in society." In this context, the commission was directed to submit to the parliament "(1) proposals for changes in the laws so that full legal equality can be realized, and (2) proposals how, apart from legal, also social equality of opportunities can be attained."(26)

The commission started its work on June 14, 1974. When it published its interim report in November 1976, it stated clearly: "Although the position of women in [West German] society has improved considerably in recent decades, the equality of men and women provided for in the Constitution has not yet been fully realized."(27) This sentiment was echoed strongly by West Germany's President Walter Scheel in his opening address to the U.N. "Year of the Woman" on January 9, 1975, in Bonn. "Girls are still being less well educated than boys," said President Scheel; "women's work is still paid less; in private and public employment, disproportionately few women have the possibility of reaching top positions. . . . Women constitute over half of the population of the FRG; but in the West German parliament, this part of the population is represented by only 5.9 percent of the delegates. . . . When one part of society, for whatever reasons, is discriminated against, the other part cannot be truly free either."(28) "The women in our society are still being discriminated against in many ways; step by step we must change this," commented Federal Chancellor Helmut Schmidt in 1977.(29) And a West German government information bulletin summed it all up: "According to the Constitution of the Federal Republic of Germany, men and women have equal rights. . . . It is up to the community and the state to make sure that equal opportunities can also be applied in practice."(30) But an article recently published in one of the FRG's leading newspapers, charging that progress has been minimal, blamed West German women themselves for the lack of it:

> For decades, women on the average have been less educated than men; they earn less than men, even if they have the same training and qualifications; as a matter of course, they themselves take over the housework and the raising of their children. . . . In major women's periodicals one still reads today: "The best social insurance for woman is marriage.". . . Women are not interested in politics, they vote the way their husbands vote; . . . they do not fight against disadvantages. They type in offices to finance the studies of their fiances and later, as wives, they represent the social status of their husbands. As long as they do not take advantage of their rights for which their grandmothers fought in the first women's movement, no law and no party can change their dependence and subordinate position.(31)

The GDR, following in the footsteps of their ideological forefathers, takes a strong and unequivocal ideological position on sex equality. "The development of women on the basis of equality of rights and their active participation in all areas of social life is one of the declared goals of socialism," explains Lilo Tappendorf, section head in the GDR's Central Statistical Administration, in a recent publication of the GDR Committee for Human Rights.(32) And at the VIII Party Plenum of the SED (Sozialistische Einheitspartei Deutschlands, i.e., Socialist Unity Party of Germany)(33) in 1971 in Berlin, Erich Honecker, First Secretary of the SED Central Committee, had this to say on the issue:

> One cannot talk about the development of socialism in our republic without recognizing the outstanding participation of women in all our achievements. It is indeed one of the great accomplishments of socialism that in our country, equality of women under the laws and in life itself has been largely realized. No capitalist country on earth can make such a claim.(34)

Western specialists do not deny that great progress in sex equality has been made in the GDR. "There is no doubt that the GDR has impressive figures to offer," writes Gisela Helwig, author of comparative books on the position of women in East and West Germany and editor in chief of Deutschland Archiv, comparative periodical for GDR and West German policies. And she points to high participation rates for women in education, even among older working women; and to large numbers of state-operated preschool facilities for children 3 to 6 years of age.(35) Yet, even in the GDR, much still needs to be done to bring about the complete emancipation of women. For example, women, on the average, still earn less than men, since they are still under-represented in higher positions and particularly in positions of real economic and political power, and since they are still burdened with most of the chores connected with housework and the raising of the children.

GDR leaders in no way deny that the end of the rainbow, even if in sight, has not been reached. "We can state unequivocally," says Inge Lange, candidate member of the SED Politburo, "that in the GDR, women have equal rights with men. This has become a reality. But in the practical application of these rights," she continues, "there are still differences between men and women. Now, in the next few years, we must see to it that conditions for the practical application of rights are made to correspond with already prevailing legal rights."(36) Erich Honecker agrees: "What matters now," says the Party chief, "is that we solve step by step those problems on which depends whether or not women can make full use of their equal rights."(37) And the SED party program pledges: "The Socialist Unity Party of Germany will do all that is required to create everywhere conditions such that women can assume to the fullest their position of equal rights in society."(38)

2 German Women Under the Law

EQUAL RIGHTS UNDER THE CONSTITUTION

The original constitutions of the FRG and the GDR, both adopted in 1949, contained virtually identical, basic equal rights provisions that proclaimed that men and women are to be equal under the law and that no one is to be given preference or be discriminated against because of sex.(1) More than 30 alterations and amendments to the West German Constitution have retained the equal rights paragraph unchanged; a separate constitution drawn up subsequently for West Berlin not only provided for equality under the law but spelled out that men and women are to have "equal rights to equal economic, social, and intellectual opportunities for development" and that "women are equal to men in all areas of political, economic, and social life."(2) The GDR revised her constitution in 1968, and the new version contained a statement that provided not merely for equal rights but, in some respects, for preferential treatment for women. The relevant equal rights paragraph stated: "Men and women have equal rights and equal legal standing in all spheres of social, political, and personal life. The furtherance of women,(3) particularly in regard to vocational qualification, is a duty for society and for the state." The 1974 alterations and partial rewriting of the GDR constitution that was tantamount to a complete revision left this paragraph unchanged.(4)

The old German Civil Code (Buergerliches Gesetzbuch – BGB), still in force in 1949, predates the turn of the twentieth century. Adopted in 1896, its important fourth book on Family and Marriage Law became effective in 1900. The equal rights provisions of the newly adopted East and West German constitutions contradicted several of the provisions of that old civil law.

Art. 144, Paragraph 1 of the 1949 Constitution of the GDR (then, in effect, still the Soviet Occupied Zone of Germany) stated clearly and unequivocally: "All provisions of the Constitution immediately become law. All [former] provisions contradicting these are hereby revoked." To emphasize even more strongly that this applies also to the new equal rights provisions, Art. 7, Paragraph 2 stated specifically: "All laws and provisions that oppose equal rights for women are hereby revoked."(5) Hence, while the old civil law remained in force for the time being, losing its influence only gradually, there was to be no doubt that wherever it conflicted with new laws, the latter were to take precedence. In the revised constitution of 1968, such clauses were no longer necessary since by then new family and labor laws had replaced the old civil law in toto.(6)

While the East Germans broke radically with the past and instituted their new laws, including the equal rights provisions, the West Germans decided to proceed more slowly to temper the shock of too sudden a break with age-old customs and deep-rooted traditions. Hence, the West German Constitution provided that any previous law that contradicted the equal rights provision "remains in force until it has been adjusted to the constitution, but no longer than March 31, 1953."(7) This amounted to an order for the lawmakers to pass all necessary laws by that date. But the time allotted proved to be too short. The Federal Constitutional Court declared on Dec. 18, 1953, that Art. 3, Paragraph 2 of the Constitution (the equal rights provision) was henceforth in force.(8) However, the new civil law on equality of the sexes dates only from June 18, 1957, and became effective on Jan. 1, 1958. Even this new law did not provide for real equality of husband and wife within the family, an issue to be taken up in greater detail below.(9)

LABOR LAW

In the FRG, claims of women to equal rights in employment, in the labor market, and in professional life in general are based primarily on the above mentioned Art. 3 of the Constitution and on subsequent court interpretations. In interpreting the meaning of Art. 3, there has never been any doubt as to the restrictions and obligations it imposes on the public sector. It obviously forbids all public authorities from passing any laws or instituting any measures that would in any way diminish women's rights to equal treatment; it mandates that agencies of government give due consideration to the equality of rights of the sexes; and it obligates the government to take positive action to bring about the equality of men and women.

As far as civil servants and other employees of the public sector are concerned, the equal rights provision of the Constitution is clearly binding on the state, as the employer; yet, criticism is frequently voiced of the practical application of the law, even in the public sector. "The problem is, of course," commented recently a senior civil servant in West Germany's Federal Ministry of Justice, "that even in this area [government employment] we are still far away from actual equality of opportunities between men and women, especially in regard to opportunities for advancement to higher positions."(10)

In the private sector where wages, working conditions, and other facets of employer-employee relations are worked out in collective bargaining sessions between management and labor, the extent of the applicability of Article 3 has been much more a point of contention. But starting in 1953, Federal constitutional courts and Federal labor courts have made it clear that the mandate for equal rights of the sexes applies also to private work contracts and private employers who, "by virtue of their social and economic superiority hold a position of power comparable to that of the state."(11) And a 1955 Federal labor court decision spelled out clearly that "wage rates must be determined only on the basis of work to be performed, irrespective of whether a man or a woman performs the work."(12)

In the GDR, the constitutional provision for equal rights was soon supplemented by numerous, more specific decrees, laws, and regulations. In the area of labor legislation, the most important were the Code of Labor Laws (Gesetzbuch der Arbeit) of 1961, now superseded by the Labor Law Code (Arbeitsgesetzbuch) of 1977 that took effect on Jan. 1, 1978, and some relevant sections of the 1965 Family Law Code (Familiengesetzbuch).

Guaranteed Employment

In the GDR, gainful employment is guaranteed to all citizens. "Every citizen of the German Democratic Republic," so reads the Constitution, "has the right to work." But beyond this mere right, it goes on to say that "socially useful activity is an honorable duty for every able-bodied citizen. The right and the duty to work form an entity."(13) Is this, then, to be interpreted as meaning that able-bodied citizens of working age, both men and women, must work in the GDR? This question is surely of sufficient importance to merit detailed analysis.

In the early days of the German Democratic Republic, it would seem that work was, indeed, considered a legal obligation. A set of legal principles distributed to GDR judges by the GDR Ministry of Justice in November 1951 postulated that "in our new order everybody who is able-bodied must work." This was subsequently interpreted as meaning that in case of couples living together, each spouse has to contribute to the family's income "according to his or her strength and ability." And the courts in the GDR did not hold that a woman met this obligation by attending to her household chores. These were deemed to be the common obligations of both spouses.(14)

East Germany's 1965 Family Law Code, still in force today, assumes no functional division of labor between husband and wife. Rather, it considers it "obvious" that both work and that both have equal rights and responsibilities to take care of home and children.(15) But the GDR's position on the duty of women to work mellowed somewhat the following year. The 1966 Commentary on Family Law, published under the auspices of the GDR Ministry of Justice, gives formal recognition to the right of wives (but, interestingly, not to the right of husbands) not to work, even where no children are involved; it "respects" an agreement between spouses to this effect; and it spells out that, in such cases, the work in the home is deemed as fully meeting the obligation of participating in the support of the family. Under this 1966 Commentary, the housewife is deemed equal to her husband as regards meeting her family obligation, "even if he alone carries the burden of financially supporting the family" (again without suggesting the possibility that the roles could be reversed).(16) The second edition of the Commentary, published the very next year, derogatorily refers to housewives who do not work as "lacking in consciousness, apart from exceptional cases."(17) But the 1970 edition reiterates the previous position and extends it to men also, spelling out that when a spouse, for whatever reasons, does not have an income, <u>be that man or wife</u>, he or she can make the proper contribution to family income by taking care of the home and children.(18)

In personal interviews in the GDR, women, without exception, told this author that work is a right, perhaps a matter of honor, but surely not an absolute duty in the GDR; several pointed out that on this issue there was a discrepancy between the Constitution of the GDR and the 1936 Constitution of the USSR, in effect until 1977, since Art. 12 of the latter stated clearly: "Work is a matter of honor and of duty for all able-bodied citizens of the USSR... the one who does not work, neither shall he eat."(19) And recent GDR publications support this point of view. In a recent book on GDR law, the authors write:

> GDR law provides for the right of women to engage in professional and social activity. But no duty for gainful employment is mandated for either spouse. Whether a man or a woman or both engage in work outside their home is left to their discretion. If the woman stays home and takes care of the home, then she makes her contribution to the family by work in the home and by taking care of the children, and she experiences no legal disadvantages. However, the overwhelming majority of women take advantage of educational and work opportunities in socialist countries.(20)

Indeed, it seems clear that most women in the GDR feel an obligation to work, surely to a great extent because there is a government and party promoted stigma attached to the woman who is or wants to be "merely a housewife." But, on the other hand, this author has not heard of a single case where, in recent years, work was forced on an unwilling woman — nor, for that matter, on an unwilling man — by GDR authorities.

In West Germany's "free market" economy, the state does not guarantee employment to anyone; nor is there a general duty or obligation for anyone, and surely not for any woman, to work. But family law used to provide for one exception from this general rule. Paragraph 1360 of the old Civil Code (as also the current, revised family law) made it obligatory for both spouses to "provide adequately for their family through their work and personal means." While it was assumed that women would usually meet their obligations by taking care of the home and the children, it was stipulated that "as far as the working capacity and the earning power of the husband are not sufficient for the support of the family, and where the situation is such that they cannot use personal means to take care of it, 'gainful employment' becomes obligatory for the wife."(21) Hardly enforceable in a free market society, this last provision has since been dropped from FRG family law.

Equal Remuneration

Fundamental for the equality of the sexes on the job market is the concept of equal pay for equal work. In the FRG, this principle is supposedly included in Art. 3 of the Constitution that guarantees equal rights for the sexes and that has been ruled applicable, as discussed above, to both the public and the private sector of the economy. Since the FRG is a federation, a great number of actual cases fall under the jurisdiction of the different Laender (roughly the equivalent of states in the United States); and many of the constitutions of these Laender have specific equal pay for equal work provisions.(22)

In the GDR, equal pay for equal work was decreed even prior to that country's official establishment, under order No. 253 of the Soviet occupational forces administration.(23) This basic principle was subsequently incorporated into the first, 1949, Constitution of the GDR,(24) clearly spelled out in the 1968 Constitution, and left unaltered in the 1974 revision.(25) Moreover, it was also incorporated into the Code of Labor of April 1950, and reiterated in the 1961 Code of Labor Law and the 1977 Labor Law Code.(26) To what extent such provisions are actually implemented, East or West, is another matter, to be taken up in Chapter 3.

Paid Maternity Leave

In both parts of Germany, expectant and new mothers are entitled to maternity leave at full pay. The pregnancy part of this leave, both East and West, extends over a period of six weeks prior to birth. Motherhood leave is eight weeks after birth in the FRG (extended since mid-1979 to 22 weeks for needy mothers) and until recently was 20 weeks in the GDR.(27) In 1976, GDR working mothers giving birth to their second or subsequent child were given the right to take additional leave, with regular sick leave pay, up to the newborn child's first birthday.(28) Since January 1, 1978, such extra leave, at full pay, is also granted on request to mothers of their first child. This "baby year" as it has come to be called, makes the GDR the world leader in extent of maternity leave; and if the mother should be unable to secure a place in a nursery for her baby, the leave is extended further, up to the child's third birthday.(29)

As is the case with working women, special consideration is also given in East Germany to female university students who are pregnant or have a baby at home. Individual "furtherance agreements" (Foerderungsvereinbarungen) are drawn up with them, according to their wishes, providing them with an opportunity to make up examinations or time lost in courses, and providing also for special financial aid, over and above the normal stipends for university students.(30) In West Germany, on the other hand, pregnancy and the need to take care of young children might be given informal consideration at universities; but there are no official, legally binding obligations for such special consideration. On the contrary, in an increasing number of West Germany's Laender, there are now stipulations that a course of study must be completed in a prescribed period of time, with exceptions being made but rarely, if at all.

The GDR lays claim to having been richly and speedily rewarded for its efforts. While, in 1977, birthrates continued to drop in West Germany, the number of births in the GDR increased to 223,100, up by 27,600 over the preceding year.(31) The GDR attributed this reversal of previous birthrate trends to the conscious efforts of the state, and particularly to the "baby year" — a view this author found to be supported by all women he interviewed, in both East and West Germany. The late, 1979 increase in paid postnatal maternity leave in the FRG is undoubtedly in part attributable to the example set by the GDR.

Time Off to Take Care of a Sick Child

In both German states, a working parent can take time off, under certain circumstances at pay, to take care of a sick child. In the GDR, this kind of legislation was first introduced in the 1961 "Decree on Social Insurance of Workers and Employees."(32) It was subsequently amended in the "Implementation Orders" of 1962, the 1967 "Decree on the Improvement of the Performance of the Social Insurance System for Workers and Employees with 2 and More Children,"(33) the "Fifth Decree on the Improvement of the Performance of the Social Insurance System" of 1972,(34) and the Labor Law Code of 1977. In the FRG, the first law that granted paid leave for parents to take care of sick children was passed by Parliament in 1973 (Law for the Improvement of Performance of the Legal Health Insurance) and took effect on Jan. 1, 1974. Although basically similar in intent, the particulars of the laws in the two German states are quite different.

A Day Off for Household Chores

The concept of a household day off dates back to the time of World War II, when a German law granted women who had their own household and who worked at least 48 hours per week a day off without pay every four weeks, or two days if they had one or more children under 14 years of

18   WOMEN IN THE TWO GERMANIES

age in their home.(35) After the war, some West German Laender introduced such a day with pay (e.g., Bremen on June 29, 1948, and Hamburg on Feb. 17, 1949);(36) but there is, at present, no such overall provision for West German female, not to speak of male, workers.

Table 2.1. Current Legal Regulations on Paid Leave
to Take Care of Sick Child

	FRG	GDR
Maximum age of child for whose care paid leave is granted	8 years	14 years
Maximum paid leave per year	one week (five working days) per child for workers; twice four days for civil servants	four weeks (six working days per week) for one child; up to 13 weeks for five or more children*
Who is entitled to such paid leave?	either parent (although in practice, mothers take it in more than 95% of cases)	single mothers or fathers, wives of soldiers and students, working wives of pensioners or disabled men, and mothers whose income constitutes the only family income. (In other cases, where both parents work, such leave can be taken without pay only.)

*The 13-week period is based on the 1967 Decree. The 1977 Labor Law Code states, somewhat vaguely, that "support in additional cases is regulated by decrees." (AGB/GDR, p. 130; also, Helwig, "Frau '75" p. 93; Statkowa, p. 46.)

Sources: AGB/GDR, 186 and 187, pp. 129-30; Familienpolitik, p. 31; So schaffe ich es allein, p. 25; Katzenstein, p. 250; Honeckers neues Arbeitsgesetzbuch, p. 52.

In the GDR, under legislation dating back to 1966, working mothers with children under 18 years of age were granted a "household day" off per month at full pay; and enterprises were given the right to allow such a special day off to all housewives employed by them.(37) Under the current 1977 Labor Law Code, this household day off has been extended to all full-time working women in the GDR who either (a) are married, (b) have children under 18 years of age in their home, (c) have a family member in their home who is in need of care, or (d) are 40 years of age or older. A male worker is also entitled to such a special day off if he is either solely in charge of a child 18 years or younger in his home, or has a wife at home who is in need of care.(38)

Childcare Facilities

To enable mothers of preschool and school-age children in the GDR to accept outside employment, governmental authorities have long assumed responsibility for providing necessary childcare facilities. Participation on the part of enterprises was until recently strictly voluntary and, therefore, restricted primarily to large-scale firms. But the 1977 Labor Law Code imposes upon all enterprises the obligation to cooperate with local political units in the establishment of nurseries and kindergartens, to assist workers in enrolling their children in these institutions, and to collaborate with local health authorities in providing necessary health care for sick children. The law also imposes on the enterprise director the duty of cooperating with labor unions and with youth and sports organizations in establishing culture, youth, and sports facilities which are placed free of charge at the disposal of school-age children for after-school, weekend, and vacation activities. Under the law, enterprises must also provide, or assist in providing, summer camps and other facilities where children can spend vacations. This is of particular importance in the GDR since workers' vacations are staggered throughout the year, so as not to interrupt production during the summer months. It is, therefore, not always possible for parents to spend their vacations with their school-age children.(39)

No similar legislation exists in West Germany. Preschool and after-school facilities are largely privately or church-owned and operated; some are under the jurisdiction of welfare or local political organizations. Nurseries for children under three in particular have been so insufficient in numbers that the Federal Ministry for Youth, Family, and Health recently introduced a new, centrally financed, system of "day mothers." Similar to baby sitters in the United States, these women take very young children into their homes during working hours, and take care of them together with their own children. These day mothers are paid at a rate of between 320 and 630 DM per month, not by the child's parents but out of social security funds. To qualify, day mothers must successfully complete short medical and pedagogical training courses.(40)

Women's Furtherance

In both West and East Germany, there are laws on the books that provide for state aid and assistance for the pursuit of education and training. In the FRG, high school students from the 10th grade on, as well as students enrolled in vocational schools and institutions of higher learning, can obtain aid under the 1971 Federal Law for the Furtherance of Education (Bundesausbildungsfoerderungsgesetz – BAfoG) varying in amounts from DM 235 to DM 580 per month. Under the Work Furthering Law (Arbeitsfoerderungsgesetz – AFG) of 1969, financial aid is available for job preparation and training, for continuing education, and for retraining in the case of professions that offer no chances for the future. Such financial assistance amounts to between 81 and 95 percent of prior net earnings, dependent on family status, plus allowances to cover tuition, school supplies, transportation costs between home and school, and health and accident insurance. Moreover, people who may be ineligible for financial aid under either of these laws and whose family income is too low to manage on while he or she is engaged full time in the pursuit of education can still apply for welfare assistance under the Federal Assistance Law (Bundessozialhilfegesetz).(41) This, of course, enables women to complete their education; and one can even find specific statements to the effect that housewives who have not previously worked and who wish to enter the labor market may make use of financial aid under these laws.(42) Still, these laws are not specifically intended to overcome previous sex discrimination in education or on the job. In other words, there are no <u>special</u> legal provisions in the FRG to further systematically the education and training of women as differentiated from men, perhaps with one exception: some emphasis is placed on the retraining of mothers who interrupted their work while raising their children. As a matter of fact, it is still predominantly men who are benefitted by these laws. The percentage of women among those furthered was 15 percent in 1968 and 24 percent in 1973; even in 1977, only one out of every four gainfully employed who were furthered was a woman.(43)

In the GDR, the situation is very different. For all practical purposes, one can speak of reverse sex discrimination – what one West German book described as "women's furtherance programs – that type of discrimination <u>in favor</u> of women so that discrimination <u>against</u> women could be eliminated."(44) Indeed, GDR legislation provides for special furtherance of women in general and of mothers in particular, with the <u>declared</u> purpose of enabling them to be fully the equals of men in education, in professional life, and in the administration of the economy of the state.

The constitutional mandate that provides for special furtherance of women has been elaborated on in numerous subsequent resolutions, ordinances, decrees, and laws. As early as 1950, women's furtherance plans were incorporated into law in the "Law on Protection of Mothers and Children and the Rights of Women."(45) Although much vaguer and less binding than subsequent laws, it did make enterprises responsible for the furtherance of women's education and their transfer to leading positions. In the 1961 Code on Labor Laws, an entire chapter was devoted to the "Furtherance of the Gainfully Employed Woman and the Problems of the Working Woman," spelling out the official position that "equal rights for women in socialist society are realized through their participation in the work process and in the administration of the state and the economy" and that "the organs of the state and the managers of enterprises bear direct responsibility for the creation of the preconditions that would enable women to participate in the work process, develop their creative faculties, and meet at the same time their vital social tasks as mothers."(46) During the rest of the 1960s and the early 1970s, a whole series of resolutions, ordinances, and laws were adopted that dealt with specific details of the furtherance of women. To name but a few:

- 1962: "Resolution on the Tasks of State Organs for the Furtherance of Women and Girls According to the Mandate of the Politburo of the SED Central Committee of Dec. 23, 1961."
- 1965. "Law on the Unified Socialist Educational System." (The preamble to this law stated clearly: "Women have equal rights [with men]. Special attention is paid to their furtherance and development, according to their important role in socialist society."(47) This was the fundamental law guaranteeing women equal educational opportunities and equal access to educational institutions.)
- 1966. "Ordinance for the Education and Training of Women for Technical Professions and their Preparation for Appointments to Leading Positions."
- 1967. "Ordinance for the Education of Women in Special Classes in Vocational Schools of the GDR." (This ordinance provided that working housewives who wanted to study for such professions as engineers or economists had to be given 20 hours per week off by their enterprises, at full pay, to pursue their studies.)
- 1968. "Resolution of the Council of Ministers on the Basic Policies and Measures for the Development and the Appointment of Women to Leading Positions in Political and Economic Life."
- May 10, 1972. "Ordinance on the Furtherance of Female Students with one or more Children and of Expectant Mothers Studying at Institutions of Higher Learning and at Vocational Schools."
- June 19, 1972. "Ordinance on the Furtherance of and Financial Aid for Mothers who are Apprentices."
- Dec. 12, 1972. "Ordinance on the Furtherance of fully-employed working Women for their Education for Skilled Production Workers." (Under this law, enterprises and agricultural collectives were ordered to enter into contracts with women employed by them [or members, in the case of collectives] before they start their training, detailing training periods and guaranteeing subsequent employment according to qualifications acquired).(48)

Finally, the Labor Law Code of 1977, currently in force, spells out in detail the intention of the GDR to continue the furtherance of women. The basic, fundamental principle is laid down in Paragraph 3:

> The socialist state guarantees that everywhere conditions be created that make it possible for women to assume evermore an

equal position on the job and in their professional development, and to combine ever more successfully their tasks as mothers and in the family. The Labor Law ... assures the special furtherance of women as they undertake and engage in professional activity....(49)

A special section of the Labor Law Code calls for the introduction at the enterprise level, of a "Plan for the Furtherance of Women" (Frauenfoerderungsplan):

(1) In the plan for the furtherance of women, there are to be laid down measures for the furthering of the creative capabilities of women in the work process, for their political and technical training and continuing education, and for the systematic preparation for appointment of women to leading positions, as well as for the improvement of their working and living conditions.

(2) The plan for the furtherance of women is to be agreed upon between the enterprise director and the local labor union leadership as part of the collective bargaining agreement.

(3) The enterprise director, in cooperation with the local labor union leadership, must make certain that the women participate in the drafting of the plan for the furtherance of women. An account on the fulfillment of the plan for the furtherance of women must be given to the women [of the enterprise].(50)

One of the seventeen chapters of the Labor Law Code of 1977 is devoted to special rights of working women and mothers. Once again, it is provided that "the enterprise is obligated to create ever improved possibilities for working women with children, by means of the development of working and living conditions, according to plan, so that they can combine their professional activity and development with their tasks as mothers and in the family."(51) And even more specifically, "For women with children under 16 years of age in their home, special measures for their furtherance and financial assistance in their education and continuing education are to be laid down in legal decrees," and "the enterprise is obligated to grant women who have children under 16 years at home whatever assistance is necessary for their education and training," with opportunities equal to those available to other workers.(52) The law specifies also that all provisions applicable to full-time working mothers in regard to working time, vacations, etc., are equally applicable to full-time working single fathers, whenever the care of a child or children demands it.(53) But such cases are rare exceptions; and they must be approved by the factory director with the consent of the local unit of the labor union.(54)

Part-Time Employment

Under the pressure of unemployment, part-time rather than full-time work is greatly encouraged for women in the FRG. West Germany has no law that deals with such part-time work in general; but there is a 1969 law that provides that female civil servants can, according to number and ages of children, work a short work week (or take a long vacation) without jeopardizing accumulated benefits. In 1974, this law was extended to cover male workers also. But in actuality, the law as a whole benefits only a small number of such civil servants since the demand for part-time positions far exceeds suitable job openings.(55)

In the GDR, where socially useful work is deemed essential both for the dignity, self esteem, and well-being of all able-bodied citizens and for the good of society, and where a labor shortage prevails, part-time work is, as a general rule, greatly discouraged. But if need be, even part-time employment is deemed highly preferable to complete withdrawal from the labor force. In this vein, the 1977 Labor Law Code decrees, for instance, that "women who, for reasons of special family obligations, are temporarily prevented from working full time are, in accordance with their enterprises' situation, to be given the opportunity to avail themselves of their right to work, for the time period required, by working part-time."(56) Part-time work is thus to be an exception rather than the rule;(57) but in reality, part-time employment is substantial.(58) To encourage women to work virtually full-time while taking care of larger families, a slightly shortened work week of 40 hours, instead of the usual 43 3/4 hours, at full weekly pay was introduced in 1972 for mothers of three or more children.(59) As of January 1977, this law was extended to all 300,000 full-time working mothers with but two children;(60) and, in essence, it was subsequently incorporated into the 1977 Labor Law Code.(61)

Protective Legislation

It would probably be difficult to find a country anywhere in the world that does not have on its books special laws reflective of society's position that women – and, even more, mothers – need to be protected from engaging in certain kinds of work deemed potentially dangerous to their (or their babies') health and well-being. Certainly all advanced Western nations and all socialist countries have such protective laws.(62) (Charges that such laws are not truly intended to "protect" women, but rather to deny them certain better paying jobs, are discussed in chap. 3).

In Germany, legislation for the protection of women has a long history. The first "Decree on provisions for the Protection of Female Workers" (Erlass der Arbeiterinnenschutzbestimmungen), adopted on July 1, 1878, restrained women from working in underground mining and related jobs, and from engaging in night work in certain branches of industry. It also empowered the upper house of parliament (Bundesrat) to forbid the employment of women in certain branches of industry "particularly dangerous to health and morals"; and it forbade altogether the employment of mothers for the first three weeks after delivery.(63)

Much of West Germany's protective legislation for women is based on sections of the 1938 Workingtime Ordinance (Arbeitszeitordnung), amended numerous times since, that provided for "increased protection for women." Today, West Germany's working women "may not be employed in particularly hard work or on jobs hazardous especially for the health of women."(64) As before, they may, for instance, not be hired for jobs in mines, nor at steel works, nor to load raw materials. Except in certain specified types of jobs, such as theater ushers, waitresses, or nurses, they may not work on Sundays and holidays after 5 p.m., nor on weekdays between the hours of 8 p.m. and 6 a.m. (although in multiple and swing-shift work places they may take the second shift, till 11 p.m., but not the night shift). On the job, they are entitled to special rest periods of at least one quarter of an hour per day if they work more than 4 1/2 hours and up to an hour for workdays of over 9 hours. Unless work in the establishment is stopped altogether during these rest periods, special rest rooms or places must be put at the disposal of the female workers.(65) And women are limited as to weights they are allowed to lift on the job. Under a December 1971 "Decree on the Employment of Women on Vehicles," for instance, they may not be hired for jobs that involve more than occasionally the lifting of weights of more than 10 kg (about 22.4 lbs) without mechanical aid.(66) The same law decrees that vehicles with female drivers be especially constructed and provided with special equipment such as seats, steering wheels, and brakes "which can be easily reached and put into operation by female operators," and which "would not give reasons to fear that their health might be endangered."(67) Such discriminatory type of legislation does not violate the constitutional provision of sex equality, so held the Constitutional Court in 1953, explaining that equal rights did not mean making all completely equal because "with a view to objective biological and functional differences...special legal provisions are permitted or even necessary."(68)

In the GDR, similarly, the present Labor Law Code that took effect on Jan. 1, 1978, provides for "special protection for working women and youths." As regards women, it decrees more specifically that (1) "the health and working capacity of women be given special consideration, (2) working conditions be created that correspond to the physical and physiological characteristics peculiar to women, and (3) that women may not be employed in physically hard work or in work hazardous to their health," (the kind of work so designated to be laid down in special decrees).(69) Types of employment specifically outlawed for GDR women under previously existing, long-established legislation are similar to those forbidden to women in the FRG. A 1951 "Decree for the Protection of Working Capacity," for instance, prohibited the employment of women in mining, as loaders, or on jobs where the temperature is above 24°C (roughly 75°F). Under current GDR post office regulations, women working at post offices are not allowed to handle packages weighing in excess of 10 kg. And, while GDR working women who are neither pregnant nor nursing a baby are allowed to work night shifts, mothers with children under 6 years of age cannot be required to do so.(70)

Neither West nor East Germany currently drafts or even accepts women for combat positions in the armed forces. Under the FRG Constitution, in emergencies, women can be drafted for hospital work;(71) but since 1968, pregnant women and women with one or more children under 15 years at home are specifically exempted from such a draft.(72) In the GDR, where no women serve in the armed forces, a change might be in the offing: compulsory premilitary defense training, including drill, marching, and instruction in crawling, creeping, protecting oneself from enemy fire, and construction of shelters, is now part of the coeducational training of all 15-year old GDR boys and girls.(73)

Special protection for mothers

In both parts of Germany, a number of laws are on the books with the declared purpose of safeguarding the health and well-being of pregnant women and new mothers. Many of these laws simply place legal restrictions on work-connected activities they might wish to or be required to engage in; others provide for special privileges extended for their protection.

In West Germany, under the present, amended version of the 1952 "Law for the Protection of Working Mothers," pregnant women or nursing mothers cannot be employed on jobs where they would be "exposed to harmful effects of health endangering materials or rays, dust, gases, vapor, heat, cold, dampness, strong vibrations, or noise," nor on jobs that entail a substantial risk of falling down, or where their duties would require them to lift regularly over five kilograms, or occasionally over ten kilograms, of weight without mechanical aid. As a general rule, they are not allowed to work overtime, nights, or Sundays (except that during their first four months of pregnancy they may in certain lines of work, such as in theater, or restaurants). After three months of pregnancy, the law prohibits their employment on any means of transportation, and after five months, on jobs that involve considerable stretching or bending down. They are not allowed to work at all during six weeks prior to and eight weeks after childbirth, when they are on maternity leave, at full pay, as discussed above. While at work, they must be given at least one hour or two half-hour periods off each working day, again at full pay, and for this time off they must be provided with suitable places to lie down and rest. If their job normally entails continuous standing or walking, they must be given opportunities to sit down and rest; and, during their period of pregnancy and for four months thereafter, they cannot be discharged.(74)

Even before the GDR was established, the 1945 "Programme of the Central Committee of the Communist Party of Germany on Restoring Democracy" called for special protection to be afforded to mothers and from the very outset, the GDR has given high priority to the protection of pregnant women, new mothers, and their offspring. The above mentioned "Law on Protection of Mothers and Children and the Rights of Women," passed in 1950 and amended in 1954 and 1958, dealt with the broad spectrum of women's rights in general, and with the rights and the protection of pregnant women and new mothers on their job in particular.(75) Other laws, decrees, ordinances, and resolutions followed. The provisions in force today are surely much more extensive than – but in substance not too different from – the protective laws for mothers currently in force in the FRG.

As has been shown, maternity leave is considerably longer in East than in West Germany (the "baby year"). Similar to West German legislation, the 1977 Labor Law Code (GDR) also provides that pregnant women, nursing mothers, and mothers with a child under one year of age cannot be employed in certain types of work deemed dangerous for mother or expected child. What types of work these are is spelled out in detail in legal ordinances; some activities are added to the list in certain cases, whenever the enterprise doctor or the physician at the prenatal guidance center determines them to be potentially hazardous under the circumstances. Where pregnant women have previously been employed at such work or in such jobs, they are to be transferred to easier, more suitable work, with at least the same average pay (this latter provision apparently not in the books in the West). Overtime work and night work is strictly prohibited for pregnant women and nursing mothers, and there seem to be no exceptions such as are allowed in the FRG. Non-nursing mothers with preschool children at home can accept such work if they want to, but cannot be required by their enterprise director to do so. Nursing mothers are to be given two 45-minute periods off per work day (two 30-minute periods in the West) at full pay; moreover, pregnant women can also take time off, again at full pay, to visit the prenatal guidance center, and new mothers to introduce their newborn at the maternity counseling center, whenever such visits cannot be arranged outside of regular working hours. And pregnant women, nursing mothers, mothers with a child under one year of age, mothers on maternity leave (which can run up to three years) and single working parents with children up to three years of age cannot normally be dismissed from their jobs. In special cases where, because of "grave violation of socialist labor disciplines or other citizens' duties" immediate dismissal is called for, the consent of the appropriate political authorities must be secured.(76)

Protective legislation: discrimination or necessary precaution?

Many if not most supporters of women's liberation in the United States would surely view most of the "protective" laws as a continuation of the age-old paternalistic male chauvinism which has always denied women access to certain types of activities under the guise of protecting them and their offspring. Surely, women are capable, such feminists angrily affirm, to determine for themselves what kind of jobs to accept, what hours to work, how much weight to lift, or what risks to take. But many (although by no means all) West and most East Germany citizens seem to look more favorably on such legislation. This position of German women is not only evident from publications on the issue; it was also verified by this author in personal interviews, East and West. "These laws protect not merely our women; they also protect our new generation," said Liselotte Funcke, liberal Vice President of the West German Parliament to this author; "Our position here and that of our Minister of Youth, Family and Health, Frau Antje Huber," commented Beate Hesse, Assistant Expert on Women at the Ministry to this author, "is simply this: We have fought long and hard for these laws; we should think it over very carefully before we give up any of them." And representatives of labor unions take the position that, in cases of such long-proven regulations as the prohibition of night work, "it is not a matter of discrimination but rather a goal all employees should strive for."(77) "Women do their job by having children, and these children have a right to protection," said Barbara von Sell, former special deputy for women's affairs of the Minister President of North Rhine-Westphalia, one of West Germany's Laender. "Women are biologically different," affirmed Dr. Herta Kuhrig, sociologist and Director of Research on "Woman in Socialist Society" at the GDR's Academy of Sciences. "Such legislation must be used with discretion," she continued, "but there are some kinds of work women simply cannot do. Protection and respect for motherhood are of utmost importance." "I used to think that women should be permitted to decide for themselves on the kind of work they want to do," said Dr. Anneliese Klenner, economist and teacher of political economy at the GDR's Berlin Party Vocational School of Economics and Market Research. "But if they are allowed to decide for themselves," she went on, "many of them would choose the harder jobs because of better pay. And there simply is no generally accepted socialist position that women have the right to ruin their health. That is an anarchist, not a socialist, position. Women are the weaker sex and they must be protected for their own sake and for the sake of their children."(78)

While, at least in personal interviews, this author found GDR women unanimous in their view, the same did not hold true for all West German women he talked to. Some of the latter felt that women should have the right to refuse certain kinds of strenuous or potentially hazardous work without jeopardizing their jobs, but should not be prohibited from taking them if they so chose; others thought that some of the protective laws had simply become outdated. "In the days before World War I, a decent woman could hardly be out alone at night. Night work for women needed to be outlawed then. But this is no longer so," commented Dr. Helge Pross, Professor of Sociology and specialist on women in the FRG at the University of Siegen. Yet others even expressed the view that more often than not so-called protective laws are used primarily to keep women off higher paying jobs and to disguise actual wage discrimination. At a 1975 labor union convention in West Germany, William Simmat, psychologist and director of the subdivision of vocational guidance at the North Rhine-Westphalia labor exchange, labeled protective legislation as pure prejudice. Arguing that the whole concept of the weaker physical condition of women is nothing but a widely accepted myth, and that ample medical testimony is available to disprove it. He commented, tongue in cheek: "Women are not supposed to come home from their jobs so tired and worn out that they are not capable of coping with their household chores, however strenuous these may be."(79) Similar views were expressed to this author, for instance, by Adelheid Koritz Dohrmann, West Berlin lawyer and until 1977 member of the executive committee of the study group of Social-Democratic women. "Strip teasers can strip, but female bakers can't bake at night," she said. "All this is hidden discrimination. It doesn't protect women; it merely excludes them." But when this author mentioned such Western criticism to East German women, the latter usually replied that this was understandable since women in Western countries need the jobs denied them by protective legislation. "But in our country, where there are plenty of jobs for all, women do not have to engage in work that is unduly strenuous or potentially harmful for them or for their unborn children."

FAMILY LAW AND SOCIAL SECURITY LEGISLATION

In ancient Rome, a "famulus" was a house slave and the word "familia" referred to the sum total of slaves belonging to a man, which, in Roman parlance, included the wife and children in his household. In more modern times, the "head of the household" no longer owns the members of his family. But until very recently, female family members, even in advanced, industrialized societies, understood that they were to obey, first their fathers and later their husbands. To this very day, one finds wedding ceremonies in Western Europe where the groom promises to support and protect his wife and children, while the bride pledges obedience to her spouse-to-be.

Until 1977, West Germany's family law was based on the fourth volume of the Civil Code (Buergerliches Gesetzbuch – BGB) that had been adopted in 1896 and taken effect in 1900. Most characteristic for the perhaps somewhat tempered but fundamentally unaltered spirit of family relationships was §1356 that allowed a wife to be gainfully employed, but only to the extent that such employment did not conflict with her "marital and family obligations." If there was any conflict, her household duties would take precedence and she would have to forego her outside work.(80) Should, on the other hand, the husband's earning power and the couple's combined means prove insufficient to support the family, §1360 of the BGB made it obligatory for the wife to find gainful employment and contribute to family income.(81) Thus, in the words of West German sociologist Helge Pross, "to stretch the point somewhat," one could say that "a wife is not allowed to find gainful employment if she wants to, and she must find it if she doesn't. Formulated as a principle: The decision concerning her own life must not be left up to her; in case of conflict, it is determined by the traditional conception of priority for family functions and of a wife's destiny to be of service to the family."(82)

Even as regards children, the old Civil Code gave the father sole parental power over their person and their property and made him their sole representative in legal transactions. In decisions concerning the children, the mother was designated merely an interested party; in case of disagreements, the father's opinion prevailed.(83) But the situation was different for children born out of wedlock. An illegitimate child had the legal status of a legitimate child in respect to the mother, but not in respect to the father; it was not even deemed to be related by blood to the latter. The mother had the right and the duty to take care of such a child; but a guardian had to be appointed, and she could represent the child only if she was appointed guardian. The father had the duty to support the child to age 16.(84) Under current laws, both East and West, the mother of an illegitimate child alone has full custodial powers.(85)

In 1957, West Germany adopted an Equal Rights Law (Gleichberectigungsgesetz) that transferred parental power to both parents "in mutual consent" and called on them to work out differences that might arise between themselves. It seemed at first that in case of irreconcilable differences of opinion, the father's view would still prevail. However, three years later, the Federal Constitutional Court declared such a position in violation of the equal rights paragraph of the Constitution, thereby finally giving both parents equal authority over their children.(86) But the Equal Rights Law did not effectively alter the sex roles in the family; for the wife, family obligations were still to take precedence over outside employment. "It is one of the functions of the husband," the introduction to the law stated unequivocally, "that on principle he be the provider and bread winner for the family, while it must be regarded as the wife's noblest task to be the family's heart."(87) Not until 1977 was this provision replaced by one that laid the foundation for full legal equality of spouses within the family.

Throughout the early 1970s, a Social Democratic-Liberal coalition in the West German government worked on a complete revision of the marriage and family law, aimed at effectuating "the full impact of the equal rights mandate" of the Constitution and at finally giving recognition to women "as partners with equal rights and on a par [with men] in all spheres of life."(88) For awhile, the attempt to revise the marriage and family code had rough going. "Opponents of the reform," reports a renowned West German research institute, "attempted to defend the old law that decreed the dominating role of the husband; and religious organizations tried — within the framework of religious communities fully legitimate and not to be questioned by the state — to impose their views on society."(89) Eventually, however, the "First Act for Reform of Marriage and Family Law" (Erstes Gesetz zur Reform des Ehe-und Familienrechts, henceforth to be referred to as new Family Law) was passed on June 14, 1976, and took effect on January 1, 1977. "For the first time, in the Federal Republic of Germany," comments an official West German publication, "equality between husband and wife in marriage and family life has been legally realized."(90) To this end, paragraphs 1356 and 1360 had been rewritten to read as follows:

> § 1356. (1) The spouses arrange the conduct of the household in mutual agreement. If only one of the spouses takes full charge of the household, then he or she alone assumes full responsibility for it. (2) Both spouses are entitled to be gainfully employed. In the choice and the performance of their gainful occupation, they are to give due consideration to the interests of the other spouse and of the family.
>
> § 1360. The spouses are obligated to each other to adequately support the family by their work and personal means. If one of the spouses is left in charge of the household, then he (or she) meets his (or her) obligation to work for the support of the family as a general rule by taking care of the household.(91)

As in other areas, so also in the area of marriage and family law, GDR legislators proceeded much more immediately and much more resolutely than their peers in the FRG. In early 1949, during the time of the drafting of the Constitution, a commission was set up within the "German Department of Justice," then operating in the Soviet Zone, with instructions to propose necessary legislation. At the same time, the Democratic Women's League of Germany (Demokratischer Frauenbund Deutschlands, DFD — see chap. 6 below) engaged actively in discussions of problems of sex equality. The results were published by Hilde Benjamin (later GDR Minister of Justice) in a brochure entitled Proposals for the New German Family Law.(92) The very first Constitution of the GDR, adopted the same year, provided for equal rights within the family (Paragraph 30); and the "Thesis on the Effects of Marriage in General," also adopted in 1949, spelled out clearly, years before the West German parliament passed similar legislation, that "all matters that affect their common life, are to be settled by the spouses in mutual agreement...."(93) The 1950 "Law for the Protection of Mother and Child" reiterated that "the hitherto prevailing right of the husband to make all decisions in all aspects of conjugal life is to be replaced by the joint right of both spouses to make decisions."(94) As to jurisdiction over children, the law stated clearly and specifically that "Parental care which includes the right and the duty to care for the children and their property, as well as the right to represent the children, is vested jointly in both parents."(95)

Prior to 1965, all family legislation in the GDR was piecemeal legislation concerned with one or a few aspects of family relations such as marriage, divorce, or child custody. The Family Law Code (Familiengesetzbuch — FGB), adopted in 1965 and still in force today, was the first comprehensive law on domestic issues in the GDR. It rescinded Book 4 of the old Civil Code in its entirety, substituting once again for its spirit of male supremacy the new code of conduct under which the care of home and children was the joint responsibility of both parents, and husband and wife were obligated to support each other's educational and career goals:

> § 7 (1) Both spouses do their share in the education and care of the children and the conduct of the household. The relations of the spouses to each other are to be so shaped that the wife can combine her professional and social activities with those of motherhood. (2) If the spouse who hitherto had not been gainfully employed takes a job, or if a spouse decides to continue his (or her) education or engage in socially useful work, the other supports with comradely consideration and assistance the intentions of the spouse.(96)

A subsequently published Commentary to the GDR Family Law emphasizes even more strongly the husband's duty to share in household chores when necessary (a point not made anywhere specifically in FRG family legislation):

> The husband may not content himself with "assisting." He must rather do his share, appropriate to the concrete family situation, in the education and care of the children and the conduct of the household.(97)

Thus, in the GDR, where outside employment is greatly encouraged for both spouses, husband and wife are supposed to share in household chores as after-work activities.

However, in the FRG, where the majority of women are housewives, housework is officially recognized as an occupation in itself. This is implicit in legislation that provides for tax-splitting of married couples (nothing like it exists in the GDR), and of divorcees' pension rights — the latter an issue discussed in greater length below. In an often cited 1970 Federal court decision in Kassel, the court stated clearly and definitely that "being a housewife is a professional activity that must be considered equal to that of a woman in business for herself." And beyond that, in cases where both husband and wife are gainfully employed but the wife does more of the housework, she is entitled to special remuneration. In two separate decisions, the Federal Constitutional Court in Karlsruhe ruled recently that if the wife does, for instance, two-thirds of the housework, she needs to contribute only one-third of her outside earnings, and he two-thirds of his, to the support of the family, thus making housework equal in value to outside employment.(98) In some civil law suits, in cases of accidents involving housewives, West German courts have placed monetary values on housework of up to 2,300 DM per month.(99) This author has never heard of any similar designation in the GDR of housework as a "professional activity," nor any monetary value placed on it.

As a fundamental principle, the FRG treats marriage and family life much more as exclusively the personal affairs of the spouses than does the GDR. In the former, the law aims merely at prescribing the legal basis for marital cohabitation; but, although the influence of "Christian morality" on family legislation is still discernible, it refuses to lay down a specific moral code for a society that claims to be "pluralistic" in nature.(100) Intervention by society is restricted primarily to cases where the rights or the safety of one of the spouses or of a child are seriously endangered, such as in the case of flagrant mistreatment of children.

In the GDR, on the other hand, the Family Law Code, dealing with rules of conduct, urges that marriage be engaged in "for life" and that it be based on "mutual love, respect, faithfulness, understanding, trust, and unselfish assistance for each other." It admonishes that, prior to concluding a marriage, "couples seriously test whether their character traits, their views and interests, and their entire ways of life provide the preconditions for the formation of an alliance for life and the founding of a family" – clearly an appeal intended to have a stabilizing impact on marital ties.(101) Beyond that, it is assumed that the state and society have the right and the obligation to exert a direct influence on marital life. "Marriage, family and motherhood stand under the special protection of the state," says the 1968 GDR Constitution in a paragraph left unchanged in the 1974 revision. And it goes on to talk about equal rights of husband and wife within the family, secured by "the social and state support of citizens in the fortification and development of their marriage and family."(102) Even more clearly, the Family Law Code proclaims that "State and society contribute to the strengthening of relations between husband and wife and between parents and children as well as to the development of the family." Apart from state institutions listed as pertinent for such tasks (such as "social organizations, labor collectives, and parents' counseling services"),(103) it also provided for the establishment of marriage and family counseling services. In 1968, moreover, state "marriage and sex-counseling services" were set up for the exclusive purpose of assisting couples with the solution of sex problems.(104) And in 1969, the GDR State Secretariat for West German Questions published an information bulletin, probably directed primarily at the FRG. In it, the right of socialist society to play a role in family life is explained as follows:

> It is not an inherently private business of individuals how to cope with marital difficulties. Whoever takes such a position decides that he will stand by and do nothing when a hitherto efficient individual gets on the downward path, and thereby endangers his existence and that of his family. . . .
>
> Moreover, it would contradict the principle of socialist society to give up, without a thought, on even one single individual.(105)

There is one family issue which is probably of primary interest and concern to the GDR and, for that matter, to any socialist society: the proper rearing of children, so that they will be brought up in the true spirit of socialism. This cannot be accomplished in schools and youth organizations alone. The home must play its part. But while in West German homes the responsibility for the raising of children falls primarily on the mother, with hardly any interference by the state, GDR lawmakers do not believe that so important a task can be left to mothers, nor even to both parents, alone. As a minimum, the state must try to inspire and guide them. Hence, both the importance of this issue to society, and the obligation of parents are clearly spelled out in paragraphs 3 and 42 of the Family Law Code:

> The bringing up of children is both the task and the concern of the society as a whole. . . . The raising of children is an important civic task of parents for which they will receive our recognition and appreciation by the state and by society.
>
> The goal of the education of children is to raise them to intellectually advanced, morally upright, and physically healthy personalities who consciously participate in the development of society. By responsibly discharging their educational obligations, by setting an example, and by adopting consistent behavior towards their children, the parents develop in them a socialist attitude towards study and work, they bring them up to respect the working person and to observe the rules of socialist life together, and they raise in them the spirit of solidarity and of socialist patriotism and internationalism. . . .
>
> In the fulfillment of their educational tasks and to ensure a uniform education, they are to cooperate closely and confidently with, and give their support to, the school, other educational and training institutions, the "Ernst Thaelmann" Pioneer organization, and the Free German Youth.

Divorce

Under present laws, in both the FRG and the GDR, divorces are granted without any attempt to establish guilt or assign blame. They are granted whenever marriages have irreparably broken down (the Zerruettungsprinzip – the irreparable break down principle). But while this kind of legislation has long been in existence in the GDR, it is relatively new in the FRG. And, once again, there is a substantial difference in the role of the state: in the GDR, the courts, as organs of the state, are to make maximum efforts to reconcile the spouses and keep the marriage intact; in the FRG, no such role is assigned to the courts or any other state organs.

In West Germany, the Fourth Book of the old Civil Code (the "Family Law"), although altered somewhat by amendments, remained essentially in force as originally written, until the new Family Law took effect in 1977. Under the old law, marriages could, as a rule, be dissolved only if at least one of the spouses was found guilty of severe matrimonial transgressions such as adultery or desertion.(106) Under supplementary legislation, divorces without establishment and proclamation of guilt had become possible before 1977, if both parties agreed and had been separated for at least three years. But in the mid-1970s, about 90 percent of all divorces were still granted for "severe matrimonial transgressions," most of them with admission of guilt and postdivorce support payments worked out in advance between the spouses themselves.(107)

The new Family Law of 1977 abolished the "guilt principle" altogether. Referring to the relevant sections of the new act as a "just divorce law," a recent official FRG government publication explains that, henceforth, "whose fault it is, is not the court's business. They [the judges] need no longer sniff around in the intimate sphere of the spouses."(108) Instead, the new law decrees a marriage can be dissolved simply if it has broken down irreparably, in other words, if conjugal life between the spouses no longer exists, and if it cannot reasonably be expected that it will be reestablished.(109) As a general rule, this is "irrefutably assumed" to be the case, when the spouses have been separated for one year and both agree to the divorce, or for three years if only one of them has filed for it.(110) In rare cases, a continuation of a marriage might (for reasons that lie with the person of one of the spouses) be deemed to constitute a hardship for the other greater than he or she could reasonably be expected to bear. Under such circumstances, a marriage can be dissolved, even if the partners have not been separated for an entire year.(111) On the other hand, there are isolated cases when the maintenance of a marriage might, for very special reasons, be considered to be of singular importance for a child from that marriage, or when a divorce would impose unreasonable hardships on the spouse who opposes it. In such cases, a divorce might not be granted. But under no circumstances can a divorce be denied if the spouses have been separated for five or more years.(112)

In the GDR, the divorce laws of the old Civil Code were revised more than twenty years before the FRG instituted the extensive reform of its family laws. In the 1955 "Marriage and Divorce Decree," the "guilt principle" in divorce cases was abolished and replaced by the "irreparable breakdown" principle.(113)

In divorce proceedings, as in other aspects of family relations, society and the state play a greater role in the GDR than in the FRG, attempting, for instance, to determine causes for the breakdown of marriage and to bring about reconciliation. Specifically, the GDR's 1965 Family Law Code states:

> (1) A marriage may be dissolved only when the court has determined that such severe reasons prevail that it is clear that the marriage has lost its purpose for the spouses, the children, and therefore also for society.

(2) If divorce proceedings have been initiated by one of the spouses, the court is to undertake a careful investigation of the development of the marriage.(114)

Marriages of long duration in which the spouses have grown old together are deemed to be in particular need of protection; judges are admonished to investigate their breakdown with special care and to explore all possibilities for the reconstitution of long-standing ties.(115) In a further attempt to prevent the break-up of marriages wherever possible, lower GDR courts were reminded by a resolution of the Supreme Court of June 24, 1970, of their "educational" duties; and, in addition to the courts' regular, obligatory reconciliation-negotiations with the spouses, new measures in cooperation with state marriage and family counseling services were decreed, in order to attempt to keep marriages intact.(116) But, says the Commentary to the GDR Family Law Code, "if the foundation for satisfactory education and development of children no longer exists, the marriage has lost its purpose for the children also."(117)

In West Germany, where courts are no longer investigating why but only whether a marriage has broken down, the GDR courts' "investigations of the development of a marriage" are nowadays viewed as undue prying into the intimate details of family life, embarassing to all involved. But GDR legislators, bent on attempting to reconcile couples on the verge of divorce whenever possible, consider the probes quite worthwhile. Official publications claim considerable success for the endeavors of GDR family courts, since differences are ironed out and divorce petitions withdrawn in one out of every four cases.(118)

Finally, we have seen that in West Germany divorces can be denied when potential harm to a child or a spouse can be anticipated. But these are rare cases, and FRG courts are concerned with such potential harm only when claims to that effect are made by spouses who oppose the divorce. GDR society, on the other hand, once again enters the picture more directly and more forcefully. GDR legislation mandates that judges find out during their investigations, as a matter of routine, "whether interests of minor children would be adversely affected by a divorce, and whether the divorce would constitute unreasonable hardship for one of the spouses."(119)

Division of property

Under the old Civil Code, the husband was in general charge of his and his wife's property. For example:

§ 1363. Upon the effectuation of a marriage, the property of the wife becomes subject to the management and usufruct by the husband.(120)

§ 1373. The husband is entitled to take possession of all things forming part of the contributed property.(121)

§ 1374. The husband shall manage the contributed property in a proper manner. He shall give to the wife, on demand, any information relating to his management.(122)

Obviously, no such provisions have been maintained in present family legislation, in either West or East Germany. Under present family law, both in the FRG and the GDR, each spouse retains title to all property brought into the marriage, but there are differences as to property accumulated during the marriage.

In the FRG, under a 1957 alteration in the Civil Code not further changed by the new Family Law, each spouse, as long as the marriage remains intact, retains title and control, including the right of disposal, even over property acquired by that spouse during the marriage.(123) While in theory this law is equally applicable to both spouses, it is actually very discriminatory against the wife since, in the overwhelming majority of cases, the husband is either the sole, or at least the major, income earner. The wife's contribution to family income more often than not consists, at least in part, of taking care of the home and the children, which does not in itself provide her with the wherewithal to acquire property.

In the GDR, on the other hand, things are different, not only because in most cases both husband and wife are gainfully employed but also because individual and separate property rights of spouses are legally much more circumscribed. With certain exceptions, such as personal presents, decorations, or inheritances left specifically to one of the spouses, all "commodities, property rights, and savings" accumulated during the marriage through the "work or work income" of one or both spouses belong jointly to both spouses.(124)

In the case of divorce, the division of property is rather similar in the two Germanies. In both, spouses are entitled to the property, or the monetary equivalent thereof, that they brought into the marriage; and property accumulated during the marriage is usually divided between them.(125) As a general rule, such property is divided equally, unless there are weighty reasons to the contrary. The GDR, somewhat more specifically than the FRG, spells out that a spouse may lay claim to a larger share because of greater need, or may be excluded from property sharing because he or she has not contributed to the creation of the common property by either gainful employment or participation in household chores.(126)

Divorcees' pension rights

Prior to implementation of the new Family Law in 1977, husbands in the FRG acquired pension and other retirement pay rights from their job activities; wives in charge of the home and the children did not. Wives who were gainfully employed had, as a general rule, lower incomes than their husbands and, consequently, accumulated less in retirement pay rights. When the marriage was dissolved and the wife was unable to work, she depended on alimony payments from her husband. But these, and even a divorcee's widow's pension, she could get only if the court found her "not guilty" of the breakup of the marriage. All this was changed under the "maintenance equalization" provisions of the new Family Law (§ 1587) which put the FRG far ahead of the United States in regard to divorced women's pension rights. As a general rule, all pensions, annuity proceeds, and retirement incomes accumulated during the time of the marriage are to be split evenly between the divorcees entitled to such income (i.e., if they are either unable to work or 65 years of age).(127) Only in exceptional cases can such equalization be denied by the court, for instance, if it would impose great hardships on one of the divorcees while the other could maintain his or her customary living standard out of his or her own income and means, or if one of the spouses during the marriage had been guilty of gross neglect of the duty to contribute to the maintenance of the family (it being understood that housework and child rearing constitutes adequate contribution to family "income").(128) "For the first time," comments an official German publication, "wives are given their own claims to the retirement and other benefits of the husband since, after all, he was able to acquire them because he went out to work while his wife looked after the home."(129) "For the first time," comments another, "the wife's work in the home and the family has been recognized for insurance purposes. This, at the same time, is the first step for women who are not gainfully employed outside the home, to get social security benefits in their own right [as housewives]."(130) In actual practice, it should be pointed out, the retirement income of the former wife still tends to be considerably lower than that of the divorced husband, since only retirement income accumulated during the marriage is "equalized" and the husband is likely to have accumulated more before the marriage than his wife. (Table 2.2 illustrates this income difference in an assumed case.)

Table 2.2. Theoretical Retirement Income of Spouses Divorced at Age 65 or Older

FRG

	Husband	Wife
Rights to monthly retirement income accumulated		
Total	DM 1,000	DM 600
Accumulated prior to marriage	700	500
Accumulated during marriage	300	100
Retirement income (income accumulated prior to marriage plus one half of combined income of both spouses accumulated during marriage)	900	700

If the couple is under retirement age at the time of divorce, the income difference is likely to become even greater because after the divorce, the husband will probably continue to earn more, and therefore to accumulate more retirement income, than his wife.

In the GDR, the problem of rights to pensions and other retirement income accumulated during the marriage is not deemed relevant. The basic assumption in the GDR is that both spouses work and that from their participation in the labor force both accumulate their own claims to retirement incomes. In the rare cases where, at the time of divorce, a divorcee does not have an independent income and is not able to provide for himself or herself, the former spouse has a support obligation — a point to be taken up in greater detail below.(131) But since, in spite of welfare measures and the subsidization of necessities, life income is still somewhat lower for women than for men in the GDR, so are therefore the retirement benefits of divorced women — surely an area, then, where improvement is necessary if full sex equality is to be established.

Support obligation

Under the old Civil Code, support payments, if any, were to be made by the party who was found guilty of the break-up of the marriage to the one who was found not guilty. But support obligations differed, dependent on who was the guilty party. If the husband was pronounced exclusively guilty, he had to support his former wife to the extent to which her own income was inadequate for her to continue living in the style to which she had become accustomed; if the wife was declared exclusively guilty, she was obligated to such support only if the former husband was unable to support himself.(132) In actual practice, the wife, more often than not, was dependent on the husband for her livelihood; and so it was he, and not she, who usually wanted the divorce. With declarations of guilt and support arrangements generally agreed on before divorce proceedings were instituted, husbands, in almost all cases, were the ones who paid alimony to their former wives. In this manner, marriage used to be a financial maintenance institution in which the wife, whether divorced or not, had a life-long right to participate in her husband's income and professional advances.

Under current family law, in both West and East Germany, spouses are to be divorced economically as well as otherwise from each other. In other words, as a general rule, each spouse is to be responsible for his or her own livelihood after a divorce. Support payments, if any, are to be based on need only and, in most cases, are to be temporary in nature.

More specifically, West Germany's new Family Law imposes support obligations upon a divorcee only if the former spouse is unable to support him or herself in the accustomed style and if the other has the means to render such support payments. Under the new law, a claim for support exists if a divorcee cannot be expected to work because of obligations connected with the care and education of the couple's children (§ 1570), advanced age (§ 1571), illness or other physical handicaps (§ 1572), or inability to find "appropriate" employment (defined as employment commensurate to the divorcee's training, qualifications, age, and health; it being understood that, where necessary, the divorcee would have to undergo the education and training necessary for "appropriate" employment) (§ 1575). In this latter case, a divorcee is entitled to temporary financial support particularly when, either in expectation of marriage or during the marriage, such education and training had been interrupted, as long as "the successful completion of such education can be expected" (§ 1575). Finally, support payments can also be requested and approved by the court for "weighty" reasons in cases where denial would constitute a gross injustice (§ 1576). On the other hand (with the only exception of divorcees who cannot work due to obligations for the care and education of the couple's children), no right to alimony exists in cases where (1) the marriage was of "short" duration, (2) the one otherwise entitled to support has been found guilty of a severe crime against the spouse or a near relative of the spouse, (3) the financial need was brought on wantonly and willfully by the one otherwise entitled to alimony, or (4) for another reason of equal gravity as those in points (1) to (3) above (§ 1579). All rights to alimony cease when the one entitled to it dies or remarries (§ 1586).(133)

If the percentage of divorced women who are paid alimony by their former spouses is much smaller in the FRG today than it used to be, this is much more the case in the GDR where the overwhelming majority of working-age women are gainfully employed, and the majority of older women receive retirement income in their own right. As early as 1955, support and alimony payments were abolished in the GDR's "Marriage and Divorce Decree," except in hardship cases.(134) In other words, similar to provisions in the FRG but in existence for 22 years longer, claims for alimony arise in the GDR only when one of the spouses, because of age, sickness, need to take care of minor children, or other weighty reasons, is unable to support him or herself. While, in theory, either spouse could request support payments after divorce, a recent article in a GDR law periodical explains that provisions for alimony are "in practice of importance only to the wife. The need for and the actual use of relevant regulations are closely tied to the specific family and social position of the wife and the mother under socialism."(135) The same situation prevails in West Germany. And it is even more realistic since, in both the GDR and the FRG, mothers are given custody over minor children in case of divorce in over 90 percent of all cases,(136) especially where very young children are involved.(137) However, in actual practice, 85 percent of GDR divorces involve no alimony payments at all; in another 10 percent, support payments are for two years or less; and in only 5 percent of all cases are they for longer duration.(138) But that in relevant cases a woman who does not work is indeed entitled to such payments of about 30 to 40 percent of her husband's income was reiterated by the GDR Supreme Court on March 26, 1976.(139)

Minimum Age for Marriage

In the GDR, the minimum age for marriage is 18, the same for men and women. In the FRG, the minimum age for men is at present also 18, reduced under the new Family Law from the previous 21; but women can now, and could also before 1977, get married at age 16.(140)

Choice of Family Name

Under the old Civil Code, there was no choice: § 1355 provided that "the wife takes the surname of the husband."(141) In the FRG, the paragraph was subsequently amended, allowing the wife, even before the mid-1970s, to append her name to her husband's.(142)

Under current legislation (in the GDR since the introduction of the Family Law Code in 1965, and in the FRG under Act of Parliament of 1975, subsequently incorporated into the new Family Law), spouses still are to have the same last name, but they can choose either the husband's or the wife's. The one whose name was not chosen can then append it to the family name. However, GDR legislation spells out that this should be done only if there is valid reason, "when, for instance, a spouse has become especially well known to the public by his or her previous name and has achieved special respect," which would, for example, be the case with individuals renowned in politics, sports, or the performing arts.(143) In actual practice, both East and West, couples almost invariably select the husband's name as the family name; and wives occasionally append their name to that of their husbands.(144)

State Child Support

In both the FRG and the GDR, state financial support for children is probably the major form of "family furtherance." In both parts of Germany, such support payments are made automatically, irrespective of family wealth or income.

Table 2.3 shows child support per month, in amounts and as percentage of workers' average wage, paid by the state for all minor children, in the FRG to age 18, and in the GDR to age 15, extended however to age 18 if the teenager is enrolled in a school.(145) In the FRG, state child support is paid to age 23 if the young adult is unable to find gainful employment and does not receive unemployment compensation, and to age 27 if enrolled in a vocational school or an institution of higher learning.(146) Such provisions are not applicable in the GDR since employment there is guaranteed to all citizens, and since students at vocational schools and institutes of higher learning are financially supported under other laws.

Table 2.3. Monthly State Child Subsidies

For the:	FRG	Total	GDR	Total
First child	50.--DM	50.--DM	20.--M	20.--M
Second child	80.--DM	130.--DM	20.--M	40.--M
Third child	150.--DM	280.--DM	50.--M	90.--M
Fourth child	150.--DM	430.--DM	60.--M	150.--M
Fifth child	150.--DM	580.--DM	70.--M	220.--M
Each additional child	150.--DM		70.--M	

As percent of workers' average wage

	FRG	GDR
1 child	2.49	2.15
2 children	6.49	4.30
3 children	13.97	9.71
4 children	22.46	16.18
5 children	28.95	23.73
For each additional child	7.48	7.55

Source: Familienpolitik, p. 17.

At first glance, it would appear that child subsidy payments are considerably higher in the FRG than in the GDR, both in absolute amounts and as percent of workers' income. But for several reasons, this impression is somewhat misleading. First, necessities of life are much cheaper in the GDR than in the FRG. Health care and education are essentially free in both, but rent, utilities, and such basic food staples as milk or bread are much lower priced in East than in West Germany; secondly, nurseries, kindergartens, and after school care centers are more plentiful, more readily available, and much lower priced in the GDR than in the FRG; thirdly, in addition to subsequent child support payments, the GDR has ever since 1950 paid mothers a substantial birth allowance which, at present (under a 1972 ordinance), amounts to 1,000 M per child;(147) and, finally, income tax payments are reduced for each child in the GDR but not in the FRG. Special tax considerations for children (similar to the tax exemptions in the United States) were a form of state child support in both parts of Germany inherited from the pre-1945 era. But in the West, such tax benefits were abolished as of Jan. 1, 1975, and replaced by higher direct child support payments. This new arrangement was deemed more equitable since poorer families, who were in lower income brackets or paid no income tax at all, benefitted less than high income families (and sometimes not at all) from tax exemptions granted for each child. The GDR, on the other hand, has maintained such exemptions, in addition to its long-standing program of child support payments. Although there,

42   WOMEN IN THE TWO GERMANIES

also, these tax advantages benefit the higher income earners somewhat more, the difference is less pronounced than it was in the West prior to 1975 since income differences are smaller, and income taxes less progressive, in the GDR than in the FRG.(148) But, if greater equality of child support irrespective of parents' income is to be the goal, the West's universally increased support payments would surely seem to be more effective.

As further encouragement to increase family size, East and West both provide numerous additional benefits for families with children. In the West, families receive, for instance:(149)

- rent allowances
- special protection on rent contracts
- government grants for vocational training of children
- national assistance benefits for low income families
- low priced, subsidized, family vacation places, with priority for young families and families with many children
- special allowances for food, clothing, and other necessities for single parents in financial need
- household help for a home with one or more children under 8 years of age, where the father works, the mother is temporarily incapacitated, and there is no other adult in the home who could take care of a child.

In the GDR, benefits for families with children have somewhat different bases, and they include:(150)

- interest-free loans of up to 5,000 M to young couples with monthly incomes under 1,400 M to outfit their apartment, repayable over 8 years, with 1,000 M of the debt cancelled when a child is born to the couple, another 1,500 M cancelled upon the birth of a second child, and the rest written off if the couple has a third child during the eight years (a law, by the way, that was copied almost to the letter by West Berlin)(151)
- 50 M per month per child in addition to regular child support payments for women who are full-time students (125 M per month more if they cannot find a nursery for a prekindergarten child; 150 M for two; and 175 M for 3 or more such children)
- increased vacation time at full pay
- special rent supplements and priority for apartments in new apartment buildings where <u>maximum</u> rent is 3 percent of family income, for families (and, since 1976, also for single parents) with three or more children
- favorable terms for the purchase of furniture, linens, and other household furnishings
- interest-free state credit, up to 5,000 M, for young couples for purchase of own home.

Both East and West Germany obviously extend substantial support to families with children; however, this author has not been able to find adequate data for the computation of total average family benefits which would enable him to arrive at a valid East-West comparison on this particular issue. (For monthly state subsidies per se see table 2.3.)

Old Age and Survivors Benefits

Social security has a long history in Germany. Comprehensive, landmark social security legislation offering workers insurance against accident, sickness, and old age had its start in the 1880s under Bismarck. New old age pensions for manual workers were introduced in 1938. In West Germany, old age assistance for farmers was added in 1957 and an "Act on the Further Reform of Pension Insurance," passed in October 1972, allowed additional groups, including self-employed persons and women who are not gainfully employed, to obtain coverage on a voluntary, self-contributing basis.(152)

West Germany's social security pension system has recently come under heavy attack, not only by interested parties but also by government agencies and by the courts, for being discriminatory against working women, even more so against housewives, and above all against widows who had not themselves been gainfully employed. As discussed below, drastic changes, particularly in the area of widows' pensions, are now being prepared.

Retirement income

In both West and East Germany, retirement income is based essentially on earnings and on number of years gainfully employed. In neither of the two are housewives covered under the regular, compulsory, retirement program. A void of much greater impact exists in the FRG where the majority of women are housewives than in the GDR where women of working age who are neither gainfully employed nor full-time students constitute less than 15 percent of the total.

Under West Germany's social security system, there are basically two kinds of old age insurance: the regular, compulsory retirement program under which virtually all blue and white collar workers are covered; and a voluntary, self-contributing one, designed primarily for self-employed individuals, but open to all applicants not covered automatically under the regular program. Voluntary insurance as a supplement to the regular program is not allowed.(153)

Under the regular retirement program, employer and employee each contribute 9 percent of wages, up to a maximum annual wage which has been increasing in regular intervals and, in 1977, amounted to 40,800 DM.(154) Annual retirement income is then computed according to the formula:

$$\frac{\text{percent of personal pension computation basis} \times \text{overall pension computation basis}}{100} \times$$

$$\frac{\text{years of insurance coverage accumulated} \times \text{augmentation rate}}{100}$$

where:

personal pension computation basis is a value reflecting the relationship between working-life-income of the insured and the average working-life-income of all insured.

overall pension computation basis is the average annual gross income of all insured which, in 1977, was 20,161 DM.

years of insurance coverage accumulated includes not only years actually worked but also additional years consisting of time spent on professional education and training, times of unemployment, illness, pregnancy, times missed because of an "act of God" such as a snow storm, and times of disability from the time of its occurrence to age 55.

augmentation rate is a multiplier fixed at 1.5 percent for the computation of old age pensions (1 percent, for instance, for the computation of disability pensions, on the assumption that the disabled can more easily earn supplementary income).(155)

In 1972, a minimum income provision was added to this computation. Of primary benefit to women, because they are more likely than men to earn relatively low wages during their working years, retirement income for low income earners has, since 1972, been computed by replacing their low incomes in the "personal pension computation basis" above with 75 percent of the average earnings of all those covered by the insurance.(156)

In regard to the computation of retirement income, West Germany's social security system does not distinguish between men and women, and makes no special allowances for housewives or mothers. Except for the pregnancy leave mentioned above, years of rearing children are not counted among years of insurance coverage accumulated (although a change in the law that would allow for their inclusion is now being debated in the FRG).(157)

Increasing segments of West German society have, in recent years, found this presumably "equal" treatment of men and women unfair and discriminatory. Official government commissions and publications are quick to point out that the system is highly disadvantageous even to working women since, on the average, they not only work fewer years but also earn considerably less and, therefore, accumulate less in retirement benefits than gainfully employed men(158) (an issue taken up in great detail in Chapter 3). Clearly, even working women would find it difficult to manage financially on their own during their retirement years. Among the majority of West German women who are full-time housewives, most depend in their old age entirely on their husbands' retirement income or on welfare.(159) Working on proposals to bring about the realization of full legal and social equality of the sexes in West Germany, the "Investigative Commission on Woman and Society," recently constituted by the West German parliament, complained that "the present system of social insurance in the FRG does not give due consideration to the changed social position of women." The commission went on to charge that "the one-sided orientation of social insurance towards the husband, who is gainfully employed, fails to consider to what extent the wife, by taking care of the home and the children, enables him to devote himself fully to his work."(160)

In the GDR, retirement income consists of a base rate of 110 M per month plus 1 percent of average earnings during the twenty years of work activity preceding retirement, multiplied by the number of years of lifetime work. For the computation of this 1 percent, a minimum monthly income of 150 M is figured, whether actually earned or not, and a maximum under the compulsory insurance system (which is paid for by the state) of 600 M. For higher incomes, the monthly earnings above 600 M are subject to additional voluntary insurance contributions, which increase monthly retirement income by 0.85 percent of the total amounts paid into the voluntary old age insurance fund of the social security system. And there is a guaranteed minimum old age pension, irrespective of lifetime income, that varies from 200 M per month for less than 15 years, to 240 M for 45 years or more of compulsory insurance coverage accumulated.(161)

In the computation of work years accumulated for insurance purposes, the GDR, similar to West Germany, gives credit for certain additional time spans, such as time spent on professional education and training, periods of maternity leave, and time lost because of illness or serious disability. Since the GDR does not acknowledge the possibility of unemployment under socialism (and for all practical purposes there is no unemployment – i.e., no people able and willing to work who cannot find jobs – in the GDR), there are no provisions for it to be counted as time worked, except prior to Dec. 31, 1945 – and for that pre-GDR period, one month of credit is given for every year of unemployment.(162) But, contrary to West German laws, the GDR's social security legislation contains several provisions that give special consideration in the computation of old age pensions to women, housewives, and mothers:

1. GDR legislation provides for a "spouse's supplement" of 75 M per month, payable if both spouses are retired and one of them has no old age pension of his or her own (or one lower than 75 M

per month), in which case it would be replaced by the "spouse's supplement."(163) Although in theory applicable to either spouse, hardly any husband would be likely to be the beneficiary. But the wives of the retired East German workers who never worked outside the home themselves, or who held only part-time jobs, can and do at retirement lay claim to the spouse's supplement.

2. Wives of pensioners, irrespective of age, who have one child under three years of age or two children under eight, and who do not have a retirement pension of their own are also entitled to the same "spouse's supplement."(164)

3. Mothers of five or more children without a retirement pension of their own receive a minimum pension of 200 M per month.(165)

4. For the computation of work years accumulated for retirement income purposes, in addition to the "baby year" off, single working mothers with one or more children under 3 years of age can count time taken off from their job or training temporarily, at regular pay, until they can find a place in a nursery for their offspring.(166)

5. One additional year is "attributed" to women for every five years above 15 of gainful employment covered by compulsory retirement insurance, up to a maximum of five for 40 years or more of work. For such "attributed" years, retirement benefits accumulated are counted at the rate of 0.7 percent, instead of the regular 1 percent of average annual earnings.(167)

6. Since 1968, GDR mothers have been entitled to another kind of "baby year" for purposes of retirement income computation whereby they get one year of "attributed" credit, as above, for every child born.(168)

In the FRG, the introduction of such a "baby year" into the West German social security system was proposed in 1972 by a coalition of the SPD and the FDP, and strongly backed by the labor unions, but failed to win the necessary votes in the parliament. However, the demand for such a "baby year," especially on the part of the labor unions, has not subsided in West Germany to this very day and some progress towards it was made in the late 1970s.(169)

Survivors benefits

Under present West German law, husband and wife are not treated equally in regard to survivors' benefits. The widower, as a rule, receives his retirement pension in toto, but does not share in his deceased wife's (except in the extremely rare case where she had contributed more to family income than he). The widow, on the other hand, receives 60 percent of her deceased husband's pension, irrespective of her age, employment status, or length of marriage (except in the case of fully employed widows under 45 with no minor children, who receive the "small widow's pension" which amounts to 60 percent of the one they would otherwise be entitled to).(170)

Under the present law, the gainfully employed widow, or the formerly employed widow who has reached retirement age, is well off indeed since she has her own earnings or pension plus 60 percent of her deceased husband's. But the housewife who lost her husband has to manage on but 60 percent of his pension; and without a pension of her own, she is not protected by accident or disability insurance either. With the increasing awareness of women in West Germany (and the rest of the Western world as well), this part of the FRG's social security laws has come under particularly heavy attack in recent years, as being unfair to the majority of West German women who are either housewives or who have very low lifetime earnings of their own. However, as this book goes to press, the details for a complete revision of the law are being worked out.

The mandate for such a revision was given on March 12, 1975, when the Federal Constitutional Court in Karlsruhe declared that the present system cannot be reconciled with the equal rights provision of the Constitution; and the court ordered that the present law be changed and discriminatory widow pensions be discontinued no later than by 1984.(171) But compliance with the court order is not considered an easy task. "It will be difficult to change a system that has been in existence in Germany for a century," commented sociology professor Helge Pross. "It is going to be very hard to alter that law, though altered it must be," said Christel Hempe-Wankerl, head of a women's study group of the Social-Democratic Party in Bremen. "The men who make the laws surely will not want to lower their own pensions; and to raise widow pensions to 100 percent of their deceased husbands', and perhaps also widower pensions to 100 percent of those of their formerly working wives, would cost a fortune," she explained.

In the GDR, individuals can generally collect survivors' benefits only when they reach retirement age. Apart from the fact that women can, as a rule, retire five years earlier than men, and apart also from a provision that allows the financially dependent widow with one child under three or two children under eight to collect survivors' benefits at any age,(172) there is no distinction between widow and widower in regard to survivors' insurance in the GDR.

In cases where widows or widowers have not been gainfully employed and are, therefore, not entitled to a pension of their own, they receive survivors' pensions of 60 percent of their deceased spouses' retirement pay, with a 200 M per month minimum. Although in theory equally applicable to either spouse, there are obviously few cases in practice where a widower would draw such a pension; and, since less than 15 percent of GDR women are exclusively housewives, even the number of widows entitled to it is relatively small. In the great majority of cases where both spouses had been gainfully employed and one of them died, the survivor, at retirement, is entitled to his or her own pension or to 60 percent of the pension of the deceased spouse, whichever is higher, plus 25 percent of the lower of the two.(173) But, once again, if it be granted that women's lifetime income in the GDR is still somewhat lower than men's, the average retirement income of widows would necessarily have to be lower than that of widowers. In any case, now and even more so after West Germany's new pension law takes effect in 1984, working women's retirement income is relatively lower in the GDR than in the FRG since the latter more fully participates in her deceased spouse's pension.

Pension supplements

In both West and East Germany, there are supplements to these pensions, such as supplements for minor children, or for children even into their twenties if they are still enrolled full time in educational institutions, for half orphans, for severely injured war veterans, and for individuals who, for health reasons, are in special need of physical care by another person. But, apart from the "spouse's supplement" discussed above, there is at least one other supplement that is unique to the GDR: all those who between 1933 and 1945 were "fighters against fascism" or "victims of fascism" (and all German Jews residing in the GDR are automatically included in this latter category) are entitled to "honorary pensions" of 800 M per month for "fighters" and 600 M for "victims," with corresponding survivors' pensions, varying from 120 M per month for able-bodied widows or widowers of working age, to 500 M for surviving spouses unable to work.(174) These "honorary pensions" are paid in addition to any other retirement income to which such pensioners might be entitled. Moreover, all "fighters" and "victims" who do not have any other pensions, are also entitled to an old age pension of 350 M per month, plus regular "spouse's supplements," widow or widower benefits of 60 percent of such pensions, corresponding child supplements, and orphan benefits. If such retired "fighters" and "victims" do have another pension, they can choose the higher of the two plus 25 percent of the lower.(175)

Retirement age

In the FRG, the normal retirement age, after 15 years of gainful employment covered under the social insurance system, is 65, reduced to 60 for individuals who have been unemployed for 52 weeks during the year and a half preceding their 60th birthday. The retirement age is 63 after 35 years of gainful, covered employment — the so-called "flexible retirement plan" — and 62 years for such persons if they are severely handicapped or unable to pursue gainful employment. All these provisions apply equally to men and women; but there is one special provision that allows women to retire at age 60 if they made at least 121 monthly contributions to the social insurance fund over the preceding twenty years (in other words in over half of the months during that time).(176)

In the GDR, as in the Soviet Union and the other socialist countries of East Europe, women can retire earlier than men. East Germany's <u>normal</u> retirement age for men is 65 and for women 60, after a minimum of 15 years of gainful employment.(177) But there are exceptions, groups that can retire earlier or after fewer years of work. Miners, for instance, can retire at the normal retirement age after five years of work in that industry, get earlier-retirement credit for additional years, and, after 25 years of work in mining with at least 15 of them underground, can retire at age 50.(178) "Fighters against fascism" and "victims of fascism," to give another example, can retire five years earlier (men at 60 and women at 55).(179) And, more important for this report, for mothers, the 15-year minimum work requirement is reduced by one year for the third child and for each child thereafter, and also by one year for every four years they gave nursing care to a member of the family in permanent need of such care, down to, but not below, a remaining minimum of five years of gainful employment.(180)

Additional earnings

In the GDR, there are no special provisions preventing pensioners from holding down part-time or full-time jobs and earning additional income. But at least some pensions are reduced if additional outside income exceeds certain stipulated monthly amounts. (For instance, the special pension for veterans injured in the war is reduced by one-half of all amounts earned in excess of 300 M per month, but may not drop below 30 percent of the full pension.)(181)

In the FRG, individuals who have reached the normal retirement age of 65 are not restricted as to additional earnings. But there are restrictions on those retiring earlier. Individuals who, for reasons discussed above, retire at age 60 (which includes women who fulfill the necessary requirements) were allowed, in 1977, to earn up to 425 DM in addition to their regular pension (up from 387.50 DM in 1976). Those who, under the "flexible retirement plan," go on pension at age 63 or 62 may earn any additional amounts for occasional work, but for no more than three months or 75 working days per year; should they choose regular employment, their upper limit of additional gross earnings permitted was 1,020 DM per month in 1977 (up from 930 DM in 1976).(182)

Laws on the Interruption of Pregnancies

Prior to the division of Germany, abortions were generally outlawed under § 218 of the Penal Code. Abortions were permitted only when there was a "medical indication," which meant that, in the opinion of qualified physicians, a continuation of the pregnancy would seriously endanger the life of the mother.(183)

In the GDR, § 218 was replaced almost from the outset by the "indications solution." Under the 1950 Law for the Protection of Mother and Child and the Rights of the Woman, a pregnancy could be legally interrupted if there was a medical, an ethical, or a social "indication."(184) An "ethical indication" prevailed, for instance, if the pregnancy was the result of rape or incest; "social indication" referred to situations where parents were not able to properly care for the child-to-be, or where it would have been unreasonable to impose such a burden on them. Although the "social indication" was always very liberally interpreted, recourse to it did not seem to solve the problem. Critics in the GDR pointed out that the necessity to justify her action before a committee of physicians and representatives of the proper social authorities was demeaning to the pregnant woman, that many women were too shy to bring their case before the committee, and that in many cases where they did, the negotiations took so long that the time for the performance of a safe abortion was missed. As a result, many women turned to illegal abortions; and in 1971, the year before the law was changed, such illegal abortions accounted for over 30 percent of all GDR mothers who died in connection with their pregnancy.(185)

In March 1972, the GDR passed the "Law on the Interruption of Pregnancy." Under it, pregnancies can be legally interrupted by any qualified physician at any gynecological institute or hospital department, during the first twelve weeks of pregnancy, with no questions asked. There are but two exceptions to this general rule: a woman can have an abortion only once during any six-month period; and an abortion may not be performed if, in the opinion of the physician, it endangers the life of the mother. Under current GDR law, the preparation for the abortion, the performance of the operation, the hospital stay, and any postoperative treatment are treated as any other illness, as far as work, insurance, and wages are concerned. In other words, the entire procedure involves no costs to the pregnant woman, and she receives her regular sick pay during her absence from work. And, finally, the law also provides for free distribution of pills and other means to avoid pregnancy for all women covered by social security.(186)

As we have seen, the GDR has long pursued the goal of augmenting population and, to this end, has introduced numerous policies aimed at encouraging couples to bring more children into the world. Why, then, should she have allowed abortions for reasons other than medical necessity, and why should she now have passed a law giving GDR women the right to have an abortion, virtually at will? There is little doubt that the decision is, to a great extent, ideological in nature. Giving a woman the right to decide on the number and timing of children she bears, although she may decide on this through a termination of pregnancy, is, in the words of a Western research organization, "consistent with GDR ideology. Communists have always defended the right of women over their own body," the organization explains.(187) But, in another publication, the same research organization sees a more pragmatic reason for the decision to legalize abortions on demand. The purpose of the new law, the organization affirms, is "to do away once and for all with illegal abortions, the consequences of which are more harmful to the economy and to the women involved than the possible utilization of legal methods to interrupt pregnancies."(188) GDR sources fully confirm that both ideological and pragmatic considerations enter the picture. The law itself states that "the equality of women ... demands that a woman has the right to decide for herself about pregnancy and whether or not she wants to bear and deliver the child,"(189) a view fully reiterated in other East German publications.(190) But GDR sources also point out that "unwanted pregnancies have always been terminated (in millions of cases in doubtful ways)" and that "the question, therefore, should not be termination, yes or no? Rather, it should be: interruption with the best possible protection of women's health: yes or no?"(191) Furthermore, there have probably been other reasons that contributed to the decision to legalize abortions, such as the example set by the USSR where abortions are legal, or even simply, as one Western source observed, "the GDR introduced, as of January 1, 1972, free travel, without visa requirements, to Czechoslovakia and to Poland; and in both of these countries, interruption of pregnancies has been legal for years."(192)

Whatever the reasons, the liberalization of East Germany's abortion laws appears to have had one immediate and highly desirable effect: maternal death rates have dropped sharply since the 1972 law eliminated the need for illegal abortions; and, as table 2.4 shows, they now stand well below those in the FRG.

Table 2.4. Maternal Death Rates
(per 100,000 live births)

Year	FRG	GDR
1968	51.6	52.0
1970	51.8	42.0
1971	50.5	44.0
1972	42.8	32.0
1973	45.9	26.6
1974	34.0	20.0
1975	N.A.	23.1
1976	36.3	22.0[a]
1977	34.0	18.0[a]

[a] Given in GDR Statistical Yearbook, 1979 as 2.2 and 1.8 per 10,000 live births for 1976 and 1977 respectively.

Sources: For the FRG, Das Gesundheitswesen, Vol. V, p. 310; also FRG Statistical Yearbooks through 1979.
For the GDR, Winter, p. 61; also GDR Statistical Yearbooks through 1979.

It is difficult to ascertain how much of an impetus GDR legislation (beamed over radio and television to the West) has given to attempts to liberalize West Germany's abortion laws. In any case, a Social Democratic-liberal (SDP and FDP) coalition in the FRG began in the early 1970s to work seriously for a repeal of what Katherina Focke, then Federal Minister for Youth, Family and Health, referred to as the "infamous paragraph 218 that has brought sorrow, desperation and misery to countless women."(193) In 1974, an abortion law was passed by the West German Parliament over strong conservative (CDU and CSU) opposition. Virtually identical in intent to the law passed in the GDR two years earlier, it would have given women the right to interrupt their pregnancy at will during the first three months of pregnancy. However, the following year this law was declared unconstitutional by a bare majority of the judges on the Federal Constitutional Court in Karlsruhe.(194) Forced to settle for less, the Social Democratic-liberal coalition introduced another, more moderate reform law, the "indications solution," very similar in concept to the GDR's pre-1972 laws on abortion. Under the new law, a pregnancy can be legally interrupted if there is a medical, psychiatric, ethical, eugenic, or social "indication" that would warrant an abortion. A eugenic indication prevails if there is a likelihood of physical or mental damage to the baby, because of hereditary factors or of an illness of the mother during pregnancy; as to "social indication," referring to the likelihood of highly adverse social effects, it was hoped that the term would be interpreted reasonably liberally, applicable, for instance, to the case of an older woman no longer capable of caring for a young child, an unmarried student who could not be expected to give a child the proper care, or a family already burdened by several children. In the case of ethical and social "indications," the pregnancy can be legally interrupted only during the first 12 weeks of pregnancy, in case of a eugenic "indication" during the first 22, and in case of a medical or psychiatric "indication" at any time.(195) To certify that a valid "indication" actually prevails, the law requires that an abortion be preceded by a "consultation" with any "physician of your choice." If approved, it can then be performed by any physician other than the consultant at a hospital or institution licensed for the purpose, and is paid for by the social insurance program.

To inform the public of the content of the new law and to win public support for it, the West German government began to publish material on the matter. By the end of 1976, literally millions of brochures had been distributed, such as <u>Before the Decision Comes the Consultation: The Reform of § 218 of the Penal Code</u> (2nd ed., 1976, 1,500,000 copies), <u>Every Child has a Right to be Wanted</u> (7,150,000 copies), <u>Every Expectant Mother has a Right to Assistance</u> (4,700,000 copies).(196) And 150,000 copies of a pamphlet entitled <u>Use of Contraceptives is Preferable to Abortion</u> were distributed to physicians;(197) but under the new law, neither oral nor any other kind of contraceptives are normally obtainable free in the FRG, except for needy mothers of several children who can apply for them through the social insurance.

Undoubtedly, the most frequent reasons why women want to interrupt their pregnancies are social in nature. But, although "social indications" have been the most frequent reasons for which abortions have actually been performed under the new law (see table 2.5), the issue has by no means been handled uniformly in the various Laender (states) and local communities. "No doubt, women have it easier today than before the reform to have their pregnancy legally interrupted," commented an official publication of the Federal Ministry for Youth, Family and Health half a year after the introduction of the indications solution, "but there are considerable regional differences." "In the North of the FRG — especially in the city states [Hamburg, Bremen, and Berlin]," it went on, "women have it much easier. In the states to the South, and particularly in Baden-Wuertemberg and Bavaria, women can count on encountering difficulties. Frequently, they have to go to large cities or to other states to succeed in getting a legal abortion. But a trip abroad, e.g., to Holland, is no longer necessary."(198) And women who this author interviewed in person in 1978 expressed the same sentiments: "In Berlin, it's merely a formality," said well-known Berlin lawyer Adelheid Koritz, "it's no real problem to get physicians to approve that there is a social indication." "In Bavaria it has always been very difficult to get abortions approved, especially for social reasons, and it's going to become worse now," said Inge Gabert, editor of the periodical Arbeiterwohlfahrt (Workers' Welfare), head of Bavaria's SPD women, and wife of a member of Bavaria's legislative assembly, after Bavaria's conservative CSU had just won a major victory at the polls. And at least ten counties in Bavaria and six in Baden-Wuertemberg have actually passed resolutions forbidding their hospitals to interrupt pregnancies for reasons of "social indications." However, the position of the Federal Government is that individuals, including physicians and nurses, can refuse to cooperate with abortions and so can private and church-owned hospitals, but that regional political units do not have the right to prohibit what Federal law has explicitly legalized.(199) Still, even in cases where the existence of a social indication has been certified, pregnant women in Southern Germany frequently have difficulties finding a physician willing to perform the abortion, or a hospital which would permit it to be performed there.(200)

Table 2.5. Reasons for Abortions Legally
Performed in the FRG
(percent of total)

Indication	First quarter of 1977*	Last half of 1976**
Social	50.5	45
General medical	33.3	36
Psychiatric	10.0	11
Eugenic	4.9	5
Ethical	0.2	0.2
Unknown	1.2	1

*The total number of abortions legally performed in West Germany in the first quarter of 1977 was 11,587, an increase of 20 percent over the last quarter of 1976.

**The total number of abortions legally performed in West Germany in the second half of 1976, the first half year after the introduction of the reform law, was 13,044.

Source: Informationen des Bundesministeriums fuer Jugend, Familie und Gesundheit, No. 27, July 7, 1977, p. 1.

3 German Women At Work

Whatever features related to the employment of women one looks at (be it job training and preparation, percentage of women gainfully employed, types of work engaged in, opportunities for advancement to high positions, equal pay for equal work or lack thereof, or just general attitude toward the employment of women), one finds considerable differences between the two German states. Even in cases where similarity of relevant laws might lead one prematurely to conclude otherwise, disparities are often very real and pronounced.

PARTICIPATION IN THE LABOR FORCE

GDR women participate in their country's labor force to a much greater extent than do their counterparts in the FRG. Without necessarily concluding at this point that the discrepancy can be accounted for by the difference in social systems, it is interesting to note that FRG participation rates, both male and female, are rather similar to those of the United States, while the GDR's are virtually identical to those of the USSR.

Significant as this difference certainly is, it actually understates the true picture. This is so because the percentage of women of working age is smaller in the GDR than in the Federal Republic. The age distribution is such that the "below working age" percentage of the population is about the same in the two Germanies; but less than 15 percent of West Germany's population is above working age, while the corresponding percentage for East Germany is above 19 percent.(1) Because of preponderately male losses in World War II and also because of generally longer female longevity, there are many more women than men in the older age groups.(2) Add to this that the "labor force" includes a substantial number of unemployed women in the West, but not in the East (a subject broached in greater length below), and it becomes clear that a comparison of gainfully employed women, expressed as a percentage of female population of working age, would have greater significance. In 1976, about 50 percent of such working age women were gainfully employed in the FRG, and over 80 percent in the GDR.(3)

Table 3.1. Labor Force*

	Total* % of total population	Men % of male population	Women % of female population
FRG (1978)	44	58	32
GDR (1977)	51	55	47
US (1977)	46	57	36
USSR (1975)	50	54	46

*For FRG and US, includes employed and unemployed; for GDR and USSR, gainfully employed only.

Source: Statistical Yearbook, FRG, 1979, p. 618.

In West Germany, women account for about 37 percent of all gainfully employed, and this percentage has remained virtually unchanged for the past three decades. In the GDR, on the other hand, the percentage of women in the actively working labor force has increased steadily, from 40 percent in 1950 to about 50 percent by the mid-1970s.(4)

To account for such pronounced differences one must look both to ideological and to pragmatic reasons.

Ideological Differences

As discussed briefly in chap. 1, West German ideology is in a sense but a continuation of the free enterprise ideology of the days of the Weimar Republic. It may have undergone some evolutionary changes entailing increased welfare measures and a somewhat greater role for government in general, but it certainly does not call for a revolutionary reconstitution of society at large. Apart from vague, general concepts of equal rights in a democracy (concepts which, for instance, have not always included women's suffrage), there is nothing specific in that ideology that would prescribe that steps be taken to integrate women into the labor force.

The architects of Marxism-Leninism and their disciples in the GDR, on the other hand, have always deemed participation in the work force

Table 3.2. Gainfully Employed
(in 1000's)

	FRG				GDR*			
Year	Total	Men	Women	Women as % of total	Total	Men	Women	Women as % of total
1950	22,074	14,125	7,949	36.0	8,477	5,090	3,387	40.0
1960	26,464	16,619	9,845	37.2	7,686	4,412	3,456	45.0
1965	26,887	17,084	9,803	36.4	7,676	4,095	3,581	46.7
1966	26,801	17,011	9,790	36.2	7,684	4,068	3,616	47.1
1967	25,950	16,566	9,384	36.2	7,714	4,072	3,642	47.2
1968	25,968	16,556	9,412	36.2	7,712	4,056	3,656	47.4
1969	26,356	16,833	9,523	36.1	7,746	4,029	3,717	48.0
1970	26,668	17,086	9,582	35.9	7,769	4,019	3,750	48.3
1971	26,725	17,132	9,593	35.9	7,795	3,997	3,798	48.7
1972	26,655	17,042	9,613	36.1	7,811	3,987	3,824	48.9
1973	26,712	16,978	9,734	36.4	7,844	3,990	3,854	49.1
1974	26,231	16,612	9,619	36.7	7,903	4,000	3,903	49.4
1975	25,323	15,957	9,366	37.0	7,948	4,002	3,946	49.6
1976	23,076	15,807	9,269	37.0	8,018	4,019	3,999	49.9
1977	25,044	15,750	9,294	37.1	8,058	4,025	4,033	50.0
1978	25,209	15,853	9,356	37.1	8,118	4,052	4,052	50.1

*Does not include apprentices.

Sources: <u>Statistical Yearbook, FRG</u>, 1955, p. 110; 1962, pp. 148-49; 1975, p. 30; 1977, p. 29; 1979, p. 29; <u>Statistical Yearbook, GDR</u>, 1956, p. 154; 1977, p. 15; 1979, p. 15.

a necessary prerequisite to women's emancipation (which, as we have seen, they have always held to be essential for the successful construction of a socialist society). "Only when women have independent positions in production," says the top leadership of the GDR's labor union, "when they are in no way economically dependent on men, and when in their work, in production, they can creatively develop themselves — only then is it possible to talk of true and complete equality"(5) — a direct take-off on virtually identical statements by Engels and Lenin [Engels: "The emancipation of women and their equalization with men is and will remain an impossibility as long as women are excluded from socially productive life and remain confined to their own home."(6) Lenin: For the complete emancipation of women and for their true equality with men, women's participation in productive labor is an absolute necessity."(7)] And, again following in the footsteps of their ideological forefathers, official and semiofficial GDR organizations hold that "only in a socialist collective of working people can women develop all their faculties and achieve complete equality."(8)

Differences in Attitudes

In part because of different ideological approaches, and in part surely also for more pragmatic economic reasons discussed below, the general attitude of German citizens, both male and female, and of German society at large toward the gainful employment of women outside their own homes is quite dissimilar in the two German states — very positive in the GDR, still relatively more negative in West Germany, despite some changes in the FRG in recent years.

In answers to questionnaires distributed in 1959 to girls graduating from a Stuttgart high school (answers deemed to "correctly reflect the situation at the time"),(9) 56 percent of those replying rejected gainful employment of married women as a matter of principle, and 93 percent considered a combination of gainful employment and motherhood "unthinkable."(10) Even in the mid-1960s, a presumably representative FRG survey still showed that 72 percent of West German men and 68 percent of West German women did not consider it "normal" for women to be gainfully employed. In the case of mothers, outside work was rejected by 90 percent of the women questioned.(11) But when the 1959 questionnaire was given to female high school graduates in Cologne in 1973, the changes were quite remarkable: 77 percent of graduating seniors said that they intended to continue working after they were married, while only two percent said absolutely "no." However, 20 percent still considered gainful employment and motherhood irreconcilable; only 29 percent held the opposite view; and the rest based their decision on the age of the children and the availability of adequate child care facilities outside of the home. While in 1959, 84 percent of the girls surveyed had answered "yes" to the question whether they saw women's real destiny primarily in marriage, and only 12 percent had answered "no," the situation was reversed in 1973: only 12 percent of the highschool girls queried answered "yes" and 73 percent "no," the rest being undecided.(12) But studies show that the less their education and training, the less skilled they are, and the lower the educational and professional background of the home they were raised in, the more likely West German women are to seek their happiness in a marriage that would not necessitate their finding outside employment.(13)

Thus, views have changed in recent years. For a woman to work outside the home has become somewhat more acceptable, not only among women themselves but also among men in West Germany. However, West German women are not expected to work; they may if they want to and if they can find jobs; but there is no social pressure to induce them to do so, and they are certainly not looked down upon if they choose to be full-time housewives. Consequently, large numbers of West German women still see it as their main — and many as their exclusive — goal in life to take care of their homes, their husbands, and their children. Just how extensive this attitude actually is, is amply demonstrated by the fact that about half of all West German women of working age are not in the labor force. Even beyond this, the view is still widespread among West Germans that a married woman who takes up outside work endangers her marriage, and a working mother of young children necessarily neglects her offspring and sacrifices their well-being to her own financial or professional ambitions. Many West German mothers fully share such views. Several of the FRG mothers interviewed by this author took the positions, widely held there, that even the best-trained teachers can never replace a mother (not, one said, "mother or father") because teachers or babysitters come and go, and young children, especially, need a "Bezugsperson," one single individual to relate to, one single individual they can always turn to, they can depend on, who will always be there for them. Hence, home, marriage, and motherhood are still major emotional hurdles in the way of the gainful employment of West German women — and, therefore, to some extent perhaps, in the way of their self-realization and full emancipation.

In the GDR, in contrast, the alternative of "marriage or job" has virtually disappeared from the consciousness of young women.(14) There, women are expected to play their part in constructive work, and over the years their participation in the country's labor force has increasingly been taken for granted. As early as the mid-1960s, in a book entitled The Miracle Over There Are the Women, two West German observers wrote: "There [in the GDR], men don't even feel discomfort that women have placed themselves next to them as equals on the job and in society, and that in some cases they have to tolerate women as bosses. Emancipation over there is much farther advanced than in West Germany."(15)

Indeed, in the GDR today, the model woman, the model wife, and the model mother is the one who can combine household and family obligations with social employment in the economy. In a recently published booklet on women in the GDR, an East German author phrased it succinctly when she wrote that a GDR woman can be exclusively a housewife, if she so chooses, "but for a healthy and able woman not to have a job without a good reason is to swim against the tide."(16) In a personal interview, Dr. Anneliese Klenner, economist and instructor of political economy at the Party Vocational School in Berlin, GDR, gave this author a real feeling for the spirit of the times. Recollecting how she stayed home with her three children in the late 1950s until the youngest was ready for school, she remembered that when she finally went back to work, "my two older children were ever so glad that they were able to say to their class mates: 'My mother has a job too.'" For the few who would like to stay home, social pressures present a dilemma. Comments one such GDR woman, mother of one child, who admits to being "old-fashioned" and not interested in being a "liberated woman," and who decided to be solely a housewife: "I understand that the times and our economy demand that women work. . . . I find it wonderful that a woman can put her talents to use, if she wants to. . . . But I want to be a woman the way I conceive a woman to be, and the way I feel right about it. You see, when a woman has five children and stays home, that is respected, that is something. But to say: 'I have only one child and want to stay home,' that is difficult to explain to people. . . ."(17)

An FRG research team, commissioned by the Federal government in 1971 to study the state of the nation, confirmed and elaborated on the difference in the two German states' official attitudes toward the employment of women. In the GDR but not in West Germany, the researchers reported, all efforts are directed toward enabling women to combine family life and motherhood with productive participation in the country's labor force. The goal is for employment to be interrupted for only short periods of time, in order to prepare for and give birth to a baby and see the child through the first few months (and now through the first year) of life. The country's laws, the educational system, the emphasis on state-built and operated nurseries and kindergartens, the attempts to ease the burdens of housework by providing increased numbers of state subsidized and relatively low priced catering services, home-delivery laundries, and other services(18) are aimed at facilitating women's participation in the labor force. In the FRG, on the other hand, the research team found that women, with official or semi-official government encouragement, were increasingly turning to the "three-phase-rhythm": a time for education, training, and some gainful employment (phase I); a time for dedication to marriage and family (phase II); and, after the children are grown, a time for resumption of gainful employment (phase III).(19) And West German laws and institutions support this attitude. While there are no other West German laws directed specifically toward the furtherance of women's work, the Work Furthering Act of 1969, as amended in 1976, does provide for the retraining of mothers who, after years of absence, want to return to productive work outside their homes.(20) An adequate number of well-run child care centers would facilitate the gainful employment of mothers, but there are not enough of them in the FRG — an issue taken up in greater detail later in this chapter. West German sociology professor Helge Pross put her finger on some of the other obstacles daily life poses for the West German working woman when she wrote: "Mailmen, repairmen and deliverymen operate 8 to 4, so working couples either miss deliveries or one of them has to take a day off to be at home when the plumber comes. Shopping hours end rigidly everywhere at 6:30 p.m., forcing most couples to face a crowded, rushed period at the end of the working day to buy groceries...."(21) Contrary to its counterpart in the GDR, the West German government has exhibited little inclination to ameliorate the service situation by direct action. In many respects, it is more limited in what it can do, because of the private ownership and operation of most of these services.

It goes without saying that women liberationists in the FRG, bent on seeing West German women more fully integrated into the labor force, are opposed to the three-phase-rhythm; while many conservatives, especially during times of economic recession, would prefer to see women back at "their place, in the home," altogether.

In any case, actual figures document the effects of the difference in attitudes. As has been shown, per hundred women of working age, roughly 60 percent as many again (80 versus 50) are in the labor force in the GDR as compared with the FRG. But in the case of mothers of working age, with two or three children at home, more than twice as many, per hundred, work outside the home in East than in West Germany (in 1973-74, 76 versus 36.5 for mothers of two children, and 69 versus 32.8 for mothers of three).(22)

Apart from any ideological considerations, there is at least one major pragmatic, economic difference that certainly accounts to some extent for the disparity in female employment statistics and for the divergence in public and private attitudes toward the productive employment of women in the two Germanies: there is a labor shortage in the East and unemployment in the West.

Unemployment vs. Labor Shortage

The scourge of unemployment has perhaps been the major economic problem in capitalist, free-enterprise nations. Socialist countries, in contrast, have generally been able to guarantee employment to all ablebodied citizens of working age; there, as a rule, the problem has been not unemployment but a labor shortage.(23)

That there has been full employment in the GDR, virtually from the outset, is readily acknowledged in the West; and that aspect of life "over there" has become the envy of workers, labor union leaders and government officials in West Germany. It is with pride that a GDR author recently wrote that "to the young people in our Republic, the word unemployment is known only from history books and from reports about everyday life in capitalist countries."(24) Similar sentiments were expressed on numerous occasions to the author of this book whenever he raised the problem of unemployment in the GDR. Such conditions and such feelings alone would inevitably have contributed to favorable attitudes toward the productive employment of women, including even wives and mothers. But the extensive employment of the GDR's female citizens was not merely desirable; the GDR could hardly have managed without it.

At war's end, there was a preponderance of women over men in all of Germany. But with 135 women for every 100 men in what today is the territory of the GDR, this disparity was considerably greater in the eastern than in the western parts of the country (see table 1.2 above). While today the greatly diminished but still existing numerical superiority of women is concentrated in the retirement-age categories,(25) the shortage of men then was predominantly in the war-decimated ranks of working-age males. Add to this that a higher percentage of the population was and is in the beyond-retirement age brackets in East than in West Germany, add furthermore the effects of the exodus to the West prior to the erection of the Berlin Wall, and it becomes obvious that the work of women was desperately needed in the GDR to rebuild the war-torn country. It is safe to say that, without the extensive participation of women in the labor force, the GDR could not have progressed as she did, could not have achieved the highest living standard among the socialist countries, and would not be among the ten industrially most advanced nations in the world today.

After a period of adjustment at war's end, West Germany's economy also had jobs for all its citizens who were willing and able to work. The rate of unemployment that had stood at 5.5 percent in 1950 was down to less than .5 percent by 1960.(26) With the exception of one single year, 1967, the rate of unemployment thereafter did not surpass 1.25 percent and was usually well below 1 percent until 1974. Job openings, again with the exception of 1967, were always far in excess of the number of Germans looking for work; and 3 million temporary workers from such countries as Italy, Spain, Yugoslavia, and Turkey, referred to as "Gastarbeiter" (guest workers), were needed to supplement the domestic labor force. But by the mid-1970s, a recession had set in and unemployment once again became a problem in the FRG.

During the 1960s, women made up only about one fourth of the relatively few unemployed in the FRG. When that percentage began to increase in the early 1970s, it was no matter of great consequence as yet, since unemployment overall was still so low. But by 1973-74, women found that they were being laid off in large numbers and, moreover, in numbers far out of proportion with the female participation rate in the labor force. After 1975, unemployment for men began to drop; but female unemployment continued to rise for another two years. In 1977 and 1978, women, while still constituting only about 37 percent of the labor force, accounted for over half of all unemployed.(27) With overall unemployment rates high for what West Germans were used to, the general attitude toward the employment of women took a long step backward. It did not, however, go all the way back to what it had been during the recession of 1919, when on March 28 the German government ordered that all married women whose husbands had jobs be discharged in order to vacate positions for soldiers

Table 3.3. Unemployment
FRG
(in 1,000's)

Year	Labor Force (Employed* + Unemployed)			Job Openings	Unemployed			Total unemployed, % of total labor force	Unemployed Men, % of male labor force	Unemployed Women, % of female labor force	Unemployed Women, % of all unemployed
	Total	Men	Women		Total	Men	Women				
1965	27,034	17,190	9,844	649	147	106	41	0.54	0.62	0.42	27.9
1966	26,962	17,128	9,834	540	161	117	44	0.60	0.68	0.45	27.3
1967	26,409	16,901	9,508	302	459	335	124	1.73	1.98	1.30	27.0
1968	26,291	16,791	9,500	488	323	235	88	1.23	1.40	0.93	27.2
1969	26,535	16,958	9,577	747	179	125	54	0.67	0.74	0.56	31.8
1970	26,816	17,179	9,637	795	148	93	55	0.55	0.54	0.57	37.2
1971	26,910	17,233	9,677	648	185	101	84	0.69	0.63	0.87	45.4
1972	26,901	17,183	9,718	546	246	141	105	0.91	0.82	1.08	42.7
1973	26,985	17,127	9,858	527	273	149	124	1.01	0.87	1.26	45.4
1974	26,813	16,937	9,876	315	582	325	257	2.17	1.92	2.60	44.2
1975	26,397	16,580	9,817	263	1,074	623	451	4.07	3.75	4.59	42.0
1976	26,136	16,374	9,762	235	1,060	567	493	4.06	3.46	5.05	46.2
1977	26,074	16,268	9,806	231	1,030	518	512	3.95	3.18	5.23	49.7
1978	26,202	16,342	9,860	246	993	489	504	3.79	2.99	5.11	50.8

*See table 3.2.

Source: Compiled and computed from Statistical Yearbook, FRG, 1970, p. 125; 1975, pp. 30 and 156; 1977, pp. 29 and 104; 1979, pp. 30 and 106.

who had come home from the war.(28) But, as West German sociology professor Helge Pross commented to a New York Times reporter in 1977,(29) and again to this author in a personal interview in May 1978, women are "the first to be fired in recession, and they are the last to be hired when it's over" (although in present-day West Germany, Gastarbeiter are likely to be dismissed even before women, when the economy is on the downswing).

There are valid economic reasons that account in part but not entirely for the disproportionately heavy rate of unemployment of FRG women during periods of economic adversity. In a personal interview in June 1978 in Bonn, Liselotte Funke, a Vice President of the Bundestag, attributed the prevailing unfavorable employment situation for FRG women largely to the fact that, on the average, they are less well trained and less skilled than their male counterparts (a fact documented later in this book), that they are less mobile (since for many "home town" is where the husband works), and many of them vie for the relatively few part-time positions available and then want to work mostly mornings when the children are in school.(30) But while pragmatic reasons such as these surely play a role, so also do age-old stereotype views that man is the "bread winner," that woman's work and income is to be only supplementary to that of the "head of the household," and that when work is hard to come by, women should not "take away" jobs from men.

A few years back, when the West German economy prospered and job openings were plentiful, no efforts were spared to integrate increasing numbers of women into the work force. In 1970, a booklet was published in West Germany by a manufacturers' research organization devoted to "the promotion of free enterprise" which presented all the well-known arguments in favor of married women's participation in the labor force: financial independence, social contacts, greater self-confidence, and enhanced respect on the part of the marriage partner.(31) There was talk then of introducing greater sex balance on jobs by training women for any kind of work they were interested in. Illustrated women's magazines showed pictures of women in bluejeans and other attire suitable for work; and cooking magazines prominently featured recipes that called for the time-saving utilization of frozen and canned foods.

By the mid-1970s, all that had changed. All West German women interviewed by this author in 1978 complained bitterly about the resurgence of a "back to the kitchen" attitude. Now, such women's magazines as Fuer Sie or Brigitte suggest strongly that woman's real job is that of wife and mother; once again, women are shown mostly in long or frilly dresses, impractical for most jobs; once again, such cooking magazines as Essen und Trinken feature almost exclusively recipes for dishes that have to be cooked from scratch, "the way mother used to do it," with hardly any references to precooked food, except those contained in paid advertisements. In the GDR, on the other hand, there is a continuous campaign in newspapers and magazines aimed at "convincing the housewife that frozen food is edible and that the best drapes are not necessarily those that have to be washed frequently."(32) Many vocational schools have discontinued their previous practice of keeping a certain number of places open for married women. Explained Olaf Sund, West Berlin senator for Labor and Social Affairs: "It would make little sense to further persistently the direction of women into traditionally male professions, if thereby the extent of training possibilities for male youths were hampered."(33) But Margaret Schaefer-Sasse, teacher for the Bremen Protestant State Association for Assistance to Women, took a dimmer view of the issue when she said to this author in April 1978: "Even in our courses that specialize in the training of women things have changed. We have to say to our students: 'Think it over carefully and then decide whether it pays for you to educate yourself, for it could lead to conflicts in marriage and, in any case, it will be difficult for you afterwards to find a job.'" And a German female journalist complained: "During periods of unemployment we are told that 'we are all in the same boat': but this is nothing but empty, hypocritical talk. When the boat begins to rock, we are among the first who have to go overboard. First come the Gastarbeiter. Then it's the women. Suddenly they are unwanted. Suddenly the place is again at home, in the kitchen, with the children, at the service of the husband."(34)

Among major political parties, the "back to the kitchen" movement seems to have the support of the conservative CDU and CSU but is widely criticized by followers and elected representatives of the governing, moderately socialist SPD. "Our minister, [Social-Democrat] Antje Huber, strongly opposes all such trends," said Beate Hesse, assistant expert adviser on women's questions at the Federal Ministry for Youth, Family, and Health in June 1978. But in another personal interview, Bundestag Vice President Liselotte Funcke, a member of the liberal but not socialist FDP, expressed the view that the Federal government ought not to take any position on the issue whether or not "women belong in the home."

West Germany's labor unions, in their officially expressed positions, would seem to be on the side of those who oppose sex discrimination on the job market. In November 1975, for instance, the DGB (Deutscher Gewerkschaftsbund – German Trade Union Federation) organized a two-day workshop on the subject "Job Opportunities – Equal Pay – Prejudices – Problems of Women = Problems of Society." Intended as a contribution to the "International Year of the Women," the declared purpose of the symposium was to bring into the open the still prevailing disadvantages women have to cope with on the labor market. At the symposium, well-qualified, invited panelists, all of them broadly classifiable as advocates of equal rights for women, were in full agreement that in regard to unemployment, "women are still those who suffer the most from business fluctuations;"(35) and the discussants did not paint a promising picture for the present, nor for the immediate future, as regards work opportunities for women in the FRG.(36) Recommendations for the "speediest possible" solution to the problem were manifold, including:

- better vocational and professional training and education
- greater diversification of fields of work for women
- more opportunities for part-time employment
- elimination of prejudices, especially on the part of employers
- alteration of attitudes of both men and women
- discontinuation of sex-directed assignment of roles for children in their parents' home.(37)

It need hardly be pointed out that many, if not most, such suggestions are more easily proposed than implemented.

But while West German labor leaders allege to be truly concerned with the problems of working women, some West German observers see it all as little more than rhetoric. "The trend is truly frightening," commented Jutta Menschik, West German psychologist and author of several books on women in East and West Germany to this author. "During a recession such as this, married women are supposed to stay home so that their men can support the family. We don't even feel anymore that we have a right to work. And it isn't just the employers," she continued. "This trend goes deep into the labor union movement itself." "Unions say they represent the interests of female workers," wrote a West German female journalist in November 1977, "but in reality they are through and through male oriented; and they surely have hardly ever given due consideration to the situation of the working women with family obligations."(38)

By United States standards the rate of unemployment (and even the rate of female unemployment) in the FRG may not seem excessive. But to West Germans, no longer accustomed to substantial rates of unemployment, it appears forebodingly high. How great a significance they attach to the solution of the unemployment problem can be inferred from a recent statement by Federal Chancellor Helmut Schmidt to the effect that full employment is the "highest economic priority of the Federal government" and that "the curbing of unemployment is not only an economic necessity but also essential for social and humanitarian reasons, for work is an all-important requirement for the self-realization of human beings."(39) Moreover, there is widespread concern in West Germany lest unemployment tip the scale of ideological competition in favor of the GDR. "Unless we succeed in abolishing unemployment in the near future," says a booklet published by one of West Germany's most renowned research foundations, "the strong position of our country in the (ideological) competition (with the GDR) could be, nay, necessarily would be, put in jeopardy."(40)

There can be no doubt that the absence of unemployment is a great economic plus for East German workers in general and for East Germany's female workers in particular. And the ready availability of employment opportunities has certainly played a most important role in whatever measures of equality and emancipation have been achieved by women in the GDR.

Why German Women Work: Economic and Non-Economic Reasons

West and East Germany may both have achieved relatively high living standards. Still, studies and surveys as well as interviews carried out personally by this author indicate clearly that, in both the FRG and the GDR, material considerations remain one of the primary if not the primary work-motivating incentives for German women. This fact is frankly and readily acknowledged in both parts of Germany. In the above mentioned West German DGB Workshop, for instance, there was general agreement that "the overwhelming majority of women in the FRG still work because the income is necessary for their own livelihood and for the livelihood of their family."(41) At a 1977 conference of Bavarian Social-Democratic women, the organization's president and editor of the periodical Arbeiterwohlfahrt (Worker's Welfare), Inge Gabert, also stated unequivocally that "more recent surveys show that most women must work, simply because it is necessary for their and their family's livelihood."(42) The GDR women's desire to earn money is readily understood and, under present conditions, neither held in low esteem nor viewed with disfavor. Here is how a recent GDR publication explained it:

> Naturally, in a socialist society as under any other system, a woman works because she wants to earn money, and in every country there are women, particularly those on their own, who have to earn money. The wish to earn money is by no means anti-socialist. After all, socialists are not pure ascetics, concerned only with the welfare of future generations. . . . That personal interests and endeavors can be in tune with those of society as a whole is one of the great advantages of the socialist system. Quality of life, therefore, as understood by a socialist, does not just mean ideal values, such as freedom from exploitation, social security, education and equality; it means, equally, rising living standards for the individual.(43)

Apart from any financial considerations, apart from ideological differences, and apart from social pressures and from attitudes of and measures taken by the leadership, there are certainly also personal, non-economic, motives that play a role in a woman's decision to seek employment. The unselfish desire to serve society seems to be of very limited influence, even in the GDR; but the desire to "get out of the house," to meet people, to be independent, the desire for self-realization, for proving oneself, and the pleasure and satisfaction to be derived from the job, per se, are surely of considerable importance. As verified by studies, surveys, and personal interviews, all of these (and especially the satisfaction derived from the work itself) are of more importance as motivating factors, the more educated, the more skilled, the better trained the woman is and the higher, the more professional, the more prestigious the position for which she qualifies. But, as will be documented later, GDR women, on the average, have much more education and training, and more opportunities to find professional employment and to advance to positions of responsibility than their FRG counterparts, so that these non-economic factors play a significantly greater role in East than in West Germany. Even as early as the mid-1960s, in a GDR survey that showed the overall preponderance of economic considerations, over half of all GDR working women contacted expressed a deeply-felt need for productive outside activity, and almost half listed the longing for contact with other people among the reasons for seeking outside employment. In a similar survey taken among FRG working women seven years later, in 1972, only 16 percent of the respondents listed satisfaction from the job, and only 9 percent the desire for contact with other people among the reasons for working.(44)

While the GDR leadership fully accepts material aspirations as a major factor motivating women to work, there is always the expectation that, in time, other factors will become at least of equal if not of greater importance. The author of a recently published booklet on women in the GDR put it into these words:

> There are women [in the GDR] who at first take on jobs only to increase the family's income. Practice, however, has shown that many of these women grow to like working. And in as far as they discover their own capabilities and prove their worth, they continue working although they may originally not have planned to do so. But what is of importance for everybody is that the work carried out by women in a socialist society finds great social recognition. The party and state leadership recognize and respect the extraordinary part that women have played in achieving our successes in building socialism; and this, in turn, reinforces their own level of self-confidence.(45)

And there is, perhaps, also a direct relationship between material compensation and non-economic motivation to work. As Dr. Ursula Katzenstein, who first introduced occupational therapy and now heads all sheltered occupational workshops in East Berlin, explained: "I have always wanted to work, have always wanted to participate in society. And one also needs recognition. Still, all over Europe, the higher the pay, the greater the prestige and the greater also the recognition...."

PART-TIME EMPLOYMENT

About one out of every five working women in the FRG work a short work week — one fourth of them more, and three fourth less, than 24 hours per week.(46) In mid-1978, 44 percent of all married women in the FRG held only part-time positions; and two thirds of them wanted to or could work only mornings.(47) Since the onset of an economic recession in the mid-1970s, many leading West Germans have not only looked approvingly on such part-time employment of women, but have actually favored its expansion among women who heretofore have held full-time jobs, as a sort of "share the work" program. Bundestag Vice President Liselotte Funcke, for instance, told this author in the summer of 1978 that more extensive voluntary part-time employment offers the best possibility for coping with the unemployment problem. While she proposed shorter workdays and workweeks for both male and female workers, the net effect would, in fact, be a reduced workload for women, since 99 percent of all part-time job openings in the FRG are aspired to by women.(48) But, as a general rule, the demand for part-time positions in West Germany far exceeds the availability of such jobs;(49) and Ms. Funcke was fully aware that most employers prefer full-time to part-time employees, and that their attitude must be changed if her remedy is to be successful.

In the GDR, part-time employment has never been intended for the convenience of women, nor as a general solution for the reconciliation of contradictions between jobs for women and their family obligations as wives and mothers. As discussed in chapter 2, it is accepted and encouraged only as a temporary solution in special situations — for instance, in cases of health problems or of mothers who, at the moment, are unable to find proper day care facilities for their young children. Yet, by the mid-1970s, about 35 percent of GDR working women worked a short workweek, two thirds of them more, and one third less, than 24 hours per week. GDR sources see this to a great extent as due to the "lack of insight" into the psychological and economic "significance of full-time vocational activity," in other words, a failure on the part of some women to realize how important productive work is for their own self-fulfillment and for the economic growth of socialist society.(50) A 1971 GDR survey verified that reasons other than those officially condoned by the GDR leadership do play a major role in motivating GDR women to work a short workweek.

Table 3.4. Part-time Work
(Summary)
(Mid-1970s)

	FRG	GDR
Percent of gainfully employed women on short work week	20%	35%
of which, working less than 24 hours/week	3/4	1/3
Official attitude toward part-time work	encouraged	accepted only as emergency solution

To overcome the somewhat lackadaisical attitude of many GDR working women toward productive full-time employment, the country's leadership has embarked on extensive propaganda campaigns, emphasizing the importance of full-time work to the women themselves and

Table 3.5. Twenty Major Reasons why GDR Women Choose Part-time Employment (Ranked in order)

1. Woman's obligations in family, home, and on the job can be combined if she works part-time.
2. Husband wants wife to work part-time so that she will have more time for the home and will not overexert herself.
3. Her state of health demands that she work only part-time.
4. A woman who holds a full-time position needs more time for relaxation than a full workday allows. It is, therefore, preferable if she works part-time.
5. School-age children are best taken care of if the mother works only part-time.
6. Children ought to be raised in the family. This is only possible if the mother works no more than part-time.
7. The spouse does not have enough time to participate in the raising and care of the children.
8. The husband's income is such that the wife does not need to work full-time.
9. There are relatives in the home who need to be taken of; part-time work is, therefore, a necessity.
10. The social condition of the family is such that the wife needs to work only so that she can buy special things she wants.
11. Not much difference in earnings between full-time and part-time jobs. It does not pay to work full-time.
12. The particular household demands the woman work only part-time.
13. It is not possible to have the children taken care of in public institutions.
14. Education and care of children in after-school-care-centers is inadequate. Family rearing is possible only if mother works no more than part-time.
15. Husband can get vocational training only if woman restricts herself to part-time work.
16. Commuting to the job is such as to make part-time work necessary.
17. It is best to work only part-time because then it is not necessary to work different shifts.
18. To have time for one's own training and education, it is necessary to work a short work week.
19. The work on the job is not so interesting that a woman should work full-time in spite of the burden of family obligations.
20. Work on the job is so burdensome, if one works full-time, that it is better for a woman, if she takes a part-time position.

Source: Sozialistische Arbeitswissenschaft, No. 1 (1971), pp. 24-25.

to society, and explaining its significance also in terms of Marxist-Leninist ideology.(51) Furthermore, a slightly reduced workweek without loss of pay was introduced in 1972 for mothers of three or more children to make virtually full-time employment more palatable for them (for details, see chap. 2 above); and steps taken to enable housewives to combine productive labor with family obligations (such as easing the burden of household chores, or providing adequate child care facilities) are also aimed in part at making it possible for them to combine full-time outside employment with their domestic obligations.

Both East and West, the extensive part-time employment of women has detrimental effects on careers in terms of lower pay, less accumulation of seniority and retirement benefits, and fewer opportunities for advancement to positions of power and prestige. In West Germany, moreover, there is also less job security for part-time employees. Thus, in a sense, the woman who, for family reasons, decides to work only a short workweek, sacrifices her career opportunities for her family.

WHAT JOBS FOR GERMAN WOMEN?

The Reality of "Equal Job Opportunities"

Apart from certain "typically female" manufacturing industries, such as textile manufacturing, German women in the pre-World War II era dominated in many service industries (as distinguished from material goods producing industries); and some of these services, such as housework, sewing, and teaching at the nursery and kindergarten level, are to some extent still considered largely "woman's work." Table 3.6 shows female participation rates in selected service industries in the immediate pre-World War II era.

Table 3.6. Participation of German Women in Selected Service Industries 1936

Job	Female, % of total
Midwives	100.0
Cleaning personnel	99.9
Kindergartner; youth leaders	99.8
Household employees	99.4
Seamsters	98.3
Typists, stenographers	95.4
Room-renters	94.3
Restaurant service, incl. kitchen personnel	91.6
Social Service workers	88.8
Sick-care personnel	88.2
Washers and ironers	84.7
Embroiderers	78.9
Sales personnel	77.9
Newspaper deliverers	77.8

Source: <u>Aufstellung des Staatlichen Reichsamtes, 1936.</u> Cited in Menschik, pp. 43-44.

Today, German women in the FRG and the GDR are, as a general rule, legally entitled to hold any job and engage in any vocational activity they desire on an equal basis with men. But, as we have seen in chapter 2, there are some exceptions in both Germanies allegedly aimed at protecting women in general, and mothers in particular, from strenuous or potentially harmful activities. As Lilo Tappendorf, Section Director of the GDR's Central Statistical Administration, so succinctly phrased it: "As a fundamental principle, all occupations are open to girls, except those that are not suited for women."(52)

East and West German women can now be found in all branches of the economy. But even abstracting from the relatively few jobs specifically closed to them by protective legislation, they are still grossly underrepresented in such more "typically male" branches as manufacturing, transportation and communication, and even more so in construction; on the other hand, the percentage of women is disproportionately high in service industries and in commerce and trade. Overall, and in each and every branch, there is a higher percentage of female workers in the GDR than in the FRG. But even in East Germany, there are still preponderantly masculine branches (and subbranches) of the economy, while others are attracting a disproportionately large number of women.

Table 3.7. Female Participation in Selected Branches
of the Economy
1976
(% of total employment in each branch)

	FRG	GDR (without apprentices)
Total, all branches	37.5	49.9
Manufacturing	28.6	38.7
Agriculture and Forestry	51.9[a]	43.0
Construction	8.2	15.4
Transportation and Communication	18.3	37.4
Commerce and Trade	55.3	72.0
Service industries	61.8[b]	72.7

[a] Includes animal husbandry and fisheries.
[b] Does not include credit and insurance where female participation in the FRG is 48.3%.

Sources: Statistical Yearbook, FRG, 1977, p. 94; Statistical Yearbook, GDR, 1977, p. 93.

AT WORK   73

Significant as female participation in broad branches of the economy may be, the difference between "men's" and "women's" work is even more evident in many individual jobs within each branch. Even among present-day trainees for skilled workers' positions,(53) bricklayers, auto mechanics, and carpenters are virtually all men, and textile workers and typists virtually all women. In some kinds of work, for instance in the chemical industry or in data processing, GDR women have a clear advantage over their counterparts in the FRG. But in the truly "male" occupations (such as the above mentioned bricklayers and automobile mechanics), GDR female participation rates, even if several times those of FRG women, have so far remained insignificantly low.

Table 3.8. Female Trainees for Skilled Workers' Positions[a]
(FRG = 1976; GDR = 1977)
(in % of all trainees)

	FRG	GDR
Bricklayers	0.1	0.3
Automobile mechanics	0.1	0.9
Concrete workers	0.1	14.1
Butchers	0.4	35.3[b]
Carpenters	1.0	3.4
Electricians	1.1	7.7
Painters	1.3	3.2
Bakers	1.9	61.0[c]
Communication workers	11.2	28.2
Cooks	13.5	26.4
Workers, chemical industry	21.9	76.0
Data processing specialists	37.8	82.4
Waiters/waitresses	66.4	76.4
Sales personnel	77.3	97.3
Hairdressers	95.3	99.0
Textile workers	96.7	90.7
Typists/stenographers	95.0[d]	99.7
Household employees	100.0	N.A.
Total, all vocations	36.1	47.5

[a] For FRG: all trainees; for GDR: trainees who have successfully completed their skilled worker qualifying examination.
[b] Butchers, meat preparers, meat processors, and, to some extent, animal and meat inspectors.
[c] Includes bakers, confectioners, and pastry cooks.
[d] Percentage of all secretaries and typists actually in labor force (Social Report, No. 1, 1977, p. 7).

Sources: Computed from Statistical Yearbook, FRG, 1978, pp. 345-347; and Statistical Yearbook, GDR, 1978, p. 291.

Specific examples abound to support the statistical evidence in table 3.8 and to illustrate further the perseverance of sex discrimination, so pronounced in the West, but still lingering also in the East, and the gradualness of change, progressing but slowly in the FRG and much more rapidly, but not as fast as desired and hoped for by the leadership, in the GDR.

A June 1978 West Berlin TV report, for instance, showed how hard it is for women to break the sex barrier in technical jobs, in a nation in which almost 99 percent of all engineers are men. Several female applicants for technical "men's jobs" in heavy industry told how they were informed that "this is not a job for a girl"; others reported that they filled out applications for apprenticeships for such jobs and received straight-forward letters in reply, to the effect that the company hired only "boys" for that kind of work. And the overwhelming majority of men in heavy industry admitted frankly that they did not consider "girls" fit for such work.(54) In spite of many female applicants, the West German Lufthansa does not have a single woman pilot, and the head of the airline company's flying school recently commented that a woman was "more likely to become a boxing champion than a chief pilot with Lufthansa."(55) A West German female journalist from Bremen told this author that she could only write on social, church, and other local affairs, but not on national or international events. "For a senator's reception, a woman is not the proper representative for a newspaper," her boss told her.

In a sample of West German institutions of higher learning checked for the purpose, 31 percent of the students in 1974 and 45 percent in 1975 majored in theology. But although 69.8 percent of all low-level service personnel in West Germany's protestant church were female,(56) only 3 percent of the ministers, and not a single one of the deans or church superintendents were women in the fall of 1976.(57) A chemical company in Gelsenkirchen, a district where more than two thirds of the unemployed youths are female, announced in 1978 that, in order to help combat the unemployment problem, it would, <u>for the first time in its history</u>, hire 15 girls for such traditionally male positions as energy-electrotechnician and technical draftsman.(58) Since 1969, West German employment offices are supposed to send applicants to job interviews, irrespective of sex; but in actual practice, women are still sent out for "women's" and men for "men's" jobs.(59) Where women do apply for jobs in "typically male" industries, their applications are often denied on the basis of such flimsy excuses as "we do not have a ladies' restroom here," an excuse which Olaf Sund, Berlin Senator for Labor and Social Problems, labeled "ridiculous."(60)

Employers' associations in West Germany are in general agreement that men are better suited for work that requires strength, knowledge, and responsibility; women, on the other hand, for job assignments that call for manual dexterity and for dull, repetitive work. Extensive tests carried out by employers have allegedly shown that women are much better fit than men for unskilled labor on the assembly line because men are supposedly too creative, always interested in carrying out new ideas, and, therefore, not well suited to cope with such dull, repetitive work. Women, on the other hand, allegedly show definite inclination for such work, are not even interested in periodic changes in job assignments to reduce the monotony, and are "as a rule satisfied with the opportunity of alternating between standing and sitting activity."(61) Indeed, women constitute only slightly more than one third of West Germany's labor force but almost two thirds of the country's 700,000 assembly line workers (although probably primarily because of inadequate education and training — an issue taken up in chapter 4 — and because of discrimination, rather than because of innate character traits). Little wonder, in any case, that, as charged by Irene Maier, Ministerial Adviser to the Federal Ministry of Justice, even during the pre-1975 period of relatively full employment, West German women did not have access to jobs on an equal basis with men. The laws are on the books, and so are Common Market equal-rights guidelines, Ms. Maier said, but they must be given "teeth so they can bite."(62)

In the GDR, by law all enterprises must actively promote the "furtherance" of women. But to provide special training for female employees takes time and money; and official GDR sources acknowledge that there are enterprise managers who hold the view that "emphasis on increased training of female production workers will tend to endanger plan fulfillment" and, therefore, postpone the legally obligatory furtherance of women.(63) At the end of the 1960s, the Berlin Philharmonic Orchestra in Berlin, GDR, did not have a single female member; as late as 1966-67, women could not even audition for it. In the mid-1970s, the first woman violinist joined that orchestra, and things are expected to change gradually over the next ten to fifteen years. But female musicians still find it very difficult to get into the Dresden Philharmonic Orchestra, and very difficult in general to make their way in the GDR in the performing arts as producers, directors, or composers.(64) According to a female editor interviewed by this author in East Berlin, most GDR reporters are men because "they find it easier to travel and to be away from home," while most desk jobs at GDR publishing houses are held by women. As in West Germany, it is next to impossible for women to get ahead in East Germany's church hierarchy; and when, in April 1976, a woman minister became superintendent of the Berlin-Brandenburg church, this was a unique event, celebrated as such by church-going Germans in the GDR.(65) Age-old stereotypes crept into a recent reply given by an editor of an East Berlin newspaper to a question by a reader as to what to do when a buyer discovers that he was given the wrong change. The editor advised that change be counted at the checkout counter and, in case of a shortage, the error be pointed out immediately to the <u>Kassiererin</u> (female cashier); and if the buyer did not get satisfaction, he should then see the <u>Verkaufstellenleiter</u> (departmental sales manager, usually implying that it is a man or, at least, as in English, not giving an indication as to the manager's sex), to request that the cash register be counted.(66) (Interestingly, in one of the major supermarkets in the author's hometown, there is a sign at each cashier's stand that reads: "Please give coupons to the cashier before <u>she</u> rings your order.")

76   WOMEN IN THE TWO GERMANIES

In the FRG, 80 percent of all women are locked into 14 typical women's kinds of jobs.(67) Even among young West German women, over 75 percent of all female apprentices in 1976 were training for but 14 types of jobs, all of them in low-level service positions (for instance, sales girl, attorney's assistant, pharmaceutical assistant, or dental assistant), or in trade.(68) In the GDR, on the other hand, less than half of all working women are in the branches of the economy (trade and services) where traditionally the percentage of women has been largest.(69) Thus, although in both Germanies women still show a preference for and have greater opportunities in traditional "women's jobs" and "women's industries," gradually increasing minorities have been forcing their way into most masculine vocations in the GDR, while in the FRG progress has been much more moderate and slower. The inroads made by GDR women have been particularly impressive in the professions, and percentagewise they have far outstripped those of FRG women. Some of the difference is certainly due to the fact that, as in other areas, so also in the area of accessibility to the professions, the party and the government in the GDR have worked for the furtherance of women virtually from the outset, while in West Germany the initiative had to come primarily from, and the struggle had to be carried on primarily by, the women themselves. Some of the difference can surely also be attributed to the greater emphasis on the education and training of GDR women (a topic taken up in length in chapter 4); and some can perhaps even be accounted for by the example set by the United States for West Germany and by the Soviet Union for the GDR. At the beginning of the 1970s, for instance, only 3.5 percent of all lawyers, 6.5 percent of all physicians, and 2.1 percent of all dentists in the United States were women; while the figures for the USSR were 36, 75, and 83 percent respectively.(70)

Table 3.9. Women's Participation Rate in Selected
Professions Other Than Government

1975-78[a]
(in %)

PROFESSION	FRG	GDR
Physicians	20.2	46.0
Dentists	17.3	45.8
Pharmacists	37.0	61.0
Teachers and educators	52.4	76.0
College and university lecturers (incl. full professors)	0.6	7.0
Lawyers	5.0	30.0

[a] Most figures are for 1977-78; some are for 1975-76.

Sources: Statistical Yearbook, FRG, 1977, p. 362, and 1978, p. 97; Statistical Yearbook GDR, 1977, p. 333; Die Frau in der DDR, pp. 13 and 49; Handelsblatt, July 27/28, 1978.

In West Germany, female teachers are concentrated in lower educational levels. In 1977, for example 63.6 percent of grade and regular high school (Hauptschule) teachers were women; but only 36 percent of Gymnasium teachers and 34.6 percent of vocational school teachers were female.(71) No comparable breakdown by sex is published in the GDR; but observation seems to indicate that there also, the higher up in the teaching profession one goes, the smaller the percentage of female educators seems to be (although at each level, the percentage is probably higher than in the FRG, if for no other reason than because the over-all percentage is so much larger).

Women in Leading Positions in the Economy

In West Germany, few women hold leading positions in any branch of the economy. In the GDR, the situation is somewhat better, but women are still grossly underrepresented in positions of economic power and control.

Estimates of the total percentage of women in leading positions vary, in part because there is no complete agreement as to precisely what constitutes a "leading" position. In a 1976 survey carried out among gainfully employed by West Germany's Federal Statistical Office, two percent of the women and seven percent of the men answered a questionnaire by stating that they held positions of "leadership."(72) Since approximately 37 percent of all gainfully employed in the FRG are women, this would indicate that out of every 10,000 such employees, 441 men and 74 women would consider themselves in "leading" positions. In other words, according to this survey, less than 15 percent of all leadership positions (74 out of a total of every 515) were held by women and over 85 percent by men. But objective studies do not corroborate even as high a percentage of women "leaders" as indicated in this self-evaluation. The Investigative Commission on Women and Society acknowledges that opportunities for the advancement of women to middle-level positions seems to have improved considerably in recent years, but sees no significant change in the sex composition of top positions in the West German economy.(73) Other West German studies conclude that, as of the mid 1970s, in the FRG, only 4.5 percent of all leading positions at the top and secondary levels of business management, and only 2 percent of "really leading positions," are held by women, and that female membership on corporate boards of directors is less than one tenth of one percent.(74) Even in such a branch of the economy as the hotel and restaurant industry where two thirds of all employees are women, the great majority of "bosses" are men.(75) "In our country," commented a leading female employee in a West German mail order house, "all better positions that entail more interesting work and require more independent decision making, more imagination, initiative, and ability to negotiate and to exert oneself are held by men. Women are not thought of as having the necessary character traits."(76) But it should be pointed out that women own a substantial percentage (given in various reports as anywhere between 12 and 25 percent) of West German enterprises. Most of these enterprises are small, and the female owners came by most of them through inheritance.(77)

In the GDR, official sources acknowledge that as late as 1969-70, only one out of every eleven leading positions in industry was held by a woman; that among those employed in GDR industry who had a degree from an institution of higher learning, one out of every three men, but only one out of every seven women held a position of leadership;(78) and that among 10,000 collective farms, the top leadership position was held by a woman in only 129.(79) But five years later, by the mid-1970s, the GDR claimed that one fourth of all leading positions in the economy, and one third in the agricultural sector, were held by women (admitting, however, that still only 183 women held top positions on GDR farms.)(80) West German sources readily concede that GDR women have made substantial inroads into middle and even upper level positions; but they emphasize that in top level positions in the GDR economy, women are still few and far apart.(81) The authors of a recent study on women in the GDR (who readily admit the "immense progress" East German women have made)(82) write:

> In spite of the impressive numbers of furtherance measures, they have not yet succeeded in elevating women to top positions in the party, the government, and the economy. There is obviously a contradiction here between official desires and unofficial obstacles. Although there are laws aimed at furthering women for leading positions, individual superiors obviously have sufficient opportunities to exert their prejudices against women. The self-confidence of women qualified for leading positinos, on the other hand, is not strong enough to withstand these prejudices.(83)

But, the authors maintain, this has been rapidly changing among younger women, and they see a new day dawning in the GDR "where no questions will be asked anymore whether someone is a man or a woman, but merely which of the two is better qualified for the job."(84)

Although numerical sum totals of different types and levels of "leading" positions held by women in the GDR are not readily determinable, considerable progress has been made, especially in recent years. Yet, GDR women still have a way to go before equality with men in positions of power and control will have been attained. To some extent, this situation is indicated by the fact that honors bestowed on meritorious female workers have increased substantially over the years, both in actual numbers and as a percentage of all such honors, but that, in this respect also, the percentage of female recipients is still far below womens' participation rate in the GDR labor force. However, if the drastic increases from 1977 to 1978 are any indication of future trends, women might be catching up with men in the not too distant future.

Table 3.10. Titles of Honor Bestowed on Meritorious Workers GDR

	1960		1977		1978		Women % of Total		
	TOTAL	WOMEN	TOTAL	WOMEN	TOTAL	WOMEN	1960	1977	1978
Hero of Labor	25	4	52	9	74	19	16.7	17.3	25.7
Banner of Labor for Individual[a]	177	16	888	148	1,059	212	9.0	16.7	20.0
Meritorious Activist	597	46	3,561	820	3,678	1,264	7.7	23.0	34.4
Activist of Socialist Labor	96,941	15,059	277,556	111,741	298,692	122,505	15.5	40.3	41.0

[a]Does not include "banner of labor" bestowed on collectives and enterprises.

Source: Computed from Statistical Yearbook, GDR, 1978, p. 104; 1979, p. 104.

Who are the "leading" women in the economy?

In the West where — as a recent newspaper article phrased it — most working women are in typical female roles of "healing, helping, learning." The relatively few who have broken through the barrier and reached leading positions in the professions and the economy come predominantly from middle class families. Except for those who are in business for themselves, most of them "are unmarried, or marry late in life, after their position has been consolidated. As a general rule, they have hired help in the home, and politically they are conservatives."(85)

In the GDR, on the other hand, women in leading positions come from all walks of life; as a rule, they do not have household help (except for an occasional live-in mother or mother-in-law, and that is getting rare, since most of those are now either working or on pension); and they are usually, but not necessarily, loyal party members. Because of the government's and the party's conscious efforts to promote the combination of motherhood and career, East German women, strongly reinforced by society's approval, find it much easier than their West German counterparts to combine family obligations with a successful career.

Several West German career women in high positions told this author that they chose to remain unmarried or at least childless, because they could not successfully have pursued their careers otherwise. But not one single East German woman interviewed by this author expressed such a view.

Why so few women in leading positions?

First, there are age-old traditions and prejudices, broadly referred to these days as "male chauvinism." Strong in the FRG but still lingering in the GDR also, such bias makes it difficult for some men (and even some women) to deem women qualified for leading positions and to accept them as bosses.

In West Germany, a mid-1970s survey among skilled workers, technicians, and middle-level government employees — all under 40 years of age — showed that 39 percent would prefer to work under a male boss and only 7 percent under a woman (the rest were either noncommittal or said they would choose on the basis of criteria other than sex).(86) Among leading executives of German corporations, asked by sociologist Helge Pross whether they thought a woman in their position could do their job equally well, 86 percent said "No." Commented Dr. Pross: "There is the stereotype view that women are good only as secretaries. Because such prejudices are strong, women can't advance; because they can't advance, prejudices remain strong."(87) And where women succeed in getting leading positions, men apparently accept them often only as a token, as an exception.(88) The proprietor of a large company, refusing to hire a qualified woman as his general manager, expressed such a view quite frankly when he said: "I've got one woman at home and two in my outer office. Three's enough."(89)

In numerous interviews, primarily with women, throughout West Germany, this author found such views generally confirmed. Some of the women he talked to would just as readily work under a female as under a male boss; but most of them thought that this did not hold true for the great majority of men (although several acknowledged that things had begun to change, if ever so slowly). "I don't mind working under a woman; as a matter of fact my chairman is a woman," affirmed a male geologist from the Technical University in Berlin. "True," agreed his wife, a free-lance journalist, "but he is the exception. My brother wouldn't even get into a taxi driven by a woman," she added. "Women can't reach high positions primarily because men are the ones who appoint them; and men don't think women are good enough," complained a West Berlin female psychologist. "If men have to work under a female boss," explained a Munich housewife whose husband teaches theology at the University of Munich, "they fear their masculinity is being threatened. My husband used to feel this way also. Now, if he were asked to work under a woman boss, he would at first say 'no'. But he would work it through and eventually accept it, I am sure," she said. "Women are a bit more accepted as bosses nowadays," remarked sociologist Helge Pross, "but men surely don't accept them gladly. And even husbands don't want their wives to hold a position of power and prestige higher than the one they themselves are holding." "A woman as a boss? Not for me," said a Bremen housewife who had worked before she got married. "I had a female boss," she went on, "and she was so mean. No man would ever be like that. Men are always polite with women." "Neither men nor women seem to want to work under a woman boss," said author-editor Gisela Helwig, explaining how she had recently been looking for a secretary, and how several men and women, both, turned down the job when they found out that a woman was in charge. And a female student majoring in Russian and Theology at the Free University of Berlin also commented that she would rather work under a man than under a woman because "there is less likelihood of conflict arising."

In the GDR, the situation seems to be better; but even there, sex prejudice has by no means been wiped out. The very fact that legislation prescribes that women's furtherance plans be incorporated into every enterprise-labor union contract is evidence not only that women are still underrepresented in leading positions but also that laws are necessary to rectify a situation that might otherwise not be corrected, or at least not with all due speed.

A survey taken in the late 1960s among male GDR workers in the energy sector showed that the majority, at least then, would rather work under a male than under a female boss. If a male and a female applicant for the top supervisory position each had minor children at home that needed to be taken care of, over three fourths of the men questioned would opt for the male applicant and only five percent for the woman (most of the rest declaring that either would be acceptable). Even in the theoretical case where the male applicant had several minor children in his household and the woman none, more of the male workers questioned opted for the man than for the woman as a boss.

The survey also broke the male respondents down according to their educational background. Interestingly, but not unexpectedly, the answers showed a greater degree of sex prejudice among the less educated than among those who had graduated from either a vocational school or an institution of higher learning.(90)

Although considerable progress has been made during the 1970s in promoting women to leadership positions in the GDR, male chauvinism still lingers on. "A woman as boss: that is by no means fully accepted yet in the GDR," wrote author-editor Gisela Helwig in the mid-1970s.(91) And personal interviews in the GDR seemed to indicate that Ms. Helwig was probably right. "Men still don't like to see women in leading administrative positions," commented a psychotherapist in East Berlin in 1978. "I could imagine working under a woman, but it would surely feel strange," said a male GDR university student majoring in architecture who worked on construction crews before entering the university. "When I became departmental chairperson," a female economist from the Party School in Berlin confided to this author, "all men but one resigned within a year. They didn't want to work under a woman, and I helped them to find other jobs. Ours is still predominantly a male society, and this will be so for another 150 years," she predicted. "True, there are still some workers who do not want to work under a female boss," admitted Helga Hoerz, chairperson of the Department of Ethics at Humboldt University, Berlin, GDR (and the GDR's representative to the UN Commission on the Status of Women). "But," she went on in a more positive vein, "this is no longer typical. It certainly has no support in our laws, in our party, or in our government."

Male chauvinism and prejudice are not the only reasons for the disproportionately low number of East and West German women who hold positions of leadership in the economy. In both Germanies, working women are also handicapped by having to work a "second shift," as the Soviets call it. In other words, they not only have to bear the children but, for better or for worse, they are also the ones usually burdened with the lion's share of household chores and of tasks connected with the raising and the care of the offspring. In West Germany, moreover, there is also a shortage of child care facilities. For these and other reasons, 83 percent of gainfully employed women in West Germany interrupt their careers for many years; most of those who remain married do not return to work at all.(92) But even if they do, the years of interruption and consequent loss of experience and seniority obviously make them less eligible and less qualified for promotions and positions of leadership than their male counterparts. And the Investigative Commission on Women and Society charges that there are virtually no provisions on the part of West German enterprises to facilitate their re-entry into the job market.(93) More dramatically and bitterly, a recent West German economic weekly complains that "young women in our country are often turned down for jobs because they might get children; older ones, who can't get any children any more, because they are too old."(94) Even if such charges were somewhat exaggerated, they are evidence of a spirit detrimental to whatever aspirations for leading positions West German women might harbor.

In the GDR, working women who become mothers interrupt their work for relatively shorter periods, nowadays usually for a "baby year." When they are ready to return to work they find excellent, free or minimally priced nurseries, kindergartens, and after-school care centers, much more plentiful than in the West, ready to take care of their children; and they can always return to their previous jobs(95) without loss of seniority. Yet, pregnancy, childbirth, and the resulting loss of experience still reduces their opportunities for promotion. When I asked a female GDR director in charge of 800 employees whether she would promote a pregnant woman, she replied: "If a woman in a position of responsibility became pregnant, I would of course keep her. But I would not promote her to such a position while she was pregnant, since I know that she would soon take off for a while." And to make things worse, GDR working women have somewhat fewer amenities such as washers and dryers in their homes than West German women, and fewer "grannies" to help them than before. With GDR husbands still reluctant to assume much of the household burden (an issue taken up in chapter 5), the "second shift" can be a special problem for women in higher positions who cannot always adhere as readily to 9-5 working hours (not to speak of part-time work) as can the lower level workers they supervise.

Finally, German working women, as working women most everywhere else in the world, are on the average less well educated than their male counterparts and are therefore less well qualified to see their aspirations for leading positions materialize. As will be discussed in detail in Chapter 4, the enrollment of West German women in high schools and institutions of higher learning still lags far behind that of men. Even in the GDR, where women of the present generation (particularly those under 30) have been receiving education and training fully comparable to that of men, there are currently still not enough women qualified for high positions. This is so because 20, 25, and 30 years ago, East German women were educationally (and also socially and emotionally) less well prepared than they are nowadays to enter the competitive race with men. But from the ranks of those who graduated from universities and embarked on their careers, then, come most of the candidates for top positions today. Hence, in days to come, the present generation of young GDR working women should find the road to leading positions easier than did their mothers and grandmothers.

GERMAN WOMEN IN PUBLIC LIFE

German women are no longer condemned to political abstinence as they were during the Nazi era; but although their participation in public life is much more extensive in the GDR than in the FRG, they still do not hold any real power in either of the two Germanies that were built on the ashes of the Third Reich.

Women in Elected Government Offices

With the exception of the Scandinavian countries, there are at least fifteen or sixteen men for any one woman in the parliaments of Western European nations. In the United States, there are roughly 30 men in Congress for every one woman (in the U.S. Senate, 96th Session, there is only one woman among the 100 senators). On the other hand, in the Soviet Union (in many respects the model for the GDR), close to one third of the members of the Supreme Soviet, the highest legislative government body, are female — in fact, there are more women in the Soviet Union's Supreme Soviet than in all the parliaments of the Western world together (although it should be pointed out that women are still underrepresented in the upper echelons of the Soviet Union's Communist Party, the real center of power in the USSR).

Table 3.11. Women in Western National Parliaments (1972)

Country	Total number of delegates	Female delegates (number)	Female delegates (percent)
Finland	200	43	21.5
Denmark	179	30	16.8
Sweden	350	49	14.0
Norway	150	15	10.0
F.R.G.	518	30	5.8
Switzerland	200	10	5.0
Austria	183	8	4.4
Great Britain	630	26	4.1
Belgium	212	6	2.8
United States	435	12	2.8
Italy	630	18	2.7
Canada	264	1	0.3
USSR	1,571	475	31.3

Source: Informationen fuer die Frau 1972, No. 9, p. 19. For the USSR, see USSR: People's Well-Being, p. 86.

West Germany's female participation rates in the Bundestag, hovering around 6 to 7 percent in recent years, are higher than those of any other non-Scandinavian, West European country. Still, they show that women play an insignificant part in West Germany's legislative decision making process. And in spite of alleged progress of "woman power," the number of female deputies in the Bundestag was lower in the 1970s than in the preceding two decades; in 1972, the percentage of women delegates was lower even than during the days of the Weimar Republic.

In the GDR, on the other hand, women participated in the first provisionary parliament in 1949 at a rate of more than twice that in the FRG; and the number and percentage of female deputies has increased continuously over the years until today they account for more than one third of the Volkskammer's total membership.

Table 3.12. Female Delegates to the German
National Parliaments
FRG and GDR
1949-1976
(percent of total delegates)

Year	Bundestag FRG	Volkskammer GDR
Both, 1949	7.1	16.1
FRG 1953; GDR 1954	8.8	23.0
FRG 1957; GDR 1958	9.2	23.8
FRG 1964; GDR 1963	9.4	26.5
FRG 1968; GDR 1967	7.9	30.2
FRG 1972; GDR 1971	5.8	31.8
Both, 1976	6.7	33.6

Sources: Zwischenbericht, p. 52; Gast, p. 165; Kurhig, p. 144; Statistical Yearbook/GDR, 1978, p. 427.

In lower legislative assemblies — at state, county, or city levels — the situation is similar: in West Germany only somewhere between 7 and 9 percent, but in East Germany over one third of all deputies and city commissioners are women; nor are matters much different in the case of mayors and judges.

There are also substantial differences between the female deputies to the FRG's and the GDR's national parliaments in respect to their professions and their age distribution. In the early 1970s, over one third of West Germany's female delegates to the Bundestag were housewives, and there was not a single industrial worker, agricultural worker, or student among them. In the GDR's Volkskammer, on the other hand, industrial and agricultural workers and students constituted almost half of the 133 female deputies; and only one woman among them was a "housewife." Moreover, East Germany's female deputies were, on the average, considerably younger than their West German counterparts: almost half of them were under 40, and well over 80 percent under 50 years of age. In West Germany, on the other hand, fully 60 percent were over 50, and well over 80 percent over 40 years of age. And there has not been any significant change since the early 1970s.

Table 3.13. Women in Elected Political Positions
(percent of total)

	FRG	GDR
National Parliament[a]	5.8 (1972)	31.8 (1971)
	6.7 (1976)	33.6 (1976)
Regional deputies[b]	7.5 (1974)	36.0 (1974)
City commissions	8.8 (1971)	34.5 (1974)
Mayors	8.3 (1974)	21.4 (1974)
Judges	10.0 (1976)	36.0 (1976)

[a] Bundestag for the FRG, Volkskammer for the GDR

[b] Landtage (state parliaments) for the FRG; Bezirkstage (district parliaments) for the GDR. (In the GDR, the five state governments and parliaments were abolished in 1952 and replaced by 14 district councils and assemblies – 15 with East Berlin.)

Sources: Sozial Report, Nr. 1, 1977, p. 7; Statkowa, p. 18; Zwischenbericht, p. 52; Kuhrig, p. 144; Statistical Yearbook GDR, 1978, pp. 166; Helwig, Frau '75, p. 98; Lange, Aktuelle Probleme, p. 12.

At first glance, one might get the impression that the relatively high percentage of women in the GDR's legislative assemblies means that East German women carry infinitely greater weight in shaping their country's political future than do their sisters in the West. But this is only true to a very limited extent. In both East and West, the higher up one goes in the political hierarchy, the smaller the percentage of women. An author of a recent book on the political role of women in the GDR summarized her findings by simply stating that "where there is power, there are no women."(96) While this might be a slight, intentional exaggeration, it is true almost everywhere that women in positions of real political power are still few and far apart. But beginnings at least have been made, even in Western Europe. In 1977, there were women in the cabinets of France, Italy, Britain, Austria, Greece, Sweden, and the Netherlands (e.g., Simone Veil, France's Minister of Health; Karin Soden, Sweden's first foreign minister; and Lina Koutzfri, Greece's Undersecretary of Education). In May 1979, Margaret Thatcher (since 1975, Britain's first woman party leader) became Britain's Prime Minister. And in the summer of 1979, Simone Veil became the first president of the Common Market countries' newly elected European Parliament.

Table 3.14. Female Members of the West and East German
National Parliaments by Professions and
Age Groups
(percent of all female members)

By Professions

	Bundestag (FRG) (1972)		Volkskammer (GDR) (1971)
Housewives	36.7	Employed in industry	24.8
Teaching professions	16.6	Agriculture	18.0
Higher public service	13.3	Education	14.3
Commercial and technical employees (non-leading positions)	10.0	Functionaries in mass organizations	7.5
		Service industries	6.0
Social workers	6.7	Arts and science	6.0
Leading employees	3.3	Students	5.3
Physicians	3.3	Commerce and banking	5.3
Lawyers and notaries	3.3	Functionaries in state apparatus	4.5
Assistants in tax matters	3.3	Party Functionaries	3.8
Editors	3.3	Medicine	2.3
		Party veterans	1.5
		Housewives	0.7

By Age Groups

40 and under	13.3[a]	47.3[b]
41-50	23.3	36.8
51-60	60.0	12.8
61 and over	3.3	3.1

[a] 10% under 35; 3.3% 36-40.
[b] 11.3% 21-25; 12.0% 26-30; 24% 31-40.

Sources: Compiled and computed from Zwischenbericht, p. 54; and Gast, pp. 178 and 183.

In West Germany, there were no women in leading positions in Konrad Adenauer's first three post-World War II governments. In his fourth government, there was a female minister, Elizabeth Schwarzhaupt; but West Germany had no female parliamentary state secretary prior to 1969. Subsequently, Annemarie Renger became the first female president of Parliament from 1972 to 1976 and Marie Schlei the first female state secretary in the Federal Chancellor's office.(97) By the mid-1970s, there were some women in high public and governmental offices (e.g., Dr. Hildegard Bartels, President of the Federal Statistical Administration; Dr. Inge-Lohre Baehre, President of the Federal Supervisory Office for Credit; Dr. Liselotte Hoehborn, Chief of the Central Employment Office; Liselotte Funcke, a Vice President of the Parliament; Marie Schlei, until 1977, Minister for Developmental Aid; and Antje Huber replacing Katerina Focke as Minister of Health in Chancellor Helmut Schmidt's Cabinet.(98)) But not only were women in high public and government positions few and far apart; even those who held such positions, had often very limited powers. The post of President of Parliament, for instance, is mainly ceremonial, and the President's main duty consists of seeing to it that members of Parliament remain civil while haranguing one another – and even this job reverted to a man, Karl Carstens, in December, 1976. Antje Huber as Minister of Health is not even in charge of the country's vast health insurance program; that is the business of the Minister of Labor, who is a man.(99) In all, in the mid-1970s, only 16.1 percent of all full-time government employees were women; among higher ranking officials such as chief clerks (counsellors) at federal ministries (Ministerialraete) only 2.4 percent were women; and at the top echelon of civil service employees (beamtete Staatssekretaere), there were no women at all.(100)

In the GDR, the percentage of women in the top echelons of government, of the civil service, and on the country's political councils is also still negligible.(101) In the mid-1970s, there was only one woman in the East German cabinet, party chief Erich Honecker's wife Margot who served as minister of education.(102) Between 1950 and the mid-1970s, the GDR's council of ministers varied in membership between 22 and 42; but there were never more than three, and usually no more than one or two women on it. The council's presidium, with 13 to 16 members, had a single woman only between 1964 and 1968. Even among deputy ministers, increasing in number from 14 in 1954 to 116 in the 1970s, there were never more than four, and usually only one or two women.(103) In 1975, there were three female deputy ministers in the GDR – Herta Koenig in the Ministry of Finance, Anneliese Toedtmann in the Ministry of Health, and Erika Lieberwirth in the Ministry for Light Industry. Even in the diplomatic corps of the recently established GDR Embassy in Washington there was in November 1979 only one single woman, the embassy's cultural attache Petra Teutschbein.

At lower levels of executive power, about 18 percent of smaller communities' city commissions were headed by a woman in the early 1970s; but only 11.5 percent of the city commissions of larger cities, less than 2 percent of county commissions, and not a single one of the

15 district commissions had a female chairperson.(104) The relatively high and rising proportion of women at all levels of the GDR's elected assemblies (tables 3.12 and 3.13) is of much less importance than it would be if it were that high in the West because in the GDR, as in all socialist countries, the real center of political power and decision making lies not in legislative assemblies, nor even in the government's executive branch, but in the leadership bodies of the Party — in East Germany's case, the SED (<u>Sozialistische Einheitspartei Deutschland's</u>), the country's Socialist Unity Party.

Women in Political Parties

In the mid-1970s, women made up close to one third of the SED's total membership of about two million. But the female membership of the Party's Central Committee hovers around 13 percent and has not changed significantly over the years. And no woman has ever been a full member of the Party's all-powerful politburo, although, in 1978 there were two female non-voting candidate members, Inge Lange and Margarete Mueller. Since the Tenth Party Congress in October 1973, Inge Lange has also been secretary of the Central Committee; but she is currently the only woman to hold this position of power in the Party's hierarchy, and she and the now deceased Edith Bauman have been the only two female CC secretaries in the Party's history.(105) The principle "the higher up, the fewer women" shows itself at the Party's district organization level also. Women normally constitute over 40 percent of the total number of candidates (consulting functions only) for the Party's district leadership, less than 25 percent of the leadership's full membership (voting power), and less than 5 percent of the leadership's secretariat (extensive decision making power), a percentage actually lower than in the 1950s and early 1960s; and there have never been any female first secretaries in SED district leadership secretariats.(106) (Candidate membership, by the way, is not an automatic stepping stone to full membership. Some candidates are not reelected at all, others are reelected as candidate members, and only a minority of candidates is subsequently elected to full-membership).

In West Germany, there is no "ruling party" in the sense in which the SED rules in the GDR. Parties assert their power only through their elected representatives and through their appointees to governmental offices. Yet, West German women are fully aware that, as in other Western democracies, the road to political potency in the FRG passes through the structure of the established political parties.

In spite of some increases in numbers, women are still outnumbered by men better than 4 to 1 in the membership of the two major political parties (the very moderately socialist SPD and the conservative CDU), as well as in the secondary parties (the liberal FDU and the CDU's super-conservative sister-party in Bavaria, the CSU). And, as is to be expected, they account for a very small part of important party positions. In 1976, there were only three or four women on each of the

Table 3.15. Female Members and Female Candidate Members of the SED Central Committee (1950-1971), GDR

	Members and Candidate Members			Members			Candidate Members		
Year	Total	Women	Women as % of total	Total	Women	Women as % of total	Total	Women	Women as % of total
1950	81	11	13.6	51	8	15.7	30	3	10.0
1954	135	18	13.3	91	9	9.9	44	9	20.5
1958	155	21	13.5	111	11	9.9	44	10	22.7
1963	181	20	11.0	121	15	12.4	60	5	8.3
1967	181	22	12.2	131	16	12.2	50	6	12.0
1971	189	25	13.2	135	18	13.3	54	7	13.0

Source: From the minutes of SED Party Congresses: 3rd Party Congress, Vol. II, p. 186; 4th Party Congress, Vol. II., p. 1082; 5th Party Congress, Vol. II, p. 1031; 6th Party Congress, Vol. II, p. 494; 7th Party Congress, Vol. II, p. 288. Neues Deutschland, June 20, 1971, p. 4. As summarized in Gast, Table 12, p. 100.

parties' governing bodies (between 7 and 12 percent of these ruling bodies' membership) and only one to four women in the leadership of the parties' parliamentary delegations (between 5 and 14 percent of the total).

Table 3.16. Female Participation in the 15 SED
District Leadership Secretariats (1949-1971), GDR

SECRETARIES

	Total	Women	Women as % of total	First Secretary Total	Women
1949-50[a]	54	8	14.8	6	0
March 1956	90	7	7.8	15	0
June 1958	92	6	6.5	15	0
June 1960	98	6	6.1	15	0
June 1962	95	4	4.2	15	0
February 1963	75	0	0	15	0
June 1964	75	0	0	15	0
February 1967	90	3	3.3	15	0
March 1967	90	3	3.3	15	0
June 1969	90	4	4.4	15	0
May 1971	90	4	4.4	15	0

[a]Secretaries of SED Land (state) leadership and of Berlin, GDR.

Source: Gast, Table 8, p. 85.

Why Fewer German Women than Men in Politics?

In its November 1976 report the FRG-parliament-appointed Investigative Commission on Women and Society discussed in some length the impediments to more active female participation in West German political life, among them primarily:(107)

1. lingering prejudice that holds that "politics is 'man's business'" (women are made to feel unfeminine if they try to find their way into politics).

Table 3.17. Women in Major West German Political Parties

Membership
(women as percent of total)

	SPD	CDU	FDP	CSU
1976	19.9%	18.5%	19.1%	11.1%
1970	17.3	13.6	15.0	10.0

Party Leadership

	SPD			CDU			FDP			CSU		
	Total	Women n	Women %	Total	Women n	Women %	Total	Women n	Women %	Total	Women n	Women %
Parliamentary Delegations 1974	242	16	6.6%	186	15	8.1%	42	3	7.1%	48	1	2.1%
Leadership of Parliamentary Delegations 1976[a]	30	4	13.3	43	2	4.7	7	1	14.3			
Party Governing Bodies 1976	36	3	8.3	33	3	9.1	33	4	12.1	44	3	6.8

[a] CDU/CSU combined totals listed under CDU.

Sources: Compiled and computed from Zwischenbenicht, p. 27; Helwig, Frau '75, p. 96.

2. the division of roles between men and women (it is "woman's job" to take care of home and family and she must not let outside activities interfere with it).
3. the usual types of low-level jobs held by working women (attendance at meetings and involvement in political activities is a liability for most working women, but the same is often an asset for men in their chosen professions).
4. inadequate job opportunities to acquire leadership qualifications (women are cashiers and secretaries rather than departmental supervisors).
5. school, job, and family experiences (they are such as to make women less interested in, as well as less prepared for, politics than men).
6. the prevailing male dominated power structure in political parties (all historical experience shows that privileged power positions are never surrendered voluntarily).

As a result of such discouraging hurdles, many West German women have become extremely frustrated. Some women interviewed by this author in the FRG strongly advocated that members of their sex become more involved in the political process. But the majority virtually threw up their hands in despair, telling of their experiences when they tried to become active in party work, of being asked to organize garden parties or to keep books, of men being willing to accept perhaps a token woman or two in an official capacity but not ready to make concessions beyond that. "A few years back, I tried to engage in party work; but all they let me to was distribute leaflets. They use women only as an adjunct working force," said a female journalist, venting her resentment. "Why should women become more involved politically? The energy input does not pay. Women do the campaigning, but the men get elected," charged a woman lawyer who for 20 years had been a relatively influential member of the SPD. "In theory, our social-democratic party believes in equal rights. But in practice, it's still male-dominated, and we have to fight them all the way," said the State chairperson of the SPD study group for social-democratic women in Bremen. "In some places, such as Berlin or Hamburg, the FDP is even more liberal than the SPD. Women have few problems rising at <u>local</u> levels. But higher up, it is extremely difficult for a woman to even get nominated for an elected office," complained a female psychologist. "In fifty years: maybe, but not now," was the comment of a Cologne translator (Dutch into German) who in 1975 had been commissioner for women's affairs under the prime minister for North Rhine-Westphalia. She had resigned in disgust when she found all doors closed, "partly because I was a woman and partly because of the improvements in the position of women I wanted to achieve. What's the use?" she went on. "My party, the SPD, talks about equality. But in 200 election districts, they nominated only 8 women as candidates for office – and, of course, not all of those got elected." And the aforementioned vice president of the FRG parliament, Liselotte Funcke, said in the summer of 1978 that she felt that West Germany's "young women, 20 to 25 years of age, are less politically motivated today than those ten years ago."

In the GDR, a woman would occasionally make a statement to this author that "this is still a man's world, even in the GDR." A female professor of jurisprudence at the University of Leipzig charged that "women still have to prove themselves more, even in our country"; and an East German psychologist explained that because women still carry the major burden of household chores and of child raising, they "don't have enough time for politics." Yet, overall, GDR women seem content and even proud of the progress they have made in the political arena. They know that "women's furtherance" is the government's and the Party's openly declared (and at least partially achieved) goal; and they are told continuously of the GDR leadership's attempts to awaken women's interests, to make them participate actively in political life, and to help them overcome the lingering prejudice that "politics is man's business." No wonder GDR women seem less concerned than their counterparts in the West with their still junior role in the political decision making process, and in general more confident that remaining discriminatory practices will be rectified with all due speed, in the not too distant future.

Women in Labor Unions

In West Germany, in the mid-1970s, only about 18.4 percent of working women, as compared with some 40 percent of working men, belonged to labor unions.(108) Female union membership has been on the rise in the FRG, constituting 15.3 percent of total membership in 1970, 17.8 percent in 1975, and 18.8 percent in 1977; but it is still only fractionally higher than during the decade of the 1950s when it varied between 17 and 17.4 percent.(109) Toward the end of the 1970s, the percentage was still barely half that of women's participation rate in the FRG's labor force. And West Germany's labor union leadership is predominantly male; there are very few women in low level leadership positions, yet fewer at high and top leadership levels.

Table 3.18. Women in Responsible DGB[a] Positions
FRG, Dec. 1974

Chairpersons	Number of men	Number of women	Women as % of total
at Kreis (county) level	225	4	1.7
at Landes (state) level	26	1	3.7
at Bundes (federal) level	8	1	11.1
Representatives at DGB National Congress[b]	478	34	7.1

[a] Deutscher Gewerkschaftsbund - German Trade Union Federation
[b] Hamburg, 1975

Source: DGB Geschaeftsbericht, pp. 44 and 46.

In the GDR, on the other hand, some 95 or 96 percent of all working women, and about the same percentage of working men, belong to the FDGB (Freier Deutscher Gewerkschaftsbund – Free German Labor Union Federation), the country's all encompassing labor union;(110) and actually slightly over half of all union members are women.(111) In 1972, women also constituted 49.2 percent of trade union functionaries; and at the 8th Congress of the FDGB, 113 women were elected to the union's executive committee, its highest leadership body, which made the executive committee's sex distribution 47 percent female and 53 percent male.(112) By 1975, women were reported to hold over half of all leadership positions in the GDR's labor union structure, including 53.9 percent at the enterprise level, and 48.2, 47.8, and 47.0 percent on governing bodies at the county, district, and federal levels respectively.(113)

There can be no doubt that GDR women play a much larger role in their country's labor union than do West German women in theirs. But it should be pointed out that East and West German unions are very different organizations. In the FRG, labor unions, similar to those in the United States, represent their members' interests against the industry's owners, and bargain collectively with management. In the GDR, as also in the Soviet Union, labor unions do not represent the interests of any particular group of workers against the "employer" since, by definition, the employer is "the workers' state." The labor union can initiate labor legislation and make its voice heard for or against laws directly affecting labor; it represents the workers in valid disputes with the managers (who also belong to the union, if they want to join). Among other social functions, it is in charge of many of the country's social welfare measures and institutions; and it plays a significant role in helping to superintend the implementation of the central plan at the enterprise level. Thus, East Germany's labor union is in some respects the representative of individual workers' interests (it would, for instance, defend a female worker's valid complaint if she had been discriminated against by the enterprise director, in violation of GDR law); but in other respects, it is an arm of the state whose interests are seen as identical with the interests of the workers themselves. Yet, although the general structure and purposes of labor unions might not be the same in the two Germanies, women's participation rates in union membership and in leadership positions is, nevertheless, a significant difference in the status of women in the two societies.

EQUAL PAY FOR EQUAL WORK?

The opportunity to earn incomes equal to those of men is of fundamental importance for the independence, the self-esteem, and the dignity of women, and for the equality of the sexes on the job market in general. Yet, as everywhere else, the income of working women in Germany has traditionally been lower than that of their male counterparts – even for equal or equivalent work.

One of the first female doctoral dissertations in Germany, submitted in 1906 by Alice Salomon at the University of Leipzig, addressed itself to the "Reasons for Unequal Remuneration for Men and Women." Among them, the doctoral candidate listed primarily:(114)

1. Women, as a rule, intend to work only temporarily, until marriage enables them to assume fully their role as wives and mothers; they are, therefore, more readily willing to accept wages which, otherwise, would be less than satisfactory.
2. Men are the primary breadwinners and must, therefore, earn higher wages.
3. Men have larger physical and intellectual needs than women and must, therefore, earn more.
4. Women, as wives, cannot legally choose their place of residence which often forces them to forego higher paying jobs.

The first two of the reasons are still accepted today, three quarters of a century later, among a substantial, although declining, section of West Germany's female population, but, as has been shown, are generally rejected in the GDR. The third reason (men have greater needs) would now find little support, East or West. As to the last reason, women in both German states certainly have as much right as men to choose their place of residence; but, in actual practice, they choose as a general rule to live and work in the cities or towns where their husbands are employed. This is not exclusively the direct result of the traditional male-female division of roles. It often also makes economic sense. Obviously, where there is only one income earner, that spouse's job will be a determining factor in the location of the family residence — and where there is only one, it is virtually always the man. Where both husband and wife work, job opportunities for the spouse who earns the higher income and who has the greater chances for professional advancement will tend to have the greater economic impact — and, more often than not, this again would be the husband, especially in the FRG but to a somewhat lesser degree also in the GDR. (An exception could be the case where a somewhat lower income for a husband would be more than compensated for by an increased income for the wife, thus making their combined income higher.) Hence, as one female author writing on West Germany recently phrased it, "the woman earns less and is therefore less mobile; and because she is less mobile she earns less."(115)

In 1949, women working in the private sector of the West German economy earned, on the average, only about half as much as men; by 1960, the difference had narrowed to 40 percent. Since then, the situation has improved further, but in the mid-1970s the discrepancy was still around 34 percent.(116) Even women who are able to reach "leading" positions, have an income 20 to 30 percent below that of their male counterparts;(117) and on the average, female managers earn DM 8,000 less per year than their male colleagues.(118)

In 1976, gross <u>hourly</u> wages of female industrial workers in West German industry were 72.4 percent of those of their male counterparts — higher in some branches and lower in others, and overall a slight improvement over 1975 and 1974, when they were 72.3 and 71.3 percent respectively.(119) However, since in the FRG a much larger percentage of women than of men work part-time only, the percentage difference in monthly income is considerably greater. In 1978, over half of all gainfully employed women, but only 12 percent of all gainfully employed men, in West Germany had monthly net incomes of DM 1,000 of less; however, at the upper end of the scale one out of every five working men, but only one out of every 29 working women netted DM 2,200 or more per month. With unemployment in the latter part of the 1970s particularly heavy among working women, no drastic improvements should be expected in the near future.

Table 3.19. Average Gross Income of Gainfully Employed Selected Branches, FRG 1978

A. Hourly Wage

	(DM) Men	Women	Women's as % of men's
Industry	12.52	9.13	72.9
Food Industry	11.80	8.25	69.9
Textile Industry	10.80	8.76	81.1

B. Average Monthly Gross Income

	Clerical Employment			Technical Employment		
	(DM)		Women's as %	(DM)		Women's as %
	Men	Women	of men's	Men	Women	of men's
Industry, commerce credit and insurance	2,805	1,912	68.2	3,214	2,167	67.4
Industry	3,072	2,117	68.9	3,261	2,201	67.5
Capital Goods Industry	3,155	2,135	67.7	3,271	2,125	65.0
Consumer Goods Industry	2,925	1,913	65.4	2,956	2,094	70.8
Food Industry	2,860	2,017	70.5	3,109	2,105	67.7
Commerce Credit and Insurance	2,621	1,799	68.6	2,683	1,888	70.4

Source: <u>Statistical Yearbook</u>/FRG, 1979, pp. 451, 457, and 458.

Table 3.20. Monthly Net Income of Gainfully Employed[a]
(percent)
FRG 1978

Income Bracket (DM)	Men and Women % of all Gainfully Employed	Men % of All Men	Women % of All Women
Under 600	12.9	7.2	23.1
600-800	5.8	1.4	13.9
800-1,000	8.0	3.4	16.4
1,000-1,200	12.3	10.2	16.0
1,200-1,400	14.7	16.3	11.8
1,400-1,800	21.2	27.0	21.2
1,800-2,200	11.0	14.6	4.5
2,200-2,500	4.3	5.9	1.5
over 2,500	9.8	14.1	2.0

[a]Excludes (a) 1,576,000 gainfully employed who are self-employed in agriculture, (b) family members who merely "help out," in all branches of the economy, and (c) 885,000 "working people" who either gave no information about their income or had no income in 1978.

Source: Statistical Yearbook, FRG, 1979, p. 97.

The discrepancy of earning necessarily reflects itself also in the pension incomes of the elderly. In 1974, 10.8 million West German senior citizens (6.2 million women and 4.6 million men) lived predominantly off their pensions. Among them, over two thirds of the male, but only 4 percent of the female pensioners had a monthly income of DM 600 or more; and the average pension income of women lagged far behind that of men.(120) Consequently, a much larger percentage of elderly women have been in need of public assistance. In 1974, for instance, 88 out of every 1,000 women, as compared with 45 out of every 1,000 men, 65 years or older were on welfare in West Germany.(121)

But all statistical evidence showing that the average take-home pay of West German women (or even their average hourly wage) is well below that of male workers may not be sufficient per se to prove wage discrimination. After all, if women are indeed less educated, less well trained, and less mobile than men, and if they are less willing or able to take on full-time jobs, they can hardly be expected to earn as much on the average as do men. Therefore, apart from the problem of equal accessibility to higher paying jobs (an issue discussed earlier in this chapter), the important question might well be whether or not West German women are receiving the same pay as men for equal or for comparable work.

Prior to the mid-1950s, there were in West Germany special "women wage categories" (Frauenlohngruppen) which provided for discriminatorily low wages for women. Numerous collective bargaining agreements spelled out that for any given job, "the wages of female employees are to be lower than those of men by x percent." In the mid-1950s, the usual reduction from the standard wage was between 4 and 15 percent.(122) In 1951, the Federation of German Employers' Associations had a legal opinion prepared to clarify whether the equal rights provision of the German constitution implicitly decreed equal pay for equal work, irrespective of sex. The "legal opinion" concluded that Art. 3 of the Constitution applied only to the relationship between citizen and state and that it was not applicable to wage settings and wage agreements in the private sector.(123) When in the mid-1950s, the courts held that the equal rights clause in the Constitution means that for equal work men and women must everywhere receive equal pay (see chap. 2), the women wage categories were abolished, with the full support of the labor unions. But they were merely replaced by the so-called "light wage categories" (Leichtlohngruppen), to this very day still the lowest paying wage categories in many collective bargaining agreements. Typically characterized as encompassing "light," "the lightest," "simple," or "the simplest" types of jobs, or jobs that entail "minimal physical exertion," or "minimal requirements," these wage categories are presumably applicable to both male and female workers. But in practice, work and wage categories are so defined that virtually all workers in the "light wage categories" are women. "In fact, the 'women wage categories' have continued to exist in the form of 'light wage categories,'" a female labor union executive charged recently.(124) Thus, although West Germany's Constitution (as interpreted by the courts) mandates equal pay for equal work, the trouble is that, more often than not, women do not perform exactly the same kind of work as men; what is therefore needed, equal rights advocates argue, is equal pay for comparable work. But this issue needs further explanation.

In collective bargaining agreements in West Germany, the representatives of labor and management settle on certain wage categories. Individual jobs are then classified under these wage categories on the basis of agreed upon criteria. In the case of unskilled and semi-skilled jobs in particular, the most important criterium is physical strength. (In skilled and professional jobs, education and degree of "responsibility" are major factors in wage category classifications.) Thus, "easy" and "simple" jobs are classified under wage categories 1 or 2, or at best under wage category 3, while jobs that call for hard physical labor are generally classified under categories 4 or 5, commanding considerably higher wages. But most of these latter positions are staffed by men, partly because the average women still have less physical strength, and partly also because "protective" laws exclude female workers from many "strenuous" and "hazardous" jobs (see chap. 2). Women in industrial employment, on the other hand, hold primarily jobs that require manual dexterity, precision, concentration, patience, and continuous exposure to repetitive and monotonous tasks (such as work on the assembly line). But these kinds of skills and stresses are given minimal consideration in the definition of wage categories. In the mid-1970s, the FRG government ordered a "scientific study" on proper criteria for job evaluations in West German industry. Although the study recommended that such job requirements as the ones mentioned above be evaluated equally to requirements for physical exertion,(125) it could do no more than provide suggested guidelines to the private sector of West Germany's unplanned economy.

As we have seen, men predominate in certain sectors of West Germany's economy (e.g., heavy industry), while in others the great majority of jobs is held by women (e.g., food processing); and even within each industry, some jobs are predominantly "male" and others largely "female" jobs. Hence, those who want to see equality of pay irrespective of sex achieved in the FRG demand that provisions for "equal pay for equal work," be expanded to include also "equal pay for comparable work."(126) Not only has progress in this direction so far been minimal, but even the constitutional mandate for equal pay for equal work has not yet been fully implemented. As an example, a 1976 international survey of several professions by the International Labor Office attested that among West German workers working on book binding machines, women received between 10 and 20 percent less than men for the same kind of work performed.(127) And the constitutional principle of equal pay for equal work is also frequently circumvented by subterfuges. A recent West German survey showed, for instance, that in a factory making kitchen furniture, both men and women were employed on the assembly lines to drill holes into cabinet doors; but women were in pay groups 1 and 2, and men were classified in pay groups 4 and 5, earning on the average 30 percent more. The official reason given for the discrepancy was that "the men drill holes into heavier and bigger doors."(128) In the case of a similarly discriminatory policy at a plant engaged in the production of radios and TV sets, a male shop steward quite frankly justified the basically illegal practice of differential pay on the grounds that "men are usually the breadwinners in their families while women are merely supplementing the family incomes."(129)

At a recent convention of the (West) German Trade Union Federation, it was charged that employers in the private sector of West Germany's economy, "for material as well as socio-political reasons, have so far put up the strongest opposition to the realization of the constitutional mandate" that provides for equal pay irrespective of sex.(130) West Germany's labor union movement itself has often and loudly proclaimed its full support of wage equality; yet, in spite of its undeniable verbal support, it has certainly not made an all-out effort. There is, for instance, not a single case on record of a German labor union ever having threatened a strike to achieve equal pay for women.(131) "Our labor unions give lip service to equal rights for women," sociologist Helge Pross told this author, "but their actions speak louder than their words. They have done nothing to abolish the light wage categories which, <u>de facto</u>, are exclusively for women workers."

By the mid-1970s, it had become clear that women workers would have to take legal action if equal pay for women was ever to become a reality in the FRG. To this end, Annemarie Renger, until the fall of 1976 president and thereafter a vice president of the West German parliament, called again and again on underpaid female workers to bring suit and, if necessary, carry the case all the way to the Federal Labor Court. She received literally thousands of letters from women who claimed to be discriminated against; but, incredible as it may seem, she was unable for years to find a single one willing to take court action.(132) Women are afraid of losing their jobs if they initiate litigation, Ms. Renger explained, pointing as an example to one of the letters in which a woman wrote her: "I know that the gentlemen earn more than I do. So I asked my boss to rectify the situation. Instead, he fired me."(133) "Where I work, women complain all the time," an unskilled female worker employed in a West Berlin paper and printing plant told this author. "But when someone tries to take up their battle, and when management then asks them what's wrong, they whisper: 'I didn't say anything,' and look away. They are afraid."

At long last, in the spring of 1978, Irene Einemann, a female baker's assistant in the North German city of Delmenhorst, filed suit demanding that her pay be brought up to the level of her male colleagues and won the case. Her wage was raised from the previous DM 6.86 per hour to DM 8.24 per hour, plus an additional supplement of DM 100 her male counterparts were earning also, and the decision was made retroactive, with back pay due her as of January 1, 1976.(134) Commented syndicated newspaper commentator Tatjana Pawlowski:

> Injustice cannot be overcome if justifiable criticism limits itself to complaining. . . .
>
> Who, until now, would have had the courage to oppose the long-established wage policies of many industrial enterprises? The women themselves were usually much too set in their roles of weak, subdued beings, devoid of self-confidence.
>
> But now? Women are hearing the signal. The first shot has apparently been fired in the final round of the world-wide struggle for equal rights. The risk seems to be much smaller than had been assumed — this, Irene Einemann's example proves. Yet, there are surely some risks involved, especially at a time when the specter of unemployment casts its spell on everyday life.
>
> But the advance guard is not alone. Behind it stand such personalities as Annemarie Renger . . . awaiting the day when women will no longer put up with discrimination.

This much, in any case, is certain: the lawmakers have created the foundation for equality; but it is up to the women themselves to stand up for their rights and play their part.(135)

"That baker has set an example that will be a model throughout West Germany," Liselotte Funcke told this author a month after the court's landmark decision. But so far in West Germany, as one labor union representative recently phrased it, "for the overwhelming majority of female workers, equal pay is yet to be achieved."(136)

In the GDR, legal provisions for "equal pay for equal work" date back to the days of Soviet military administration in the immediate postwar era. Unfortunately, the GDR has neither published nor even compiled separate wage and income figures for men and women since the 1960s ("one of the best kept secrets in the GDR," a recent study called it,(137)) so that de facto wage equality cannot be readily proven or disproven statistically. Under the law, GDR women are guaranteed equal pay for equal work. The provision is certainly fully supported by all state and party organizations, and this author has not encountered any allegation that it is being violated in the GDR. However, this does not mean that GDR women actually earn as much on the average as their male counterparts, since in the GDR also, a greater percentage of women than of men work in lower-paying industries and hold lower-paying jobs in each industry. The last usable official table on women's wages in the GDR was published in 1968 and dealt with wages in industry in 1962. It showed that 80 percent of all working women, as compared with 30 percent of men, were then in the lower four of East Germany's eight wage categories.(138)

Because of the labor shortage, the continuous, conscious, efforts to "further" women, the ever-increasing educational qualifications of women, and also because of the abolition of private property and of its concomitant personal interest of employers in paying lower wages, sex-based wage differentials in the GDR are surely now much smaller, on the average, than in West Germany;(139) but there are differences nevertheless. A law professor at the University of Leipzig told this author that she did not know of a single case where a woman in East Germany was paid less for the same work than a man; but she readily acknowledged that branches of industry, and jobs within each branch, that require hard physical labor tend to command higher wages; and, she admitted, women hold few such jobs. On the average, for instance, construction jobs (held mostly by men) pay some 20 percent more than jobs in trade and commerce (where the majority of employees are women).(140) Workers in heavy industry earn considerably more than those in light industry (about 50 percent of all female, but only 26 percent of all male industrial workers are employed in the textile, food processing, and light industry in general).(141) In metallurgy, the highest paying of all GDR branches of industry, only 25 percent of all employees are female; and industry as a whole pays more than the service sectors of the economy which employ 75 percent of all women with college degrees or vocational training.(142) Moreover, as we have seen, there is still a preponderance of men in leading, and therefore high-paying, positions in the GDR. Add to this that a substantial number of women (but few men) hold part-time positions only, and it will come as no surprise that even in the GDR, the take-home pay of female workers is on the average still well below that of their male colleagues.

Since the 1960s, the FDGB has been working on proposals for a revision of the entire remuneration structure for East Germany. New wage calculations are to evaluate more highly such "typically female" characteristics as manual dexterity and precision, as compared with mere physical strength. Upward wage revisions in the predominantly female-staffed trade and health sectors that took effect in 1974 are steps in the right direction; but the revamping of the wage structure as a whole is still in the discussion and drawing-board stage.(143)

Overall male-female wage differentials are certainly smaller in East than in West Germany, and are likely to continue diminishing. But, at this time, the sectors in the GDR economy that employ the most women still carry the lowest pay scales.

AND WHAT TO DO WITH THE CHILDREN?

If German mothers are to have an opportunity to accept productive outside employment, their children must be properly cared for. Unless there are "built-in" or readily-available, competent baby-sitters, this necessitates a network of low-priced nurseries and kindergartens. Moreover, since in both the FRG and the GDR most elementary schools are operated on a morning-only, half-day basis, there is also a need for day-camp type, after-school facilities for younger school age children.

Child Care Facilities: Availability and Cost

In West Germany, child care facilities for children under 3 and after-school child care centers for young school-age children are extremely scarce. Day nurseries are a rarity in small communities and rural areas; not even in most larger cities is there one in each city district.(144) Labor unions complain that they have hardly been expanded at all in recent years;(145) and they are attended by less than 1.5 percent of West German children in the under-3 age group. Even counting all facilities for prekindergarten children, including infant care homes and other institutions where they can be housed and spend nights also, there is barely 1 for every 15 children under 3 years of age. And after-school child care centers, generally operated for children in grades 1 through 4, cannot even accommodate one such young elementary school child in 33 on school day afternoons.

The number of kindergarten places for West German preschoolers above 3, on the other hand, has increased rapidly during the 1970s and, by 1976, there was one place for every two children in that age group, probably sufficient to meet the demand of middle and upper income families. But, a recent survey has indicated, the lower the parents' income and the greater the need for both to be gainfully employed, the smaller is the likelihood that their children will find an acceptable kindergarten place. This is so because the great majority of West German kindergartens are not public institutions; hence, many of them are rather expensive or are organized cooperatively, requiring that each mother assist on a part-time basis in taking care of the children – a requirement often impossible for working mothers to meet.(146) As the number of kindergarten places continues to increase, this situation can be expected to improve (and to some degree, it has improved already). But in the meantime, in rural areas in particular, most kindergartens are still operated on a morning-only, half-day basis(147) – of but limited help to families where both parents need to hold full-time jobs or to single parents in similar financial situations.

Table 3.21. Places Available in West German Child Care Facilities
(As % of all children in respective age group)

	1973	1974	1975	1976
All child care facilities for prekindergartners[a]	6.4	6.6	7.0	7.2
Day nurseries[b]	0.9	1.3	1.3	1.4
Kindergartens[c]	39.6	43.5	48.3	52.2
School-attached kindergartens[d]	2.3	2.6	2.9	3.0
After-school child care centers, grades 1 to 4[e]	2.3	2.6	2.7	3.0

[a]Includes day nurseries for children under 3 as well as different facilities where children under 3 are also housed overnight, such as infant care homes, and special "observation" homes.

[b]For children under 3.

[c]For preschoolers, 3 and over, computed as percentage of children 3 to 6 plus 9/12 of children in the 6 to 7 year age bracket. (This method has been used to keep percentages comparable with GDR figures where kindergarten attendance percentages are computed in this manner.)

[d]Kindergartens attached to regular schools and therefore definitely school preparatory. Mostly for children 6 years old who are not quite ready for school. However, percentages computed as for all kindergartens above.

[e]Computed as percentage of all children 6 to 10. (Difference from children actually enrolled in grades 1 to 4 is minimal and would lower the percentage figures very slightly.)

Sources: Statistical Yearbooks, FRG, 1974-1978. Computed from enrollment figures and population tables, broken down by age. (Earlier yearbooks give number of institutions but not number of places available.)

In an effort to help the mothers of hundreds of thousands of West German infants and young preschoolers who have been unable to place them in appropriate day care centers, West Germany has launched a controversial, social security financed, "day mother" program. First tested in 1974 in the Stuttgart area, the program has met with the opposition of some West German psychologists and child behavior specialists, such as Cologne's Dr. Emil Schmalohr and Freiburg University's Bernhard Hassenstein, who hold that very young children, especially under two, should not be exposed to the shock of even temporary daily separation from one single "person of reference," generally the mother. For similar reasons, such separation has drawn vehement criticism from conservative Christian Democrats and from the churches. Women liberationists have also opposed the program because, they charge, it is demeaning to day mothers who are relegated to the role of "glorified nannies and wet nurses." Yet, in spite of such objections, the program has apparently found widespread popular response and approval.(148)

In the GDR, the high rate of female participation in the work force makes an adequate supply of low-cost day care centers a matter of great urgency. (With the exception of the baby year, most mothers, even of young children, have outside employment in the GDR; while in West Germany, only about 40 percent of mothers with children under 15 hold outside jobs.(149)) With ever increasing numbers of GDR "nannies" either gainfully employed or on pensions, built-in baby sitters are extremely hard to come by in East Germany.

The all-out efforts of East Germany's ruling authorities have paid off: By 1977, six out of every ten children under 3 whose mothers were not on paid maternity leave were in nurseries, almost nine out of every ten 3 to 6-year olds were in kindergartens, and more than seven out of every ten school children in grades 1 through 4 attended after school child care centers. With ever-improving housing facilities, most preschool children are now in day care centers, and the previously more popular child care facilities where children could be housed overnight also, usually to come home on weekends, are being phased out. Also phased out are seasonal child care facilities which are open only during farmers' busy season, usually from May to October, and which were more prevalent during an era when fewer GDR mothers were gainfully employed on a year-round basis. While, for instance, in 1960 over 10 percent of all prekindergartners in GDR nurseries stayed in sleep-over institutions and almost 11 percent were cared for in seasonal facilities, these percentages had dropped to 4 and 5 percent respectively in 1970, and to 2 and .33 percent by 1977.(150) Similarly, in 1960 almost 12 percent of all preschoolers over 3 enrolled in GDR kindergartens attended a seasonal kindergarten that was open only during part of the year; by 1970, that percentage had dropped to 5 percent and by 1977, to barely over .5 percent.(151) (Sleep-over kindergartens, where children come home on weekends only, are not listed separately from day-care kindergartens in the GDR. But it can be safely assumed that their number and percentage of all kindergartens has also dropped drastically in recent years.)

Table 3.22. Places Available in GDR Child Care Facilities
(as % of all children in respective age group)

	1955	1960	1965	1970	1972	1974	1976	1977
All child care facilities for prekindergartners[a]	9.1	14.3	18.7	29.1	35.9	47.8	57.0	60.1
Regular day nurseries[b]	6.8	11.1	15.4	26.5	33.7	45.9	55.5	58.7
Kindergartens[c]	34.5	46.1	52.8	64.5	73.0	80.4	87.4	89.2
Kindergartens, excluding seasonal facilities	30.4	40.7	48.5	61.1	70.5	79.0	86.7	88.7
After-school child care center, grades 1-4[d]	N.A.	N.A.	40.3	47.9	55.3	62.8	69.3	70.8

[a] Includes day nurseries for children under 3 as well as facilities where children under 3 are also housed overnight, and "seasonal" facilities, usually open only from May to October, during the farmers' busy season. Percentage computed as percentage of all children under 3 who are "under consideration," i.e., all children under 3 except those whose mother (or, in very rare cases, father) is on maternity leave at full pay, to take care of the infant.

[b] For children under 3. Excludes facilities where children are housed overnight and excludes also "seasonal" facilities.

[c] All school preparatory, for preschoolers 3 and over. Includes regular day care kindergartens, installations where children stay all week long and come home on weekends, and "seasonal" facilities, usually open only from May to October, during the farmers' busy season. Computed (as for the FRG in table 3.21) as percentage of children 3 to 6 plus 9/12 of children in the 6 to 7 year age bracket.

[d] Computed as percentage of all children 6 to 10. (This method has been used to keep percentages comparable with FRG figures in table 3.21. Differences from children actually enrolled in grades 1 to 4 is small and would lower the percentage figure but slightly. For 1972, for example, the percentage would be 54.5 instead of 55.3.)

Sources: Statistical Yearbook, GDR, 1978, pp. 35, 36, 284, 285 and 334. For population figures by age brackets, needed for computation, Statistical Yearbooks, GDR, 1966 through 1978.

AT WORK   107

Official plans call for enough places in GDR nurseries by 1980 to accommodate 75 percent of all children under three. Places in kindergartens and after-school child care centers were, by 1977, deemed virtually adequate to meet existing needs; even in rural areas, such facilities, staffed and equipped at least as satisfactorily as in the cities, have become a matter of course.(152) Still — especially in light of anticipated continued increases in birthrates and decreases in infant mortality rates(153) — further additions to such facilities have been planned, to assure that by 1980 no child 6 to 10 years of age who needs a place in a kindergarten or an after-school child care center anywhere in the GDR will be found wanting. Although no steps are contemplated to make attendance at either of these facilities mandatory, it is anticipated that nearly all parents of children in these age groups will want to make use of them, once they are readily available.(154) That there be adequate facilities for all children is of utmost importance to society in general and to working mothers in particular, Party Central Committee member Inge Lange emphasized, so that no woman would have to interrupt her professional life even temporarily because she can't find a satisfactory place for her child while she is at work.(155) (Note that even a female GDR Central Committee member, in charge of women's affairs, still foregoes ideological purity for lingering, traditional reality by talking about the "woman" and not about "one of the parents," having to stay home with a child, if no appropriate accommodations can be found.)

All East German child care facilities are heavily subsidized by the state, and costs to parents are very low. In fact, as GDR publications correctly phrase it, "the children are cared for free of charge . . . parents merely make a contribution to the costs of their food."(156) Day nurseries cost up to 1.40 M per day, about the average wage for one and a half hours of work for a week's care. Nurseries where children stay all week and come home only on weekends cost 2 M per day, kindergartens a mere 35 pfennig. Almost two thirds of East German youngsters, up to 18 years of age, participate in school lunch programs (virtually nonexistent in West Germany), at a cost of 55 pfennig per meal. Attendance in after-school care centers where no meals are served is free.(157)

Quality of Child Care Facilities

Apart from number and costs, GDR institutions also seem to offer much better quality of child care than do West Germany's. All East German kindergartens are school-preparatory in nature. In the West, this is the exception rather than the rule most anywhere outside of Berlin.(158) Most of them are essentially supervised group baby sitting facilities for 3 to 6 year olds. Many of West Germany's child care centers are staffed by overworked and not always well-trained teachers, in some places assisted on a cooperative basis by parents. A highly critical 1977-78 West German TV program showed an example of such a facility: 27

children in a crowded home, under the supervision of a single teacher who charged that the children could not even play outside because the neighbors complained.(159) And the Federal Ministry for Youth, Family and Health charges in a 1980 publication that nurseries for small children under 3 in particular are not only extremely scarce but their quality "must be improved" also.(160)

Most West German women interviewed by this author also cast aspersions on the quality of their country's child care facilities and especially on nurseries. "I would never put any of my children into a nursery," commented the wife of a West Berlin psychology professor, a non-working mother of two. "The ones that I saw," she elaborated, "were terrible, with 30 to 40 children to a teacher. The teachers were so busy, they even tied the kids down on the potty because they didn't have time to stay with them!" "I have no children of my own," said a West Berlin female psychologist, "but if I did I would never put any in a nursery. They do not get enough personal attention there. Some of the kindergartens in Berlin are all right, though." "Nurseries are much too crowded; only if absolutely necessary would I ever have considered putting any of my children in one of them," remarked one of two Bremen housewives interviewed together by this author, and the other agreed: "Our nurseries are generally used only in emergencies, or by women who absolutely have to work and who have no other way out – if they can find a place for their kids in one of them, and at a price they can afford." But an unskilled, female factory worker in West Berlin had more pleasant experiences: "I had my daughter in a small, very good nursery school in this city," she reported, "and it wasn't expensive either. But I realize that this was an exception; I was much luckier than most other mothers I know. Over there (in East Germany), facilities are much better. Before the wall went up, one of my female co-workers used to commute, just so that her kid could be in one of their child care centers." "Here in [West] Berlin, some private child care facilities are quite acceptable; but reports we get from the rest of the country and especially from Bavaria are not so good," a West Berlin female lawyer, very active in the then governing Social Democratic party, whose husband was a high government official, summed it up. And as regards the few West German after-school child care centers: "Not too terribly expensive, but lousy," Gisela Helwig, Cologne magazine editor and author of books on West German women, labeled them.

In the GDR, on the other hand, party and government have put a great deal of money and effort into what one West German author called a "widespread network of inexpensive, scientifically run child care centers."(161) Teachers (mostly women) are well trained, and the number of children per teacher has been declining and is much lower than in West Germany. In the case of kindergarten, the only kind of pre- or after school facility attended by substantial numbers of West German children, there are actually less than half as many children per teacher in the GDR.(162) Men and women interviewed by this author have been unanimous in their praise. Yet, an East German psychologist points out, traditional values are hard to erase. If a child who regularly attends one of these child care facilities develops an illness or an emotional problem which children taken care of in their homes by their own mothers can and do develop just as readily, he writes, "a feeling of maternal inadequacy is apt to develop," and mothers often take off from work under such circumstances to personally attend to their youngsters.(163)

4 The Education and Training of German Women

"The problem of women's equality is above all a problem of women's education," said former West German Minister of Health Katherina Focke.(1) The statement may be too categorical. Yet, it is obvious that the emancipation of women cannot be successfully achieved unless a new approach to their education breaks with the traditions of yesteryear. There are two aspects to the problem: First, the educational <u>level</u> of women must be raised to that of men as an absolutely necessary step without which neither equal job opportunities nor equal political representation nor even women's own self-realization can ever become reality. And secondly, there must be a change in what the famous French existentialist and passionate scholarly opponent of sex-stereotyping, Simone de Beauvoir, referred to as "the primary obstacle to women's equality," namely "the <u>kind</u> of education that forms women in the traditional image of wives and mothers."(2)

During the past three decades, women's education has surely made progress in both German states. But it is probably correct to say that in no other area of women's struggles for equal rights are the differences between West and East Germany as enormous as in the area of education — especially in the field of higher education and particularly as far as the present generation of German youth is concerned.

As has been shown in chapter 2, East German laws amount to an all-out effort to legislate for the educational furtherance of women. While there are no comparable laws in West Germany, FRG legislation, nevertheless, provides basically for equal educational opportunities, irrespective of sex. But a book on GDR women recently published in West Germany clearly delineates the fundamental difference: West German women "are in principle permitted to achieve educational goals equal to those of men, but in practice they don't." In the GDR, age-old traditions have not been wiped out overnight either, and older women have not been able to catch up completely with men; but "the young generation has already achieved equality of qualifications for boys and girls."(3)

EDUCATION AND TRAINING   111

West German government authorities are well aware of existing deficiencies and of the need to remedy them. "Schooling and professional education of girls remains less adequate than that of boys. We must realize that traditional sex-role concepts frequently prevent girls from utilizing existing educational and training opportunities to the same extent boys do," concludes the FRG parliament-established Investigative Commission on Women and Society. Although noting a slight improvement in the area of schooling proper in the past few years, the Commission points out that a considerable percentage of girls enter the job market immediately after completion of the minimum number of years of school required by law. As a result, 70 percent of all unskilled workers are female, "and this percentage has remained fairly constant in recent years."(4) And there is official recognition of the need for a "reform of the educational system, so that boys and girls, men and women, would be prepared equally for tasks in the family, profession, and society, and so that they would be able with equal abilities and knowledge to shape their lives and participate in social processes."(5) But West Germany's Federal authorities are much more handicapped in their efforts than their counterparts in the GDR because, apart from constitutional guarantees, there is no one, single, ideologically "correct" standard in the FRG. To make matters even more difficult, some of the country's primary and secondary educational system is privately, cooperatively, or church operated and controlled; and most of the rest is under the control of the municipalities or of the Laender which constitute the Federal Republic of Germany, and which vary greatly from one another in the degree of political and religious "conservatism" of their citizens, their governments, and hence their educational authorities.

EDUCATION STARTS IN THE FAMILY

"Give me the children during the first seven years and you can have them for the rest of their lives," is an axiom attributed to one of the major Western religions. There is much truth to it. Western psychologists, surely, are convinced that the earliest years of childhood play a significant role in shaping the behavior, the attitudes, and the character traits of individuals. Undoubtedly, much of the predisposition, much of the predilection of adults, much of their prejudice or lack thereof toward the equality of the sexes can also be attributed to the home environment, the conduct of their parents, and the way they and their brothers and sisters were brought up during their early youth.

In West Germany, some progress may have been made in recent years. But it is probably correct to say that the average West German family still contributes more to the maintenance of the status quo in sex-role stereotyping than to the emancipation of women. Such, in any case, seems to be the view of virtually all observers and investigators, private as well as governmental. This includes, of course, the conservative elements in West German society who approve of it, convinced that long-standing, sex-based differences in the education of children are in conformity with natural laws and, therefore, fully justified and justifiable. The problem is clearly and succinctly outlined by the Investigative Commission on Women and Society:

> Education for partnership [of the sexes] must start as early as possible in other words already with the education of the toddler at home.... Frequently [in West Germany] the early education of the preschool child in the family is still extremely onesidedly oriented towards sex differentiation. A different behavior is expected from girls than from boys, and such different behavior is also actively promoted. Toys also prepare children for different functions in life, according to sex. For instance, by playing with dolls and small household appliances, the girl develops nursing-type abilities ... the boy plays with technical toys and thus he learns to build things and to develop his imagination....(6)

A recent publication of the Federal Ministry for Education and Science expresses virtually identical sentiments. Pointing out that the division of labor which prescribes that "woman belongs in the home and the man outside, in the hostile world" is still deeply embedded in the consciousness of West German men and women, the booklet also finds that sex-differentiated toys "reinforce some and suppress other talents and interests," depending on the child's sex:

> Little girls play with dolls, dress and undress them, wash them, lovingly put them into their doll beds....
>
> Construction toys, conducive to the imaginative erection of structures, Indian equipment, cap-guns, rifles prepare boys for life's struggles, for having to prove themselves in the outside world.

And the booklet further notes:

> A girl is supposed to be pretty and neat. A boy who does not come home once in a while dirty and with torn pants and who shies away from fights with other kids is "not a real boy."
>
> Even parents — and their numbers are increasing — who would like to raise their daughters and sons equally find it difficult to escape such standards.(7)

At a recent DGB conference on women's problems in the FRG, a speaker charged that "the realization of equal opportunities for women is interfered with in many ways: It starts virtually at birth. In the home, in kindergarten, in school, in their daily environment, women are so role-educated that they do not even aspire to equal opportunities."(8)

Although the new generation of West German girls is surely somewhat less marriage and somewhat more career oriented than their mothers and grandmothers, a recent New York Times article, tellingly entitled "West German Women: Few Gains Since the War," finds that in the FRG "many parents still think education for daughters is a luxury."(9)

In East Germany, for a number of reasons, parents are personally motivated and feel strong social pressure to avoid sex-discriminatory upbringing of children:

1. In the GDR, all means of communication and information, including newspapers, magazines, radio and TV programs, and works of art and literature are committed to the eradication of sex-differentiated childrearing; opposing views are generally deemed unacceptable and hence not publicized.(10)
2. Society plays a somewhat greater role in child rearing than in the FRG. It imposes on parents the obligation to raise future generations not in the traditions of yesteryear, but in the "spirit of socialism."(11)
3. Parents are somewhat more limited in their ability to make choices for their children. For instance, they cannot choose to have children educated in private or parochial schools, and they have, at best, limited opportunities for exposing their children to books other than those officially approved.
4. A much greater percentage of GDR than of FRG mothers have outside employment, so that a much greater percentage of GDR children are exposed to a somewhat different sex-role model in the home than the one that sees the mother's job exclusively as that of homemaker. Since, moreover, GDR society tends to hold non-working mothers in low esteem, East German families could hardly be expected to discourage their daughters from pursuing an education or seeking outside employment – and school enrollment figures and job participation rates would appear to indicate that they don't.
5. In any case, a much greater percentage of GDR than of FRG children attend nursery schools, kindergartens, and after-school child care centers (see tables 3.21 and 3.22) which somewhat lessens the parents' influence on young children (and in the GDR, all kindergartens and grade schools are coeducational; and educators, from nurseries through the universities, have been trained and are under orders not to allow discriminatory sex differentiation).

It would be reasonable to assume that for reasons such as the ones above, non-sexist upbringing of children should have made more progress in the GDR than in the FRG – and there is evidence that indeed it has. (For instance, the very fact that the father is no longer the sole breadwinner in the typical GDR family reduces sex discriminatory attitudes; the view that "the woman belongs in the home" is necessarily foreign to children in a society where, as a general rule, both parents

114   WOMEN IN THE TWO GERMANIES

are gainfully employed.) But after all has been said, it remains true, nevertheless, that the problem has by no means been solved entirely in East Germany as yet either. In a research project on "sex and personality," GDR psychologist Heinz Dannhauer asked over 300 East German third and fourth graders whether they would rather be boys or girls. He reported that 92 percent of the boys and 84 percent of the girls chose their own sex. But when asked why, a substantial minority gave sex-identification answers which, according to one Western analysis of Dannhauer's project, "follow almost the same pattern as they do in capitalist countries."(12) About 20 percent of the boys said, for instance, that they preferred to be boys because boys are stronger, have greater professional opportunities, don't have to help as much in the home, and because girls play boring games and are scaredy-cats. Among girls, 8 percent said they wanted to be girls because girls are treated better (4 percent because they are whipped less frequently), 17 percent because they can dress nicer, and 36 percent because boys are "fresh and ill-mannered."(13) In a similar study of several hundred GDR kindergartners, 3 to 6 years of age, Dannhauer found a wide prevalence of lingering sex stereotypes (for instance, whether right or wrong, the great majority of the children perceived of boys as stronger and of girls as more obedient and more ready to help in the home).(14) From his research, Dannhauer reached the conclusion that "the furtherance of sex-oriented play behavior of boys and girls (in the home) still follows outmoded traditions and circumscribes unnecessarily the children's range of experiences." And he recommended that "within the family there be no differentiation in the rearing of boys and girls. . . . Boys are not to be less burdened with household chores than girls."(15) Other studies carried out in the GDR in the early 1970s reached similar conclusions.(16)

To give one more example, a study of 540 children age 4 to 6, carried out in the mid-1970s by GDR sociologist Prof. Schmidt-Kohner, showed no basic intellectual differences between boys and girls; but there were noticeable differences in concept formation. In tests administered, boys responded more positively to "vehicles," girls to "vegetables." Also, girls were better in tying ribbons, boys in making bows and arrows. The investigator attributed the differences to lingering "outdated ways of upbringing according to sex."(17) And in a personal interview, the GDR representative to the UN Commission on Women, Humboldt University Professor of Ethics Helga Hoerz, frankly stated: "We have come very far, but we have not yet reached in all families our goal of equal rearing of young children, irrespective of sex. In their homes, both boys and girls should, for instance, be taught to cook. But there are still parents who teach it just to girls. . . ."

CHILDREN'S BOOKS

Books to which young children are exposed in their most formative years are very influential in shaping their attitudes toward the world, and hence also toward male-female roles in their society. This holds true for picture books read to the very young, for reading books they read on their own, and more even for school books. These latter tend to make the greatest impression since they are likely to be accepted as "official" and, therefore, unquestionably "correct."

In West Germany, a 1969 survey carried out under the auspices of the Cologne Institute for Mass Communications checked 85 reading books from various parts of the country, among them 65 used in grade schools and 16 used in high schools. In only 10 percent of these books did the main female character have a profession or a job of her own; in only 1 percent did she show any political interest. Motherhood, friendliness, and willingness to make sacrifices for her family were the characteristics for which she was lauded. Asserting that such sex stereotyping amounts to an attempt to "integrate the youth of today into a society which no longer exists," the authors concluded that it "unavoidably creates danger zones, not only for the relationship between men and women but also for their entire approach to society and thereby for the contribution women can make in the diverse areas of social life."(18)

While some different, emancipation-oriented children's books are available in West German book stores, little overall change has taken place in recent years, especially in regard to school books. Children's reading books, used in West German schools in the 1970s, contain such sentences as: "Father knows everything." – "Wait till Dad comes home; he'll be able to explain it to you." – "A girl is almost as good as a boy." – "It's all right for a little lady to be scared at times." – "Hanna comes home from school. She helps mother. She carries the wood to the kitchen. She shines the shoes; she waters the flowers." And in the same first grade reader used in Munich grade schools, which features the above, it also says: "Peter comes home. 'We have learned something really interesting in school,' he says. 'I can build an airplane now.'" In general, such grade school reading books show the woman as working in the house, cooking, cleaning, taking care of the children. She lives for her family. In her free time, she knits or embroiders. The father, on the other hand, is depicted as the head of the household. He goes to work, earns the money for all, comes home to prepared meals where his family eagerly awaits him. In his free time, he reads the newspaper.(19) In 1979, the North Rhine-Westphalia Emancipation Group (AEM) produced a study of 42 picture books available in West German public libraries. Although there was some progress (for instance, two girls were shown getting angry and one boy crying), the traditional role image of girls and women persisted in general. Fifty-three male professions were depicted – from king to farm worker. Women, on the other hand, were shown in only 17 professions and they were usually those regarded as typically female: doctor's receptionist, secretary, kindergarten teacher, etc.(20)

West Germany's Federal Ministry for Education and Science charges that children's reading books repeat and reinforce stereotyped views on men's and women's functions in society and on "proper" behavior for boys and for girls.(21) More specifically, the Investigative Commission on Women and Society lists the following deficiencies as characteristic of school books used in the FRG in the 1970s:

- They do not take note at all — or, if they do, at best extremely inadequately — of the fact that a substantial percentage of FRG women is gainfully employed, nor of the double burden of job and of housework and child rearing such working women are forced to live with.
- The model of "only-mother" or "only-housewife" is often idealized.
- The unmarried woman is treated in an antiquated and stereotyped manner as less worthy than her married counterpart.
- The family is idealized in a fashion that no longer corresponds with reality. No note is taken of the fact that today more families than in the past are also interested in a variety of activities outside of the home. . . .(22)

And, so charges the Commission, such stereotyping enters into all kinds of school books, including mathematics books where one can find it integrated into mathematical problems children are to solve.(23) ("If mother needs two eggs, two cups of flour and two cups of milk to make 20 pancakes and if eggs cost DM 1.80 per dozen . . . ," "If Hans drives at a speed of 80 km. per hour. . . .")

In East Germany, children's books tend to be much more oriented toward sex equality; but they do not yet present the picture of the fully emancipated woman and the household-chores-sharing husband so strongly advocated by GDR authorities. In 1970, Erna Scharnhorst, member of the GDR Academy of Sciences' Scientific Council on "The Woman in Socialist Society," surveyed reading books used in grades 1 to 4 in GDR schools. She found that working-age women portrayed therein were not housewives only; virtually all of them held outside jobs also. But with few exceptions, they were shown as employed in "traditional women's work." As to the distribution of roles in the family: In the more than 60 reading and picture books which focused on domestic situations, the mother or grandmother was outstandingly the most visible character. In only 10 of them did the father play any role at all, and then only as contact person for the child. "Such a selection," the author complained, "does not even correspond anymore with the reality of our younger families, and much less so with the requirements of the future."(24)

The trend of demonstrating greater equality of the sexes in GDR children's books made further progress during the 1970s. Fathers nowadays are, for instance, shown more frequently caring for young children or pushing baby carriages. Yet, even in recent books, soldiers are still virtually always men, and it is usually still the mother who prepares the breakfast and sees the child off to school.

West German and, to a lesser extent perhaps, East German children's books often still present a somewhat outdated sex division of roles. But if the former frequently show the woman as housewife and mother without a career of her own, and the father as provider, they paint a picture of life as to a great extent it actually prevails in the FRG. By the same token, if GDR children's books show women at work, but only occasionally in hitherto virtually "all male" occupations, and if more often than not the albeit <u>working</u> wife is shown as the one who also does most of the work in the home, this too is reflective of real life as to great measure it exists in the GDR today. (For more details on division of labor in the home, see chapter 5.)

West Germany's Investigative Commission on Women and Society called on official school book commissions to see to it that in revised and in new school book editions "the position of the woman in the family and in society be portrayed factually and realistically."(25) Maybe both parts of Germany need to go somewhat further. If future children's books are to be conducive to instilling in the minds of new generations the spirit necessary to the furtherance of what is broadly referred to as "women's liberation," they should selectively deemphasize lingering sex-role divisions of past generations; and they should perhaps put greater emphasis on developments in the "right" direction (female law enforcement officers, fire fighters, and university students in laboratories; husbands and wives together doing the dishes, etc.), but without going to extremes. Mother a truck driver and father cleaning the house and preparing the meal while waiting for her to come home from work, even if true in rare instances, would probably still seem too detached from reality to have the desired effect on the young child.

PRESCHOOL AND GRADE SCHOOL EDUCATION

As discussed in chapter 3, the overwhelming majority of West German kindergartens are not school preparatory.(26) Proper preschool kindergartens, a recent publication of a prestigious West German foundation explains, would be instrumental in introducing equality of opportunities for children from widely different social and educational backgrounds. But, so the publication charges, "conservative forces in the Federal Republic strongly reject the implementation of such equality of opportunities, advocating instead 'justice of opportunities' by which they mean that existing differences between the privileged and the underprivileged correspond to a principle of natural selection and are therefore justified."(27) While this statement refers primarily to social differentiation, it applies equally to sex discrimination. As has been shown in other parts of this book, West Germany's conservative forces, strong throughout the Federal Republic and particularly powerful in some of the <u>Laender</u>, such as Bavaria, have been opposed to many aspects of women's struggle for equality, from the introduction of relevant laws to the equal participation in their political parties' leadership, irrespective of sex – and they are opposed to sex equality in the schools as well.

Because most of West Germany's kindergartens are not schools proper but more or less refined babysitting institutions, the old pattern of "dolls for girls and trains for boys" is continued in many if not most of them. In any case, there is certainly no general, centralized effort to fundamentally alter the status quo at the preschool level.

At the grade school level (and into high schools), West Geman boys and girls until recently had different curricula. Although the educational system varies from Land to Land, this generally is no longer the case. Girls nowadays have at least the same choice of curricula as boys. This presents an improvement over the past but does not solve the problem. What it amounts to is that girls are no longer automatically assigned to cooking and sewing classes and boys to shop. Each child can choose "freely" now. But, commented the head of Bavaria's SPD women, Inge Gabert, to this author, "they feel like outsiders if they do not go the traditional 'normal' way. Hence, 'free choice' does not alter the fact that there are still few boys in home economics and few girls in shop. What we need is an end to curriculum choice and the adoption of identical compulsory curricula for both sexes. The SPD is surely for it; the conservatives obviously not." And the West German author and publisher, Gisela Helwig, in an interview with this author, added to this criticism that the changes heretofore introduced are of such recent nature that even where curricula are similar and curricula choices the same for all, "the teachers are still the old ones with their old prejudices and background, and not much has actually changed as yet."

In the GDR, the "democratic school reform" that decreed identical educational curricula for boys and girls dates back to 1945, the time immediately after the war when East Germany was the Soviet-occupied zone of Germany.(28) The GDR's long-standing efforts toward non-sexist education start with the young child. For a generation these efforts have included conscious policies to promote the non-sexist education of the teachers as well. "In our nurseries," proudly asserts a GDR publication on Women in Socialist Society, "many girls are astronauts and many boys bathe dolls and feed teddy bears."(29) In East Germany's state-controlled kindergartens, boys and girls are taught — and apparently with considerable success — to play the same games and enjoy the same toys; and they undergo equal preparation for grade school. In primary and secondary schools, the curriculum is the same for all children. Boys and girls take, for instance, both needlework and shop. But cooking is no longer taught in regular schools at all because, as several GDR interviewees told this author, "we don't cook much any more. Our children get their noon meal in school and we, the parents, have it at or near our place of work. At night, it's mostly cold cuts."(30) Even occasional hot evening meals are usually not prepared at home; more often than not, they are taken by families at the omnipresent food stands, cafeterias, and restaurants, or are catered at costs purposefully kept low by the state.

Yet, after all has been said, there is no denying that lingering prejudices are not easily eradicated in toto, not even in the GDR. So, there are occasional (although in recent years very infrequent) reports, especially from smaller towns in East Germany, about teachers of the "old school" who would say to kindergarten or grade school girls that they must set the right examples for boys. As girls, they must always be good, never fresh, never sloppy, never loud.(31)

SECONDARY EDUCATION

In the FRG and the GDR both, grade schools are basically uniform throughout the respective country; but there is a choice among different types of high schools in West Germany, while virtually all GDR high school students attend the same kind of secondary-level educational institution.

Upon completion of 4th grade, West German youngsters can enroll in the regular five-year high school (Hauptschule), the somewhat more intensive six-year Realschule, the college and university preparatory nine-year Gymnasium, or they can choose a two-year "orientation level," the equivalent of 5th and 6th grade, and postpone the final choice for two years. Table 4.1 briefly describes each type of school in the West German school system.

Table 4.1. West German Schools[a]

(Brief Descriptions)

Elementary Level. Kindergarten for preschoolers over 3. Voluntary.

Primary Level. Grade school; grades 1 through 4. Uniform.

Orientation Level. Voluntary stepping stone to high school subsequently selected, but counted as part of years required for graduation from that high school. 5th and 6th grade. Designation varies from Land (State) to Land, e.g., orientation level, observation and furtherance level, proving and testing level, etc. Intended to give student two extra years to decide which high school to enroll in — if qualified.

Hauptschule. Regular high school; through 9th grade, with a 10th grade optional. After 9th grade, students who do not wish to proceed with one more year of regular high school can enter a traineeship (formerly referred to as apprenticeship) for a skilled worker's position; alternately, they can enroll in certain non-college level vocational schools (Berufsfachschule). Graduation from 10th grade is preparatory for certain advanced non-college level professional and vocational schools (Fachoberschule); the latter in turn is preparatory for college level professional and vocational schools (Fachhochschule).

Realschule. Somewhat more intensive high school than the Hauptschule. Through 10th grade. Generally, basis for higher, non-academic professions of all kinds. Graduation considered equal to that from secondary level vocational schools. Graduates wishing to continue study can proceed to certain types of advanced non-college level professional or vocational schools (Fachoberschule and hoehere Berufsfachschule). With evidence of necessary ability, they can also transfer to upper-level Gymnasium classes or enroll in a Gesamtschule.

Table 4.1. (Cont.)

Gymnasium. Most intensive type of West German high school, with classical orientation. Through 13th grade. Graduation from the Gymnasium, including a school-leaving examination, (Abitur) entitles recipient to attend universities or any type of institution of higher learning selected.

Gesamtschule. Combination high school (not separately shown in Fig. 4.1). High school that combines the various different types of high schools. Can be "cooperative" which means organized as a unit but with each type of high school separated within it, or "integrated" with the different types united and the curriculum overlapping. As the orientation level above, the purpose is to leave students as many avenues open as possible.

Berufsschule, Berufsaufbauschule, (hoehere) Berufsfachschule, Fachschule. Types of non-college level professional and vocational schools, part-time and full-time, often combined with apprenticeship-type on-the-job-training, and usually leading to some kind of skilled worker's certification. 6 months to 3 years, or part-time equivalent where applicable, depending on type of school, course of study, and previous preparation. Intended either (a) as preparatory for more advanced schools, or (b) for acquisition of necessary skills, for better preparation, or for advancement in various trades, vocations, and professions, such as electrotechnic, agriculture, business administraiton, textile and clothing, or health care. Fachoberschule, for instance, covers also such fields as engineering, economics, and education. Fachschule, in particular, is intended to further the students' careers in fields for which they have already been prepared in previous schools and/or for which they have already attained considerable experience (e.g., in the field of health care, a career as children's nurse or occupational therapist). Berufsschule is a lower level vocational school which can be a stepping stone toward admittance to a Berufsfachschule, Fachschule, or alternate road to education. Graduation from Berufsfachschule, Berufsaufbauschule, or Fachschule is equivalent to graduation from Realschule. Graduation from hoehere Berufsfachschule or Fachoberschule is preparatory to enrollment in Fachhochschule (see below). Prerequisite for hoehere Berufsfachschule or Fachoberschule: graduation from Realschule or equivalent.

Fachgymnasium. Vocationally-oriented upper-level Gymnasium. 11th through 13th grade. Graduation entitles student to enroll in Fachhochschule. Prerequisite: graduation from Realschule or equivalent.

Hochschule. Institution of higher learning. Usually 3 to 4 years, leading to the equivalent of a U.S. bachelor's degree. Includes such institutions as Universitaeti (university), paedagogische Hochschule (school

Table 4.1. (Cont.)

of education), Kunsthochschule (school of fine art), theologische Hochschule (schools of religion), Fachhochschule (see below), and Gesamthochschule (combination-institution of higher learning – see below).

Fachhochschule. Vocational College. 3 year program. Encompasses primarily the former schools of engineering and higher vocational schools. Reaching specific levels of educational training at Fachhochschule entitles student to change to a university. Prerequisite: Graduation from Fachoberschule, hoehere Berufsfachschule, or equivalent (e.g. Fachgymnasium).

Gesamthochschule. Combination-institution of higher learning. Combines various colleges and schools. As in the case of the high school level Gesamtschule, it can be "cooperative," i.e., organized as a unit but with each type of school such as paedagogische Hochschule or Kunsthochschule separated within it; or "integrated," with the curriculum drawing from a variety of schools for a broad general education.

Alternate Road to Education (2. Bildungsweg). Infrequently used path available to qualified students who have not gone through a Gymnasium or Realschule to prepare themselves for entrance into an institution of higher learning. First, intermittent, degree is Realschule graduation equivalent; second, final, degree entitles student to enroll in institution of higher learning. This educational route requires several years of study after graduation from Hauptschule to earn a college preparatory degree. Only one Hauptschule graduate in 500, as compared with six out of every ten students who finish the Gymnasium-Abitur, eventually enroll in an institution of higher learning.

---

[a]Special schools (Sonderschulen) and special forms and arrangements in the various Laender (States) not included.

Sources: Above description based mainly on Frauen und Bildung., pp. 60-77. Also Statistical Yearbook, FRG, 1978, pp. 335-336 and Bildungs-und Weiterbildungsbereitschaft, p. 265.

Even today, the course of study pursued by West German high school students depends to a great extent on the class in society they come from and on their parents' income. Among qualified youngsters, three-fourths of those from middle and upper income classes, but less than one-fourth of those from working class families, attend a Gymnasium. And the child's sex also plays a major, even if diminishing, role. For a girl, "all classes in [West German] society tend to value the traditional role of housewife and mother more highly than schooling and professional training," writes Gisela Helwig in her 1975 study of German women. And she points out that this tendency is particularly strong among lower income families; if they decide to send one or more of their children to more advanced schools, "they clearly give preference to the sons."(32)

Not only parents, but even some school authorities themselves take similar sex-discriminatory positions. North Rhine-Westphalia, for instance, issued guidelines for <u>Realschulen</u> in 1973 which state: "The peculiar characteristics of the sexes and their different tasks in life must be given due consideration in curriculum choices and in the organization of instruction methods." Nor is this an isolated incident. Many observers report that the attitude that, because of different abilities, boys and girls must be taught differently is still widespread and that it is only gradually being abandoned in the Federal Republic.(33)

In recent years, there have been some improvements. As mentioned before, all high school courses are now open to boys and girls alike (although curriculum choices, wherever available, still leave boys tending toward different subjects than girls); the great majority of formerly sex-segregated high schools have become coeducational; and female enrollment in the prestigious, university preparatory <u>Gymnasiums</u> has made considerable progress and by 1976 it almost equalled that of boys. Yet, even in 1976, <u>Gymnasium</u> (and college) dropout rates for girls were still twice those of boys, and one out of every five girls (as compared with one out of every 15 boys) who go to work after finishing their required schooling wind up as unskilled workers. (In West Germany, high school through 9th grade <u>and</u> school attendance to 18 years of age is compulsory; those who do <u>not</u> go on in high school must attend a vocational school to age 18, either full-time or part-time while training on a job.) Hence, so concludes an official 1977 FRG government report, "even the statistically evident progress cannot deceive us; we cannot talk about an actual equality of educational opportunities for girls"(34) – a statement, as we shall see, true even more at the college and university than at the high school or vocational school level.

In the GDR, for their years of compulsory grade and high school attendance (through 10th grade), all children are enrolled in a virtually identical curriculum of required courses,(35) leading to graduation from the general-education high school (<u>polytechnisches Oberschule</u>). Only since the late 1970s has there been a limited alternate choice for upper grades of enrolling in a special vocational program or in a curriculum preparatory for two years of advanced high school (<u>erweiterte Oberschule</u>), leading to the <u>Arbitur</u> – the type of graduation degree which, East and West, entitles the holder to enroll in a university. But, contrary to the arrangement in the West, there are several ways accessible to all high school students to attain the educational prerequisites for admission to institutions of higher learning, including universities (for instance, via an <u>erweiterte Oberschule</u>, a <u>Fachschule</u>, a school of engineering, a special <u>professional-vocational training course</u> with <u>Arbitur</u>, evening courses while holding a job, with a qualifying examination at the end). Since curricula are virtually uniform, and since selection of students admitted, for instance, to the erweiterte Oberschule is objective, there is no difference in theory or in practice between the education and preparation of boys and girls at the grade or the high school level in the GDR.

Table 4.2. Girls Enrolled in West German Schools
(as % of total enrollment)

Types of Institution[a]	1960	1965	1970	1976	Total enrollment 1976
Grade Schools and Hauptschule	49.3	49.2	49.0	48.2	6,277,564
Realschule	52.0	51.5	52.9	54.1	1,248,652
Gymnasium	39.9	41.3	43.9	48.4	1,913,954
Fachschule	46.4	50.2	55.2	63.4	91,754
Berufsfachschule	68.4	65.3	60.7	66.9	279,205
Berufsschule (mostly part-time)	44.1	44.1	41.9	40.2	1,629,460
Berufsaufbauschule		25.3	32.6	28.4	22,588
Fachoberschule[b]			20.3	31.6	121,834
Institutions of Higher Learning (Hochschule)	23.5	23.7	30.7	33.5	913,308

[a]For description of types of institutions, number of years necessary for graduation, prerequisites for enrollment, etc., see Fig. 4.1 and Table 4.1.

[b]Fachoberschulen were started in 1969.

Sources: From Grund-und Sturkturdaten, 1977, in Frauen und Bildung, pp. 62-63. Total enrollment figures in last column from Statistical Yearbook/FRG, 1978, pp. 339-49.

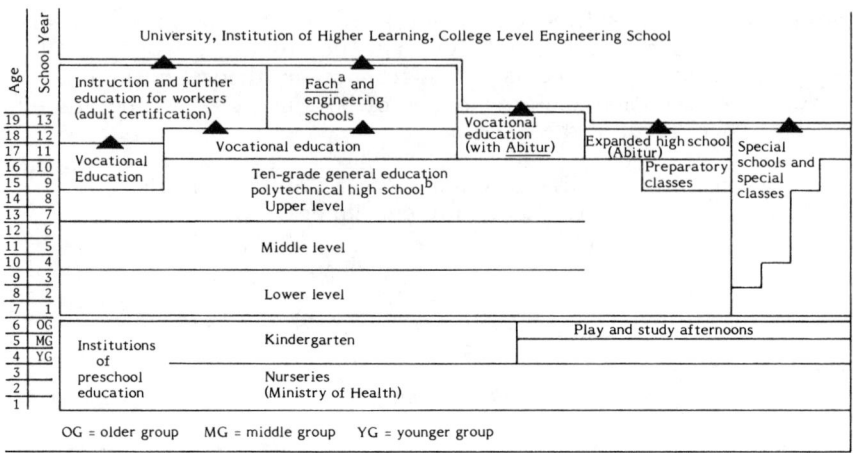

OG = older group   MG = middle group   YG = younger group

[a] In the GDR, a more advanced type of professional-vocational school than the Berufsausbildung, translated in this table as "vocational education."

[b] A "polytechnische Oberschule" is a modern, general-education, non-classical, secondary-level school.

Source: DDR Handbuch, 2nd ed., 1979, p. 294. Reprinted by permission.

Fig. 4.1. GDR school system.

VOCATIONAL TRAINING AND EDUCATION

At the trade school level, differences between the two German states are considerable. "It cannot be denied that in the development of a vocational school system — as regards financial funding, modernization, balancing of theoretical and applied instruction, and breadth of offerings — the GDR is ahead of us," says a study on "Vocational Training and Vocational Guidance in Both German States," published under the auspices of the Friedrich-Ebert Foundation. And it goes on to caution: "Vocational education will be the decisive factor as to whether we shall be able to prevail tomorrow in the competition of social systems with the GDR, as well as in the competition with other Western industrial nations."(36) In a similar vein, Helmut Rhode, Federal Minister for Education and Science, warns: "In the future, the Federal Republic will not be able to hold its own as a coalition of unskilled workers on the one hand and academicians on the other. For survival as an industrial country, and in light of new economic challenges, it needs new blood in its rank and file of skilled workers."(37)

Since in West Germany many more young men than women attend college and university (more details in the chapter), the latter predominate as a whole in below-college-level vocational and professional schools. In 1976, about two thirds of the student body of West German Fachschulen and Berufsfachschulen was female; but female enrollment in the Berufsschulen (mostly part-time, usually connected with on-the-job training), the less popular Berufsaufbauschulen (less than 23,000 students in the entire FRG), and the more advanced Fachoberschulen (prerequisite: graduation from a Realschule or a 10th year of Hauptschule) was much lower, percentage-wise (see table 4.1).

Under West German law, all youths who enter an on-the-job training program (formerly referred to as apprenticeship – and still called so today in the GDR) must spend at least one day a week (20 percent of their total training time) in a vocational school until they are 18 – although in some of the Laender there is such a shortage of Berufsschulen and of Berufsschul teachers that this law cannot always be fully enforced.(38) But universal, compulsory vocational education (leading to skilled worker's certification or to professional degrees for all who can pass) could probably not be legally adopted in the pluralistic Federal Republic, since "the freedom of choice of occupation, provided for in Article 12 of the Constitution, precludes that a vocational education be imposed on anyone who does not want it."(39) Actually, in 1976, 20 percent of West German girls (but a much lower percentage of boys) neither finished high school nor learned a trade.(40)

In the GDR, on the other hand, Article 25 of the 1968 Constitution provides that "all youths have the right and the obligation to learn a trade or profession"; and the 1974 revision of the Constitution left this sentence unchanged.(41) Since, traditionally, the vocational education of girls had lagged behind that of boys, and since the constitutional provision applied equally to both sexes, it had the greatest impact on female enrollment in the GDR's vocational schools.

During the first half of the 1960s, the total number of students enrolled in East German vocational schools actually declined by 10 percent. Female enrollment dropped also, but proportionately less, so that girls constituted a slightly larger percentage of the student body in 1965 than in 1960. Between 1967 and 1977, total vocational school enrollment rose, but by less than 30 percent for the decade, while female enrollment expanded almost two and a half fold. By 1978, over 70 percent of all students, and over 80 percent of all regular, day-time students, enrolled in vocational schools in the GDR were female – an enormous increase from the 36 and 47 percent respectively, 11 years earlier. And by mid-1978, two thirds of all female GDR employees in industry and agriculture had attained skilled worker's certification or a higher diploma or degree (as compared with only 50 percent in 1971).(42)

As we have seen, extensive legislation provides for the active furtherance of women's education in East Germany (without anything comparable on the books of the Federal Republic). Since the mid-1960s, such legislation has included provisions for special Fachschule classes made available for GDR working wives and mothers ("the most far-reaching measure for women's furtherance," one West German study calls it),(43) enabling them to attain, for instance, a diploma in engineering or economics, "even if they have a family to take care of," with schedules tailored to their individual needs.(44) They can keep their jobs but work only two to three days a week and go to school two to four days (depending on the kind of program and on whether or not their studies are college-preparatory), while earning their full, regular

Table 4.3. Enrollment in Vocational Schools
GDR
(in 1,000)

	1960			1965			1967			1970			1978		
	Total	Women	Women % of Total	Total	Women	Women % of Total	Total	Women	Women % of Total	Total	Women	Women % of Total	Total	Women	Women % of Total
Vocational Schools (total)[a]	126.0	36.0	28.6	113.6	34.6	30.5	126.0	45.6	36.2	167.2	81.2	48.6	164.6	116.1	70.1
Regular Students	47.3	15.5	32.8	50.8	19.9	39.2	55.1	25.7	46.6	62.8	37.8	60.2	99.9	81.5	81.1
Correspondence	30.5	5.6	18.4	37.6	9.2	24.5	44.2	13.9	31.4	64.4	30.4	47.2	53.4	29.9	56.0
Evening	25.6	2.2	8.6	23.4	5.4	23.1	24.8	5.9	23.8	37.4	12.7	34.0	11.2	4.6	41.1

[a]Subparts do not include all students. For instance, students enrolled in special study programs are not included.

Source: Compiled and computed from Statistical Yearbook/GDR, 1979, p. 296.

wage. Or they can attend school for three years on a full-time basis and draw 80 or even 90 percent of their average net wage as a stipend.(45) The sponsoring enterprises with which the students sign a contractual agreement guarantee them not only continued financial support but also a position corresponding to their newly acquired qualifications upon completion of their studies.(46)

Even as early as 1964, 85 percent of those female high school graduates in the GDR who did not immediately pursue further studies in a <u>Fachschule</u> or work toward a college or university degree started to learn a trade and prepare themselves for at least a skilled worker's certification; by 1968, when the new constitution made vocational or professional education mandatory for all, that figure reached 97 percent.(47)

In theory, West and East German youths – both male and female – are essentially free to choose their own trade or vocation, based on their individual ability and inclinations. In practice, the GDR has an advantage since its labor shortage gives young people a greater opportunity to locate a position in their preferred line of work. This is of even greater benefit to women than to men since the former are disproportionately strongly affected by West Germany's unemployment. Among employees under 20, the unemployment rate in 1975 was 14.1 percent for young women and 11.1 percent for young men. (48) Still, official GDR sources do not deny the possibility of a conflict between society's needs and individual preferences: "There has never been an absolutely free choice of careers anywhere. For instance, only as many people can earn their livelihood as barbers and hairdressers as there is hair that can be cut."(49)

In the choice of vocational training and education, young women in both East and West Germany still tend to turn toward traditional female careers (see table 3.8 and relevant discussion). But there are substantial differences in degree.

Although in the Federal Republic all fields of study and training except those specifically prohibited to women by protective legislation are open to male and female students alike, enrollment to a considerable extent is still along traditional male-female lines. Of all those preparing themselves for industrial-technical occupations, 91 percent are boys; in commercial fields, two thirds are girls (but in business schools, most girls study two years and become office helpers, while most boys study three years and earn a diploma as "industrial-businessman");(50) and in vocational preparation for health care, social welfare, and domestic employment, virtually all students and trainees are girls. A 1977 Federal government publication explains:

> Nothing is more stubborn than the prejudice that girls are less intelligent than boys (but more industrious), that they have no talent for natural sciences (but they do for languages), that they are no good in abstract thinking (but they are better in health care) – in short, that they are simply more sensitive, more tender, and more adaptable. But numerous studies, and not

merely in the Federal Republic, have proven that there are no innate sex differences in intelligence, mind, or spirit. Only education in a child's world of doll houses and knitting needles prevents the development of tastes for, for instance, technical and natural sciences.(51)

In the GDR, the 1970 decree on vocational counseling imposed on all schools the obligation to awaken students' interest in "crucial vocations," and to induce more women to embark on a curriculum of technical education.(52) Together with numerous other laws, decrees, and ordinances, and supported by far-reaching efforts of society and of individual enterprises to further women and to encourage them to enter formerly all-male careers,(53) this law has had its effects. While even in the GDR some jobs are still predominantly male and others predominantly female (see table 3.8), the new trend is definitely noticeable. By 1974, over 30 percent of all regular, **full-time** students at GDR vocational schools who majored in technical sciences were women, and so were 49 percent of those majoring in mathematics and in natural sciences; and for newly enrolled students, the percentages were substantially higher, i.e., 35.4 and 61.7 respectively.(54) (Figures, although showing similar progress, would be somewhat less impressive if computed as percentage of all, not merely of regular, full-time, students, since relatively fewer women are enrolled in evening and correspondence programs.) Yet, even within the technical sciences, there were still lingering, sex-related differences. For instance, most of the students who in 1974 decided to major in "machinery" were male, while more than four out of every five who opted for "textile-, clothing-, and leather technology" were female.(55)

HIGHER EDUCATION

For centuries, higher education most everywhere had been men's domain. Not until the first decade of this century were any women admitted to German universities. Without access to institutions of higher learning, women are effectively barred from most of the professions, from most better paying jobs in the economy, and, in general, from the opportunity to choose their own careers and to take their places in society as the equals of men. Hence, the extent to which women have made inroads into this men's world of higher education, or have failed to do so, is a most telling aspect of women's progress, not only in the field of education proper, but in the job market and in society as well.

At the end of the 1940s, around 18 percent of all German college and university students were women. Three decades later, women constituted somewhat over one third of the student body of institutions of higher learning in the Federal Republic; but female college and university enrollment in East Germany had by then almost reached a par with that of men. By 1977, over half of all regular, full-time GDR college and university students were female (in 1978, it was 51.8 percent); but among the 11.4 percent of students classified as "correspondence students," only one fourth, and among the one eighth of one percent classified as "evening" students only slightly over one third, were women.(56)

In the FRG, perhaps nowadays young women may be somewhat less restricted by the prejudices of the past than previous generations of prospective female students; but, nevertheless, they are still held back not only by the lingering stereotyped sex-role attitudes of their parents and society but also by the persisting negative frame of mind of West German college and university faculty.

Table 4.4. Female Students Enrolled in German
Institutions of Higher Learning
(as % of all students)

YEAR	FRG	GDR
1949[a]	17.7	18.6
1960	22.4	25.2
1965	22.9	26.1
1970	30.2	35.4
1972	29.0	40.7
1975	33.4	48.2
1976	33.8	47.7
1977	34.4	47.5
1978	35.3	47.6

[a] For winter 1949-50, exclusive of Schools of Education and of West Berlin.

Sources: Compiled and computed from Statistical Yearbook, FRG, 1952, p. 70; 1962, p. 103; 1967, p. 95; 1975, p. 106; 1977, p. 334; 1978, p. 348; 1979, p. 348. Statistical Yearbook, GDR, 1979, p. 35.

Faculty Attitudes Toward Female Students

In 1960, an inquiry among faculty members at Western German institutions of higher learning found that, of those asked, 64 percent expressed opposition to women studying, 4 percent were neutral on the issue, and 32 percent vacillated between neutrality and opposition. While not denying that female students did just as well as their male counterparts, they attributed this fact merely to greater industriousness and willingness to undertake additional assignments; but they remained firm in their view that "female students, in spite of greater diligence, have less ability."(57) And they saw women "by nature" as lacking (in order of frequency of replies) in ability to think, ability to analyze critically, intelligence, creative-productive abilities, fantasy, initiative, self-confidence, independence, physical sturdiness, and conviction.(58)

In the two decades since the publication of this study, little seems to have changed. Young West German women may have begun to gradually push their way into institutions of higher learning but, in words well-couched by an American observer, "this invasion of the cobwebbed hallowed halls of higher education seems not to have changed the traditional attitudes of the ossified, hierarchical, professorial caste. Taken as a group, they (still) hold the view that coeds really have no place in their lecture halls. They frankly regard women as less capable...."(59) According to a recent survey of West German faculty attitudes, the majority sees female students as probably more diligent than male students, more eager to learn, meticulous, conscientious, receptive, and equipped with better memory. But they regard these attributes as less important for professions that require a higher education than logic, intelligence, critical observation, or ability to think independently and to take the initiative — and they consider men superior to women in all of these. West German faculty members are reportedly tougher on female than on male students; at large, they seem to believe that women enter universities primarily to obtain an "MRS" degree; and their general attitude certainly contributes to the higher female dropout and failure rates, which they, in turn, view as proof that women are less well suited for a higher education than men.(60) Thus, the fact that, in spite of such obstacles, West German women have achieved proportionately larger roles in some professions such as medicine or journalism than women in other West European countries or in the United States is certainly to their credit. But with such obstacles in their path, it would have been virtually impossible for them to keep up with the progress of their peers in the GDR.

Nowhere in East Germany can anything like the attitudes of such West German faculty toward female college and university students be found. On the contrary, all-out efforts to encourage qualified women to enroll in institutions of higher learning and prepare themselves for professional careers receive the full support of college and university faculty and administrators. And if there were any older faculty members in the GDR who still harbored negative views on the subject, it would surely be the better part of wisdom for them to keep such views to themselves.

Who Decides Who Goes to College and Who Doesn't

Whether or not to give a child the opportunity to attain a higher education is a decision still left in the main to the parents in West Germany; in the GDR, on the other hand, parental guidance has been replaced largely by a more objective, sex-neutral (if not discriminatory in favor of women) selection process. West German parents are, for instance, the ones who determine whether or not an otherwise qualified child is to be enrolled in a university preparatory Gymnasium — and, as we have seen, many such parents still consider the education of daughters a luxury. In the GDR, on the other hand, it is usually not the parents who decide to enroll their children in 9th and 10th grade preparatory classes or in the college-preparatory 11th and 12th grade expanded high school (erweiterte Oberschule), although they do have the right to petition for such admission. As a rule, it is the school principal who recommends students to the county school board for admission, for instance, to the erweiterte Oberschule, on the basis of scholastic achievements, "faultless behavior," and "close affiliation with the state." Lack of sex-based discrimination seems rather evident since as early as 1971, about half of all those who took and successfully completed their Abitur were girls.(61)

Who Pays for a College Education?

In both West and East Germany, institutions of higher learning are tuition-free. But there are substantial differences in the extent of financial assistance and particularly in special aid to female students.

In West Germany, stipends are available to needy students, depending largely on their parents' income. (In 1973, for instance, 47 percent of FRG college and university students received some financial aid.)(62) Still, the parents of most West German students pay at least part of the considerable expenses connected with a college education. Counting needed supplies and living expenses, a multi-year college program costs tens of thousands of DMs.(63) This is of particular disadvantage to young women because, as previously discussed, whenever West German parents feel that they cannot afford to send all children to college, they virtually always tend to finance their sons' rather than their daughters' college education.(64) And it is even more to the disadvantage of young mothers. The birth of a child is one of the main reasons why female students in the FRG interrupt their studies much more frequently than men. Unlike the GDR, there is no obligation on the part of FRG college and university administrators to minister to their particular needs: low-cost child care facilities are rarely available, and special financial aid is not provided to help defray expenses. Apart from motherhood, among factors contributing to high female college dropout rates, a recent student also lists marriage, inadequate motivation, financial difficulties, and special psychological problems, all factors "linked more or less directly to the prevalent expectation of role division according to which the sphere of domestic and family obligations is primarily women's responsibility."(65)

In the GDR, on the other hand, over 90 percent of all students, male as well as female, receive monthly stipends in addition to tuition-free education. In the mid 1970s these varied in amount from 50 M for grade school students to 270 M for good, full-time university students — surely at the university level adequate to manage on while living either at home or in the extremely low-rent student living quarters. Only children of very high income families can be denied such stipends; however, students are granted stipends irrespective of family income if they have served in the armed forces, have held a job for five or more years prior to enrollment, or are single parents — this latter provision of special benefit to mothers who, in most cases, have custody of their minor children.(66) Women's furtherance programs assure qualified women that their college education will be adequately funded. And there are special provisions for mothers to enable them to pursue their studies. Financially, they, just as working mothers, receive maternity grants and children allowances.(67) Moreover, since 1972, mothers who are full-time students receive an extra 50 M per child per month, in addition to the regular stipend; for single parents or parents whose spouses are also students and who are unable to find a place in a nursery for their children, this amount is raised to 125 M for one child, 150 M for two children, and 175 M for three or more children.(68) Finally, a special study program for mothers enrolled in institutions of higher learning was introduced in 1970 (for mothers in vocational schools in 1967). Such women "who have proven themselves in the construction of socialist society and who because of the need to care for children in their home are burdened with special family obligations" are paid by their enterprises 80 or even 90 percent of their average net earnings(69) to enable them to pursue studies "which will qualify them for leading positions."(70) (Eligible women not currently working can apply for such a special study program to enterprises where they were previously employed or to social organizations.)(71) The institution's administration is under obligation to work out with such students a program of study which meets their special needs, enabling them, for instance, to catch up with lectures missed or to postpone examinations.(72) No wonder that with such special assistance, GDR coeds find it easier and more to their advantage to pursue advanced studies than their counterparts in the Federal Republic.

West German authorities have become increasingly conscious of the lack of any special measures and facilities in the Federal Republic that would enable women there to pursue their education while meeting, simultaneously, their family obligations. Recently, the Federal Ministry for Youth, Family and Health commissioned an "inquiry into the readiness of women under 45 to advance their education and continuing education." The inquiry pointed to the inadequacy of existing measures and the need to remedy the situation:

> The prevailing offerings of measures for continuing education minister to the needs of but a small part of the population.... Measures are necessary that would enable women to meet their immediate and long-run needs and to combine them with opportunities for education and continuing education.... Those responsible for adult education must be ready to offer practical living assistance primarily to women from lower social levels, and to assist them in the articulation of needs and the solution of conflicts.(73)

But, so far, no new special provisions have been introduced in the Federal Republic to assist women, and especially mothers (financially or otherwise)(74) in their endeavors to attain a higher education while coping with their maternal duties. In this respect, certainly, young female students in the GDR are far ahead of their peers in the West.

And What Do Female German College Students Study?

West German female students enrolled in institutions of higher learning still tend to concentrate largely in traditionally female areas of study. So, for example, two thirds of all students enrolled in West German schools of education in 1978-79 were women (most of them studying to become primary grade school teachers), and so were almost 60 percent of those majoring in linguistics and the humanities. On the other end of the scale, less than 8 percent of engineering students, and among them less than 2 percent of those studying electrotechnology, were female.

Table 4.5. Enrollment in West German Institutions of Higher Learning 1978-79

Types of Institutions	Total	Men	Women	Women as % of Total
Universities	637,542	412,746	224,796	35.3
College Level Professional & Vocational Schools	172,773	127,263	45,510	26.3
Schools of Fine Arts	16,228	8,917	7,311	45.1
Schools of Education	55,481	18,343	37,138	66.9
Combination Institutions of Higher Learning[a]	61,714	42,904	18,810	30.5
Schools of Religion	2,159	1,607	552	25.6
Institutions of Higher Learning: Total	945,897	611,780	334,117	35.3
Major Disciplines and Groups of Disciplines[b]				
Humanities & Linguistics[c]	217,301	94,162	123,139	56.7
Social Sciences	218,195	153,428	64,767	29.7
Mathematics and Natural Sciences	145,495	97,147	48,348	33.2
Medicine and Dentistry	62,052	43,036	19,016	30.6
Veterinary Medicine	3,915	2,469	1,446	36.9
Agricultural, Forestry, and Nutritional Sciences	23,638	13,339	10,299	43.6
Sports: Physical Education	18,225	10,598	7,627	41.8
Engineering	171,776	158,377	13,399	7.8
Electrotechnology	48,678	47,835	843	1.7

[a] Gesamthochschulen. See table 4.1.

[b] Winter Semester, 1977-78.

[c] Includes, among other disciplines, theology, philosophy, history, library sciences, general and comparative linguistics, classical philology, psychology, and educational sciences.

Sources: Compiled and computed from Statistical Yearbook, FRG, 1979, pp. 348 and 350; also Sozial Report, Nr. 1 (1977), p. 13.

Detailed enrollment statistics for specific disciplines in GDR colleges and universities, broken down by sex, are more difficult to come by. Whatever figures are available indicate that with the active support of society, female GDR college students have penetrated more deeply than their West German peers into traditionally male areas of study; yet, they are still concentrating heavily on "women's work," preparing themselves for careers in teaching (especially kindergarten and grade school levels), nursing, and social work – all areas in which the great majority of students are women. But in that society in which just about half of all students enrolled in institutions of higher learning are female, 35.8 percent of students in mathematics and the natural sciences in 1974 were female, varying from 27.6 percent in mathematics proper to 41.8 percent in biology and 45.2 percent in chemistry; and in the technical sciences, 32.8 percent of students were female, ranging from 24.8 percent in machine-building to 61 percent in city planning and architecture(75) – percentages slightly higher in mathematics and the natural sciences and significantly higher in the technical sciences than in the FRG, but not at par with men as yet. Statistics published for Leipzig's Karl Marx University show that in 1978 out of 1,300 students majoring in natural sciences, 510 (39.2 percent) were women, and so were 2,800 out of 4,600 social science majors (60.9 percent) and 1,500 out of 2,500 medical students (60 percent).(76) Finally, a set of figures for 1971 gives some indication of the rapid penetration, even then, of East German female college students into various groups of related disciplines.(77) Comparing the sex distribution of all gainfully employed college graduates with that of recently graduated job holders, it shows substantial increases in the percentage of women in all professional lines of endeavor (see table 4.6).

Table 4.6. Gainfully Employed Female College Graduates in Selected Disciplines, GDR, 1971

Disciplines	Gainfully employed female college graduates as % of all gainfully employed college graduates	Gainfully employed female college graduates under 30 as % of all gainfully employed college graduates under 30
Mathematics; natural sciences	25.5	35.7
Engineering and architecture	5.6	9.9
Medicine and pharmacy	41.9	53.2
Agriculture and forestry	12.8	23.5
Economics	16.6	37.2
Philosophy, history, political science, and law	19.0	44.0
Art, education, and sports	32.5	48.4
Language and literature	55.5	73.9

Source: <u>Volks-, Berufs-, Wohnraum-, und Gebaeudezaehlung am 1. Januar 1971</u>, Berlin (GDR): Central Statistical Administration, 1972, p. 117.

5 German Women in the Home and Family

TO BE OR NOT TO BE A "MERE" HOUSEWIFE? – AND WHO SHOULD DO THE HOUSEHOLD CHORES ANYWAY?

If women are to achieve de facto equality with men in education, on the job market, in government, and in society at large, the age-old division of roles in the family must be abolished — that division that makes the man the "head of the family," and the woman first and foremost the housewife and mother, even if she does hold an outside job as well. If women are to be truly emancipated, the new family must be one in which both spouses have comparable rights, obligations, and power to make decisions.

Recent West German family legislation provides that the household management be carried out "in mutual understanding" between the two spouses; but it also spells out specifically that one spouse (in practice, almost always the wife) may take sole charge of, and assume full responsibility for, the operation of the household. But in East Germany, where it is virtually taken for granted that husband and wife both hold outside jobs, family legislation calls on both spouses to do their fair share of household chores; and it specifies that the husband may not content himself with merely "assisting" his wife in the home.

The laws may be on the books. Still, if there is any one aspect of sex relations and sex equality that cannot be effectively legislated, it is the division of roles in the family. And it is probably in this area that the least progress toward sex equality has been made, East or West. Yet, there are noticeable differences between the two Germanies in the extent to which sex roles within the family have been altered in recent years. These differences can be accounted for to a great extent by the very high percentage of married women in the GDR, and the relatively low percentage in the FRG, who are gainfully employed outside the home, and by the different attitude of society toward such working wives. In the GDR, the model woman is increasingly one who can successfully combine professional competence and achievement with her functions as a wife and mother. But in West Germany, official sources report that some 14 million housewives "have not worked since marriage or have left their jobs."(1) There, as a recent book entitled The Double-Role of the Woman in the Family and on the Job expresses it, "the housewife who works hard in her home, and the lady of society, still correspond to the mental image of men as well as of countless women as to what an exemplar woman ought to be."(2) As German sociologist Helge Pross elaborates:

> The average West German housewife does her own housework without outside help. She prepares the meals every day. She cleans the home thoroughly once a week, does the washing twice or sometimes three times a week. She goes shopping three times a week. The windows are cleaned once a fortnight. . . . We know from surveys that most young girls of today orientate themselves to a future with the family as their main occupation, and employment as a supplementary job. With very few exceptions, they were also trained for an existence in which the family is the focal point. Basically, hardly anything has changed since grandma's times. For this reason, the mass rejection of the role of housewife cannot be anticipated.(3)

An extensive "empirical survey" on the "role relations of husband and wife in marriage and family [in the Federal Republic] and the resulting opportunities for the wife to achieve greater equality in the family, on the job, and in society" was undertaken in 1975 by the Bonn Institute for Applied Sociology, under the auspices of the Federal Ministry for Youth, Family, and Health. The results of the survey, reported in some length below, confirm that in actuality there have been no far-reaching changes in the traditional roles of spouses in West German families:(4)

1. Partnership is the generally valid image for role relations of spouses.

   The patriarchal family principle according to which the husband has the power to make decisions and the wife subordinates herself to it is no longer accepted as a valid image by the majority of marriage partners. . . . 88 percent of wives and 92 percent of husbands declare themselves satisfied with the division of roles in their marriage. . . .

2. Behind the proclaimed partnership, the traditional division of roles shines through: The wife remains responsible for the internal sphere of the family; the domain of the husband lies in the outside world.

   In spite of proclaimed partnership, decision making power is sex-specifically differentiated. If for certain areas only one spouse is responsible, it is the husband for major, in the long-run important, and the wife for minor, every-day decisions. When it comes to contractual agreements, the husband decides by himself in 41 percent of all marriages, the wife in only 4 percent. Decisions on larger purchases are made by the husband alone in 22 percent of all cases, but wives hardly ever decide on them by themselves (1 percent). . . . Twenty five percent of husbands, but only 9 percent of wives, decide by themselves which TV programs to watch in the evening. . . . Wives have greater influence on decisions regarding the purchase of minor household utensils (24 percent as compared with 12 percent of husbands). . . .

3. The duty of the husband to be the provider for the family remains untouched.

The sex differentiation between the wife's and the husband's role becomes particularly clear when we look at the division of duties of the spouses. The model has remained unchanged: the wife is responsible for the internal affairs of the family, the husband for the external affairs. Seventy percent of all married women and 69 percent of all married men see it as the main task of the wife to take care of the family. . . . Only 2 and 3 percent respectively are of the opinion that there is no "main task" for either wife or husband; 37 percent of married men and 29 percent of married women are even of the opinion that, by nature, the woman is here to take care of home and family and that she should stay away from outside employment and public life. The primary task of the husband, on the other hand, is seen as that of provider for the family's livelihood: 78 percent of wives and 77 percent of husbands hold this view, while only 19 and 24 percent respectively see non-material concerns for the family as one of the husband's main tasks. The husband's role as provider is deemed not only a burden but also a privilege. . . .

4. The husband's employment is his own affair, the wife's employment is the business of both spouses.

. . . 43 percent of all married men completely reject outside employment of their wives. And where it is accepted, it is viewed as supplementary activity which is not equal in importance to the husband's occupation, as far as planning for the couple's future is concerned.

5. The wife's primary responsibility for the education and care of children is the main, but not the only barrier to her activities outside the home.

The mother-role of the wife is the pendant to the provider-role of the husband. So far, both spouses have considered it a matter of course that the care of the children is primarily the wife's, and only secondarily the husband's concern.... As the number of children increases, the division of tasks between the marriage partners becomes more clearly separated. Among husbands in childless marriages, 52 percent help in the home; where there are children over 18, 47 percent of husbands help with household chores; in families with one or two children under 6, it is 44 percent; with three or more children under 6, 38 percent; with children between 6 and 18, 27 percent....

6. The wife's outside employment does not alter the structure of decision making in the family.

Even in marriages in which both spouses hold outside jobs, the husband tends to assume authority over major decisions and outside matters, and the wife to take charge of internal affairs. In 31 percent of such marriages, also, the husband alone decides on contractual agreements, while this is the case for wives in only 4 percent of all instances. And as regards major purchases, the decision rests with the husband alone in 18 percent of such marriages as compared with 3 percent for wives.... Two thirds of the husbands of gainfully employed women are ready to help their wives with household chores.... Among husbands whose wives do not work, barely one third would do so....

7. The wife's outside employment brings with it great additional burdens for the wife, but few additional burdens for the husband.

Working wives are certainly not relieved by their husbands' help to such an extent that they really have to take care of only half of the household chores and family obligations.... Twelve percent of husbands still refuse altogether to help in the home, even if the wife is gainfully employed. The double burden of the gainfully employed wife shows itself very clearly in the manner in which the spouses use their free time. While the husband uses his free time primarily for entertainment and relaxation, free time for the working wife means catching up with previously postponed household chores. Sixteen percent of husbands and 72 percent of working wives use free time for housework. On the other hand, 43 percent of husbands but only 23 percent of wives take time out in the evening to watch TV, 23 percent of husbands and 13 percent of wives occupy themselves with reading, and 18 percent of husbands but only 5 percent of wives with activities outside the home....(5)

8. As the relative educational level of women increases, so does their influence on decision making in the family.

The more advanced the husband's education as compared with that of his wife, the more pronounced is his dominancy. On the other hand, the wife's influence over decision making increases in proportion with her relative educational level as compared with that of her husband. . . .

9. Women are more strongly inclined toward an alteration of existing role relationships; men insist more strongly on a continuation of the prevailing model.

Although the prevailing structure of relations between spouses is accepted by the great majority of husbands and wives, one can, nevertheless, notice a slight tendency on the part of wives toward alteration. . . . Wives are less satisfied than husbands with the division of labor in marriage (88 versus 92 percent); the desire to have some relief from household chores by the husband (23 percent of all married women) is greater than the readiness of husbands to undertake such chores (9 percent of husbands undertake frequently, and 43 percent once in a while, some of the wife's household chores).To improve opportunities for women it is not enough to motivate and activate wives. It is also necessary to call more attention to the role of the husband and redefine it to the same extent.

Other surveys, studies, and reports may come up with slightly different figures, but the general picture they portray is very similar. The Hamburg Sample-Institute, for instance, reported the results of a 1972 survey of West German working women age 25 to 44, carried out under the auspices of the DGB, which showed that 36 percent of these women's husbands helped occasionally with housework and 34 percent with specific chores. Only about 25 percent of housewives age 25 to 34, and less than 15 percent in the 35 to 44 age group, said that they shared household chores with their husbands on a partnership basis.(6) According to a 1971 report, one of every four husbands of working wives did not help in the house at all(7) — and this in a society in which (so says the FRG Ministry for Youth, Family and Health) five hours of work are performed in the home for every six hours of gainful work in the economy.(8)

Occasionally, a West German researcher will report that some of West Germany's housewives who do not work outside the home grope with feelings of emptiness and are unfulfilled.(9) But such dissatisfied housewives seem to be the exception rather than the rule. Most observers and studies corroborate the above-mentioned findings of the Institute for Applied Sociology, that the great majority of West Germany's nonworking wives like their role. Helge Pross, for instance, concludes that "they like to be there for their families. Their thoughts are centered on family subjects — the household and bringing up of the children. . . . These family women are quite satisfied with their husbands — most of whom do not help in the house."(10) And a West German government information bulletin which describes the average German housewife as working a 60-hour week "looking after her family and doing housework," notes that only 25 percent of the "housewife-only" group would like to have a part-time outside job, while 26 percent of those who hold full-time jobs would prefer to stay home.(11)

An extensive survey among 14 to 16 year old teenagers in Hamburg finds that even West Germany's youth of today still holds largely to the traditional sex role division in the family. Fully one-third of the male and one-fourth of the female youths interviewed were not in favor of wives holding outside jobs; 90 percent of them said that the women should wash the laundry, 70 percent that cooking and cleaning were "woman's work." The Hamburg psychologists Karin Schoof-Tams, Leonhard Walczak, and Juergen Schlaegel who reported on the survey conclude: "Today's girls are more inclined to accept the double burden than young men give them credit for."(12)

In spite of all that has been said, some progress has been made in recent years in changing the attitudes of both men and women in the FRG toward wives seeking gainful employment and toward husbands helping with household chores. Surveys show, for instance, that in 1964, only 25 percent of West German men and 28 percent of West German women regarded it as "normal" for wives to hold outside jobs. But by 1976, 48 percent of married men and 65 percent of married women considered it "right" for wives to have careers of their own.(13) And Elisabeth Noelle-Neumann, head of the Allensbach "Institute for 'Demoscopy'," who with 80 co-workers has been analyzing German opinions since 1947, reports that as late as 1960, fully 43 percent of West German housewives did not want to see their husbands in the role of a "dishwashing simpleton"; but in 1970, 84 percent said that they like it if their husbands helped them occasionally with the dishes and two thirds of all married men owned up "more or less gladly" to some service in the kitchen.(14) (But interestingly, a cartoon ridiculing women's liberation accompanies the above referred to article in Die Welt. It depicts a demonstration for women's rights. In it, two women carry signs that read "Partnership not only in bed," and "An end to the slave labor of the housewife." And one of the women is shown turning her head to the other asking: "How do you manage it that your blouse is always whiter than mine?").

Extensive interviews carried out by this author generally confirmed such findings and observations as the ones reported above, and showed particularly strong feelings on the perceived duty of mothers to stay home and take care of their young children. Several childless West German career women, including previously cited sociologist Helge Pross, explained that they had no children because they could not combine motherhood with successful pursuit of their professional work. Working women with children usually related how they interrupted work for several years until the youngest child had reached a certain age – in most cases, they said three years. Most nonworking mothers expressed contentment with their role, although one of them, the young wife of a theology professor at the University of Munich, said: "I am fulfilled as a housewife; but sometimes I feel like an exotic being. It isn't supposed to fulfill me." Most such nonworking mothers strongly defended their "housewife and mother only" status. "If I had an outside job," said the wife of a Berlin psychologist, "I would need a teacher as kind of substitute mother for my children. Then I couldn't understand my children, and they would not have the right childhood memories." But one divorced mother who had been a housewife for 23 years and who is now employed by a Protestant women's aid organization attributed her divorce largely to her lack of fulfillment as a "mere housewife" and to her husband's refusal to let her take a job, even after the children were grown. Yet she, as all others, expressed the firm view that when a child comes into the family, "the mother herself must take care of it for the first few years."

As regards husbands' participation in housework and child-rearing, this author did not come across one single wife in West Germany who felt that her husband fully shared household and parent responsibilities. The pair that came closest to equal sharing was a university student couple with two children, where she acknowledged that he "can and does help me in the home and even watches the children when I am in class." (Although she did attend a few classes a week, she, too, was steadfast in her conviction that, except for such very brief absences, "the mother should stay home with her children, at least until they are three. I wouldn't have enrolled at the university at all if my husband couldn't himself mind the children while I am out of the house.") Several other West German housewives interviewed by this author asserted that their husbands were <u>willing</u> to do their fair share, but for one reason or another they didn't. Professional women, themselves very busy, told this author that their husbands wanted to lend them a hand at home but often didn't have the time, and couldn't be expected to "after a hard day's work." Others explained that they could do it "faster and better" themselves; and when their husbands wanted to do their part "in theory," but in practice "it is very difficult for them because they were raised with the view that housework is a woman's job." Many reported from their own and their friends' experiences that when a husband helps he does what he likes, while the wife has to do whatever else needs to be done. "This is the difference," said a West Berlin journalist whose husband is a well-known author and TV script writer, "he'll play with the children, but I have to take them to the doctor and have to attend parent-teachers meetings." And many women remarked that their husbands did contribute, but that who did what was still decided automatically along traditional sex-lines. "I cook, but my husband does the taxes, and he takes me shopping whenever we need to buy a lot and the bags are heavy, because I do not drive," said the wife of a geologist who had been a seamstress, secretary, and free-lance writer. "I cook and do the garden but my husband takes care of all repairs and recently even did an extensive renovating job on our home," proudly boasted a Bremen housewife and mother of one whose husband is a printer. "Once in a while, he'll even take the laundry to the laundromat; but husbands usually turn the care of children over to us, and we women like it that way," said the mother of one who is employed as an unskilled laborer in a paper and printing plant.

Some women, to be sure, emphasize that things have improved. "Twenty or twenty-five years ago, no German man would even have carried a shopping bag. Nowadays my husband often picks up a few groceries on his way home from work, or carries heavy bags up the stairs for me when he is home," said one. "My husband often sets the tables, helps dry the dishes, and occasionally even puts our daughter to bed. In the 1950s, he would have been considered henpecked," commented another.

In West and East Germany alike, the small family consisting of mother, father, and children is the basic social and economic unit. Extended family units which include grandparents and/or other family members are no longer common and are becoming more and more the exception, particularly in the cities. Cohabitation of couples not legally married is somewhat more prevalent in the West and is becoming more accepted, at least in theory, among West German youths. (A recent survey among FRG teenagers found that 87 percent of the male and 92 percent of the female youths saw nothing wrong with it.)(15) Premarital sex is fairly widespread in West Germany and is not uncommon in the GDR either(16) – the relatively high and increasing percentage of babies born out of wedlock testifies to that. Still, only a very small percentage of West German and a yet smaller percentage of East German households actually consists of unmarried couple. Other forms of basic social units, such as communal living arrangements, are rare in the Federal Republic and nonexistent in the GDR.

Table 5.1. Children Born Out of Wedlock
(as % of total number of births)[a]

FRG and GDR

Year	1965	1970	1972	1975	1976	1977	1978
FRG	4.7	5.5	6.1	6.5	6.3	6.5	7.0
GDR	9.8	13.3	16.2	16.1	16.2	15.8	N.A.

[a]GDR figure include still-births, FRG figures do not.

Source: Statistical Yearbooks through 1979, both countries.

As previously observed, West Germany treats the family and family life as a private affair; the state merely sets the legal framework (divorce laws, inheritance laws, etc.) and otherwise enters the picture only in extreme cases (e.g., child neglect). In the GDR, on the other hand, the family is intended to have a social function also, and there is a closer link between the family and society at large. In a court decision of the early 1950s in which a divorce was granted to a wife because her husband refused to let her accept outside employment, the judge explained that "the living conditions of spouses are inseparable from those of the society in which the spouses live. Since the defendant is violating the vital interests of society, he therefore also violates the vital interests of his spouse."(17) In another GDR court decision of the same year in which it was ruled that the right of a daughter to a dowry — a right previously provided for under German law (<u>BGB</u>, §1620) — could no longer be legally upheld under conditions of socialism, the judge elaborated: "Marriage . . . has lost its character as an economic maintenance institution. It has become a relation of two economically equal partners <u>to whom our state offers every opportunity</u> to build their life and their household together to the best of their own ability."(18) A recent West German study on women in the GDR describes the relationship between the family and socialist society: "Although intimate relations are to be considered a private family affair, the family is nevertheless understood as an institution in which each member has a responsibility to the entire society while society on the other hand must give due consideration to the family sphere. . . .(19)

In part because of East Germany's active attempts to promote equality of the sexes in the family as elsewhere in society, in part because women there participate in such large numbers in the labor force, and in part because the educational level of GDR women has been rising so rapidly, one would certainly expect to find that the sex-based role division in the GDR family has been altered drastically. Undeniably, progress has been made; and GDR reports as well as personal observations seem to indicate that progress has been more pronounced than in the Federal Republic (see a few examples below). Nevertheless, there is clear evidence that East German women also still have a long way to go before they can claim full sex-equality in their family relations and status.

GDR authors often express pride in the progress toward sex equality within the family which, they assert, has been achieved there. An East Berlin psychologist, for instance, recently wrote that the "new family and the new trends in school education" have influenced young people to "take the social equality of men and women for granted." And he goes on to say that, although young men do want to advance in their professions, they nevertheless "show more concern and more interest than any previous generation in matters of homemaking and family life. They consider it perfectly natural to prepare a meal and to play with and take care of their small children. Twenty-five years ago, a man would not appear in public pushing a baby carriage, while today it has become commonplace."(20) There is surely a certain amount of truth to such a contention, especially as it applies to the better educated strata of young people in the GDR today. But the careful reader will note that the statement by the East Berlin psychologist does not suggest that GDR husbands are nowadays doing their fair share of housework and child rearing. As a matter of fact, that psychologist himself had to admit later in the same article that the division of labor within the home was still in a state of flux. While reiterating that East German husbands have been increasingly willing to take over a large share of domestic chores, he acknowledged that there are still those who resist this trend and that, therefore, wives "in some cases" are still at a disadvantage in vocational development. And although he pointed out quite correctly that few GDR women would want to be full-time housewives, even if they could afford it, he also found that "marriage and motherhood remain the center of their attention."(21)

Leading GDR experts on women's problems also see sex-equality within the family as still wanting in the GDR. For instance, Herta Kuhrig, head of the study group "The Woman in Socialist Society" at the GDR Academy of Sciences, writes: "Without wanting to belittle the ever-increasing participation of husbands in the family, the primary burdens are still borne by the wife";(22) and Inge Lange, Central Committee Secretary on Women's Affairs and the highest ranking woman in the GDR party hierarchy, agrees. More specifically, Lange points to a frequently cited study by the GDR Institute for Market Research which found that, in 1970, participation of men in domestic chores amounted to only 13 percent of the work done in East German households — in spite of all governmental and party efforts, an increase of only 1.4 percent (barely more than half an hour per week) over 1965.(23) In 1970, GDR women over 18 reportedly spent one fifth more time on their households than on all their outside employment.(24) A West German study reports that, in the mid-1970s, East German women still did 84 percent of the cooking, 78 percent of the cleaning, 90 percent of the laundering, and 76 percent of the shopping.(25) And a 1978 West German TV documentary, tellingly entitled "All is Not as it is Supposed to Be: Women and Emancipation in the GDR," gave the average weekly number of hours of housework performed in GDR homes in 1978 as 5.5 for husbands and 37 for wives (which would leave husbands at 13 percent of the total of 42.5 hours — less, if other members of the family contribute additionally to domestic chores).(26)

Table 5.2. Distribution of Household Chores in Multiperson Homes, GDR

	1965		1970	
	Hours per week	%	Hours per week	%
Wife	37.7	79.4	37.1	78.7
Husband	5.5	11.6	6.1	13.0
Others	4.3	9.0	3.9	8.3
Total	47.5	100.0	47.1	100.0

Source: Lange, Aktuelle Probleme, p. 25. Also, for instance, see Helwig, "Frauenfoerderung," p. 56; Die Wirtschaft, Berlin (GDR), # 22, 1974, p. 12; and DDR Handbuch, p. 272.

Once again, personal interviews generally confirmed the findings of such studies and surveys. Even professional women acknowledged that their husbands did not fully share in household chores. Famous Jewish GDR folksinger Lyn Jaldati observed that "some men do help, but among the older especially, women still do more." Leipzig university professor Traute Schoenrath told this author that her husband, also a Leipzig university professor, "does what I ask him to, <u>if he has the time</u>." Some of the women interviewed even defended certain traditional views. Editor Suse Nehritz, for example, expressed strong convictions on the issue of child care: "Of course, the mother belongs with the young child; it would be insanity if it were the father. The mother has a more intimate relationship to the baby: it came out of her body. When a child gets sick, it is almost always the mother who takes off from work...." But the great majority of those interviewed took pains to point out progress and what they see as rapidly changing attitudes of the younger generation. "Years ago," said one of East Berlin's leading occupational therapists, Ursula Katzenstein, "no German man would have wanted to be seen taking care of a baby. Now, fathers bathe their babies, diaper them, drive them to day care centers...." "In my own family," said GDR economist Annelise Klenner, "my husband [a professor of philosophy] and I worked it out over the years. What one of us doesn't like, the other one does. He makes good spaghetti; but when we have guests, I always cook — I do it better — and he bakes. It used to be, however, that my husband wouldn't touch a baby carriage. Now, many men take their babies for a stroll." Folk singer Jaldati even found remarkable differences between the more "old fashioned" attitude of her 36-year old son and the "more modern" approach of her 30-year old son, the former more hesitant to share domestic chores, the latter gladly ready to "help" and even watch the two young children while his wife is at work. Suse Nehritz, with her conviction that the <u>mother</u> must attend to the young or the sick child, related that when her little grandson took ill, her son, rather than her daughter-in-law, once took off from work to take care of the sick child. And two young GDR university students, interviewed together (she studying to become an engineer, he an architect), both stated that they expected to share domestic chores "fifty-fifty" with their future spouses. But both, and most others this author interviewed in East Germany, readily acknowledged that in GDR families at large, <u>equal</u> sharing of domestic chores would still be some time in materializing. The students attributed the delay primarily to lingering aspects of traditional upbringing in the home which can be changed only gradually.

West and East German observers generally agree. Cologne author and editor Gisela Helwig, for instance, sees the attitude of young GDR men and women toward housework still greatly influenced by the behavior of their mothers and fathers, as they witnessed it in their own home during their childhood;(27) and recent GDR surveys among teenagers, 16 to 18 years of age, find that such teenagers still base the model for their future family to a great extent on the division of labor actually practiced by their parents in their home.(28) Even among younger couples who share household obligations much more readily than did their parents, GDR studies show, "boys are still less frequently called on to help with domestic chores than girls," a fact which is perceived by GDR analysts as an "indication of weakness in present family education."(29)

In relentless effort to promote full sex equality in the new "socialist" family, including joint responsibility for household chores and for the raising of the children, the GDR has not merely passed relevant legislation. Aware that laws can only provide the legal basis for such equality within the family, the GDR leadership, virtually from the outset, has imposed upon the country's media the obligation to lend its support to the cause. Hence, authors, journalists, artists, motion picture producers, song writers, and educators have long been addressing themselves to the problem. East German men and women are called upon by them and by the authorities to abandon their "traditional thinking about predestined roles" and to "so completely change the upbringing of their children that boys receive the kind of training in their home which would make them as fit as girls to do housework."(30) A recent book on women in the GDR properly describes the situation: "In the family, two people make the decisions, the man who is privileged because he has tradition on his side and the woman who has propaganda and the law on her side."(31)

The GDR has undertaken a wide variety of measures aimed at easing household burdens, still borne mostly by women — and in East Germany mostly by working women at that. While such measures do not in and of themselves _directly_ promote sex equality (after all, there are more household appliances in West than in East Germany), they at least make it easier for women to accept outside employment and combine family obligations and a career. Toward this end, the GDR's state economic plans have been providing for the construction of ever more restaurants, cafeterias, and work place canteens and of other service establishments such as caterers, laundries, and dry cleaners. Increasing numbers of grocery stores have introduced preprinted lists of available groceries to be checked off and left at the store by customers for home delivery during early evening hours. Moreover, production plans have been calling for increased output of vacuum cleaners, refrigerators, washing machines, and, to a lesser extent, dryers and dishwashers; and, today, the GDR leads all socialist countries and approaches the Federal Republic in the percentage of families who have such household appliances. (In 1977, for instance, 73 percent of East German homes had washing machines and 85 percent had refrigerators.)(32) In recent years, East German shoppers, especially in larger cities, have been able to find in the stores growing numbers of precooked and semiprepared foods and textile items that need little care; and finally, to help working mothers, the number of child care centers has been expanded rapidly (nurseries, kindergartens, and after-school care centers, discussed in chapter 3) and so have kitchen and dining room facilities in schools where children now can partake of hot lunches.(33)

Actually, all these measures undertaken by the government and the Party are supposed to do more than just ease the workload of East German women (and, to a lesser extent, of other members of GDR families). According to Party chief Erich Honecker,

> Overcoming some of the burdens which still have such an influence on the life of women will also make an important contribution to the development of a new socialist life style. Above all, it will reinforce young people to display in their personal life-sphere an attitude free from outmoded traditions and habits, which corresponds fully to the new social position of the woman in socialist society and also to her great responsibility as a mother.(34)

And Honecker calls for the continuation of "step-by-step measures in the formation of a mature socialist society that will enable the working mother to meet, as an equal member of society, her obligation on her job and also as a mother."(35)

But Central Committee member Inge Lange warns that nothing will be of any avail unless women change their own attitudes:

> The woman must free herself from old habits as well as from a certain feeling of guilt that because of her professional activity she neglects her family. Otherwise, all our efforts to reduce housework will be but a bottomless pit, expensive for our society but of little assistance to women.(36)

And Lange reminds us that "as socialist society develops, so do accordingly the expectations of individuals for better foods, greater comfort, and more hygiene" (for example, more frequent changing of clothing and bed linens). Consequently, she cautions, the attempts to satisfy the new demands could "devour" the benefits gained from providing the means for reducing household chores.(37)

There is substantial evidence that Lange's concerns are not unwarranted. In spite of all measures taken, average time spent on housework declined by only half an hour per week during the five-year period from 1965 to 1970 (see table 5.2). To cope with the problem, Lange gives friendly advice: Be less fastidious when it comes to housework. Adopt a new attitude: Change, as she says she has, from "I'll keep my house as good as possible" to "I'll keep my house as good as necessary."(38)

MORE MARRIAGES END IN DIVORCE

Whenever sex-based role division in the family is such that the man is the sole breadwinner, wives are under strong <u>economic</u> pressure to hold on to marriages even if they are highly unsatisfactory to them. These wives are also under strong <u>social</u> pressure, for in such a socio-economic environment, a divorced woman tends to be looked upon with disapprobation and treated as a social misfit, a failure as a wife and mother in what was her primary responsibility in life: to provide a warm and loving home for and take care of her family. Even today in West Germany, according to an official FRG information pamphlet, "the married woman is most highly respected, while divorced women have the lowest rating."(39)

In recent years, there have been marked changes in the stability of marital relations in both West and East Germany. In West Germany, the number of new marriages per 1,000 population declined steadily during the 1960s and the 1970s. A recent West Berlin TV documentary, explicatively entitled "Is Marriage Still Attractive at All?", reported increasing skepticism among West Germans toward the institution of marriage.(40) In the GDR, on the other hand, the rate of new marriages dropped during the early 1960s but has been on the rise rather steadily ever since. But neither East nor West German marriages are as stable as they used to be. In both Germanies, divorce rates per 1,000 population have doubled during the past two decades. However there are almost half as many divorces again in the GDR (where most wives are financially independent) than in the Federal Republic (where a substantial percentage of housewives are still almost totally economically dependent on their husbands). But since new marriages have been on the decline in the FRG and on the increase in the GDR, divorces expressed as percentages of new marriages have, to be sure, been rising more rapidly in the former than in the latter and are currently approximately at par in the two Germanies, totaling about 30 percent of new marriages in each.

Table 5.3. Marriages and Divorces
(per 1,000 population)
Selected years

Year	Marriages		Divorces	
	FRG	GDR	FRG	GDR
1960	9.4	9.7	0.9	1.4
1965	8.3	7.6	1.0	1.6
1970	7.3	7.7	1.3	1.6
1975	6.3	8.4	1.7	2.5
1976	5.9	8.6	1.8	2.7
1977	5.8	8.8	N.A.[a]	2.6
1978	5.3	8.4	N.A.[a]	2.6

[a] The 1979 FRG Statistical Yearbook gives divorce figures for 1977 only for divorces "under the old law." The new divorce law came into effect in mid-1977. No figures for 1978 are available.

Sources: Statistical Yearbook FRG, 1977, p. 68; and 1979, pp. 67 and 75. Statistical Yearbook GDR, 1977, p. 396; 1978, p. 349; and 1979, p. 351.

Table 5.4. Divorces
(% of population and marriages)
1976[a]

	Divorces	Population	Existing Marriages	New marriages of same year	Divorces % of population	Divorces % of existing marriage	Divorces % of new marriages of same year
FRG	108,363	61,531,000	15,165,000[b]	365,728	0.18	0.71	29.6
GDR	44,803	16,786,057	4,195,000[b]	144,590	0.27	1.07	31.0

[a] 1976, rather than a later year was chosen because adequate figures for the FRG were not available (see footnote to table 5.3).

[b] Roughly averaged and rounded off from Statistical Yearbooks since slightly different figures are given for "married men" and "married women." (It can be assumed that a person widowed during a year is counted as married for that year.)

Sources: Computed from Statistical Yearbook, FRG, 1978, pp. 50 and 62, and 1979, p. 75; and Statistical Yearbook, GDR, 1978, p. 345 and 1979, pp. 347 and 351.

Taking note of the rapid increase in divorce rates (and also in the percentage of babies born out of wedlock), a recent Friedrich-Ebert-Foundation study holds that in both the Federal Republic and the GDR "a connection between these developments and the growing emancipation of women can be assumed as certain." West German author, TV producer, and member of West Germany's Communist Party, Erika Runge, goes even further, concluding that "apparently marriage and emancipation are mutually exclusive."(41)

Most observers would surely consider Runge's appraisal too extreme; but there seems to be general acceptance of the notion that the economically independent working woman is much more likely than her "housewife-only" counterpart to resent the burden of having to take care of home and children virtually by herself. Hence, the rebellion against the "double shift" appears to be much stronger in the GDR (where most working-age women hold outside jobs) than in the FRG. "There still seem to be quite a few men in the GDR who, spoiled in their parents' home, want to become the pasha in their new home," writes a West German author of a book on the family in East Germany. "But," he continues, "few women in the GDR will stand for that; about one in three puts a stop to the marriage when she feels hampered in her personal development."(42) And an East German author of a book on women under socialism agrees:

> If a woman is emancipated both professionally and socially, she tends to feel it all the more if her husband regards her as little more than a servant. The desire for a full and happy family life which takes due consideration of a woman's work outside the home is growing far more rapidly than the capabilities on both sides of shaping their lives together as harmoniously as possible.(43)

Statistical evidence seems to support such views. Not only have divorces in East Germany increased so rapidly that next to the United States the GDR has today the world's highest divorce rate,(44) but there has also been a more than proportionate increase in the number of divorce proceedings where the woman was the plaintiff. In 1958, wives filed for divorce in 53 percent; in 1965, in 59.6 percent;(45) in 1972, in 64.8 percent;(46) and in 1977, in about two thirds of all cases.(47) Moreover, the husband's reluctance to help in the home nowadays is mentioned as a factor in more than half of the divorce cases in East Germany.(48) In West Germany, throughout the 1970s, over 70 percent of all divorce proceedings were initiated by the wife.

Table 5.5. Divorce Proceedings Initiated
by the Wife

FRG

Year	Total Divorces	Divorce proceedings initiated by wife[a]	Divorce proceedings initiated by wife[a] as % of all divorces
1970	76,520	53,747	70.2
1972	86,614	61,418	70.9
1974	98,589	70,735	71.7
1976	108,258	76,947	71.1

[a] Does not include divorce proceedings that did not end in actual divorce granted.

Source: Statistical Yearbook, FRG, 1972, p. 51; 1974, p. 62; 1976, p. 75; and 1978, p. 75.

6 Women's Organizations

West Germany has a wide variety of women's organizations, among them regular women's associations and groups open to women in general, religious women's organizations, various professional women's organizations, women's groups within and as part of political parties, and radical women's groups which West Germans refer to as "feminists." Yet, as a recent New York Times article correctly observed, "West Germany has no powerful women's liberation movement like the one in the United States."(1) Indeed, West German women's organizations generally are not, and at this stage mostly do not try to be, effective political pressure groups. A recent publication by the Federal Ministry for Youth, Family and Health, which focused largely on the activities of FRG women's organizations in the "Year of the Woman," 1975, observed that, to bring about concrete improvements in the position of West German women, it is necessary first to create "the basic preconditions: to intensify public realization of the problems, to change the population's general attitude, and to encourage women to make use of their rights and opportunities."(2) It is toward these ends, above all, that the efforts of West German women's organizations are directed.

REGULAR FRG WOMEN'S ORGANIZATIONS

The German Council of Women, located in Bonn, is the umbrella organization to which belong over a hundred womens' federations, organizations, and associations with a total membership of about ten million. The Council has the declared goal of "focusing public attention on the situation of women as a social and political problem – of awakening the consciousness of politicians as well as of individuals to this problem." To this end, the Council organizes meetings, workshops, seminars, and talks with people in politics and with representatives of the general public, the media, and feminist groups "to whom it must be made clear, above all, that without women sharing the thoughts and the responsibility in all areas and at all levels, neither national nor international problems can be solved in the future."(3) And as this book goes to press, the German Council of Women is preparing somewhat more drastic action: a demonstration for Nov. 5, 1980 in Bonn to lead off a campaign against "the distorted depiction of women in the media." The Council is planning to ask support for a boycott of newspapers which use cartoons portraying secretaries as employers' playthings or those which run advertisements featuring housewives as not-very-bright endorsers of products.(4) The women's organizations that are members of the Council, so explains a summary report of the Federal Ministry for Youth, Family and Health, "focus their activities primarily on direct assistance to women...." The Kronberg-based "German Women's Ring," as an example, organizes meetings, discussions, and workshops to motivate girls to complete their schooling, to induce female students to choose traditionally non-female occupations, to help women who want to remain housewives to overcome feelings that it is demeaning to be exclusively a mother and a housewife, and, on the other hand, to help women who want outside work to organize their household to enable them to combine their family obligations with a career. Other women's organizations have established counseling centers which render assistance to women in divorce and conflict situations, concern themselves with foreign women and children residing in West Germany, and offer support to foreign girls in their professional education.(5)

In the political arena proper, the German Council of Women advocates greater political engagement of women under its slogan "more women in politics, more women into the parliament." But the Council does not seem to consider the furtherance of this goal one of its current priorities. In any case, it expresses full awareness of the fact that even its occasional lobbying efforts with party leaders can, at this stage, have but "a very limited impact" on the selection of candidates.(6)

WEST GERMAN RELIGIOUS WOMEN'S ORGANIZATIONS

The Catholic, Protestant, and Jewish denominations all have their women affiliates in West Germany; the last, the "Jewish Women's Association in Germany," is obviously small and relatively unknown.

The "Workshop of Catholic Women's Organizations" claims 2 million members for its affiliated Catholic women's organizations such as the "Union of Catholic Working Women" and the "Catholic Women in the Economy and Administration." It is a member of the "World Association of Catholic Women's Organizations," organizes meetings, publishes pamphlets, holds seminars, and engages in other types of activities to promote the interests of Catholic women within the framework of its religious orientation.(7)

"Protestant Women's Work," the parent organization of West Germany's Protestant women's groups, claims a membership which encompasses roughly "those adult women who belong to the Protestant church and in one way or another (a) are professionally active or hold an honorary office, or (b) can be reached through community work." It proclaims that "it has become evident in the church and in the world that adherence to obsolete traditions and to a division of roles between the sexes which emanates from a patriarchally imprinted culture stands in the way of the real emancipation of women," but it has to admit that its efforts have not yet shown wide success. Nevertheless, and although its advocacy of emancipation "publicly and in the media undoubtedly causes irritation," it intends to persist on its course of informing the public and raising women's consciousness in the hope that it will "enhance the realization of just how socially important the emancipation of women really is."(8)

ASSOCIATIONS OF WEST GERMAN PROFESSIONAL WOMEN

In many professions, FRG women have organized their own groups to advance their respective interests. As examples of some such organizations and of some of the work they do, the "Association of German Female Academicians," with some 1,750 members, encourages research on women's problems, prepares relevant bibliographies, and organizes conferences dealing with specific scientific themes and also, more generally, with "basic problems concerning the social position of women." The "German Female Physicians' Association" sponsors projects on "the possibility of combining the medical profession with family obligations." The "League of Female Jurists" (which includes among its members female economists and business administrators as well as women in the legal profession) hosted and chaired the 1975 conference of the "International Federation of Women Lawyers" in Hamburg, which focused on the legal position of women in the family, on the job, and in society, and advocated an enhanced role of government to promote women's interests and sex equality. Governments should, for instance, "seek to solve the problems of families by promoting means to strengthen family-ties and to resolve family disputes; . . . provide incentives for industry and management to train and promote women for positions in areas where women have been underrepresented; . . . and cooperate with women's organizations . . . to promote the advancement of women in all fields of endeavor." And there is even a "German Housewives' Association" which concerns itself with problems of interest to the German housewife, holding seminars and workshops, for instance, on independent social security benefits for nonworking FRG housewives, recognition of the value of the work of housewives in the FRG's gross national product, and, more generally, the position of the housewife in West German society.(9)

WOMEN'S GROUPS IN WEST GERMAN POLITICAL PARTIES

Three of West Germany's four major political parties(10) have their own women's divisions: the SPD's "Working Team of Social Democratic Women" (ASF), the CDU's "Women's Association of the Christian Democratic Union of Germany," and its Bavarian sister party's "Women's Union of the CSU." Only the FDP does not have and never has had its own women's affiliate. Representatives of the SPD, the CSU, and the CSU explain that their women's groups are necessary as a "basis for information and training and as a pressures group"; but, according to then FDP candidate Otto Graf zu Solms, there is no need for a separate women's organization in the FDP because "there are no women's problems that are not social problems."(11) In a personal interview, FDP member and vice president of the FRG parliament, Liselotte Funcke, explained that even a women's committee, formerly active in the FDP, has now been abolished because when anything like that exists, "male delegates or party leaders whom we approach with women's problems refuse to listen and tell us instead to take the issue up with the women's committee."

The women's groups in West Germany's major political parties are primarily discussion and study groups: they organize meetings, seminars, and workshops. The ASF, undoubtedly the politically most active of all, also makes some attempts to exert influence on its own party and, through it, on the legislature and government, trying to persuade them to give favorable attention to matters concerning women's rights. It has, for instance, issued demands for the rejection of school books which portray traditional sex-role images, for special educational consideration for women, and for shortening the workday and improving working conditions so that "women will be able to better dedicate themselves to the education of children and other social tasks." Some of the ASF's proposals — such as its proposals for equal school curricula for boys and girls — have actually been enacted into law, although not necessarily only because of its efforts. In 1975, the ASF succeeded in having the party add to its program a rather general section on "equality of women," which demands of its own party that it "get serious as regards equality of position of women in its own ranks, for only then can the policies of the SPD be believably represented."(12) Yet, on the whole, the ASF's influence as a pressure or lobbying group is still minimal, as evidenced by the small number of female party functionaries, and by the small number of women put up by the party as candidates for elective office or appointed by the party to government posts it controls — an ineffectiveness ASF members are the first to admit.

The CDU's and the CSU's women's organizations seem to be much less politically involved than the SPD's. They focus their attention more on encouraging discussions "at all levels about the position of women in our society," and on "awakening the interests of men in the problems of women."(13)

WEST GERMAN FEMINISTS

Women who belong to "feminist" organizations are widely regarded by West Germans as "left-wingers, radicals, lesbians, or simply idle dreamers."(14) Actually, there are three different types of feminist movements in the FRG; all relatively small but more aggressive than other West German women's organizations; they differ in their approaches to the achievement of women's emancipation for which they are striving.

The largest feminist group in the Federal Republic, with a membership of 300 in the mid-1970s, is the Munich-based FFP ("Furtherance Circle for the Formation of a Feminist Party," formerly "Women's Forum") whose declared purpose it is "to help women find their own identity in free democratic self-determination, without tutelage by male ideologies, dogmas, institutions, and organizations." To accomplish this goal, the organization's head and founder, Hannelore Maybry, favors the formation of an independent women's party that would compete with the existing major parties; but with her present following, this is still only her dream and goal. Her movement has been labeled by some as "Marxist"; but she rejects such designation as a "final patriarchic subterfuge." Her opponent, she says, "is not capitalism but patriarchy."

Other feminist organizations, such as the "Socialist-Feminist Action" in Cologne, want to make women's emancipation an adjunct to a socialist revolution so that women in the FRG can be freed from their "double oppression: oppression by capital of those who depend on wages and oppression by the patriarchy which subordinates women to men."

There is a third type of feminist movement which calls itself the "autonomous feminist movement." It rejects large central women's organizations altogether; and its founder, Alice Schwarzer, perhaps best known since 1977 as publisher of the radically feminist monthly _Emma_ (a "newspaper by women for women"), advocates, instead, the formation of independent, individual local women's groups. Such groups have, indeed, sprung up under various names (e.g., Women's Group, Emancipation Group, Workshop Group, Women's Liberation Action, Bread and Roses) in all major West German cities and universities. These groups each have their debates, seminars, workshops, and discussion evenings; above all, with the U.S. women's liberation movement as a guide, most of them have their regular consciousness-raising sessions aimed at helping women to "find" themselves. They do not want to fight seriously _against_ men; but at this stage most of them believe that they can solve their problems better _without_ men. However, so far, they have not had any major impact on women's emancipation or lack thereof in the Federal Republic.(15) Here is the way a recent article on the FRG's feminist movement, published in one of West Germany's leading newspapers, summarized the present condition of West German women and the immediate goals feminists have set for themselves to alter the situation:(16)

For years the [West German] statistics have remained unchanged: Women are on the average less well educated than men, they earn less than men even if they are equally qualified, they undertake by themselves as a matter of course the housework and raising of children. As long as they are not gainfully employed, they do not have their own social security for their old age. In major women's periodicals one still reads, even today: "The best social security for a woman is a marriage that works." Equally unchanged, women are not interested in politics, they vote the way their husbands do, only rarely do they take advantage of their opportunities in enterprise committees and in parties, and they adjust and do not fight against discrimination. They type in the office to finance the fiance's studies and later as wives they represent their husband's social status.

As long as they do not take advantage of the rights their grandmothers fought for in the first women's movement, no law, no party can change their dependence and lack of self-reliance. But this is precisely what the feminists want: encourage women to become independent, help them to become self-reliant.

Apart from religious and professional women's organizations that focus mostly on their own members' religious and professional interests, West Germany's women's movement is still largely in its formative stages. In personal interviews throughout West Germany, this author has found women much more often than not reluctant to subscribe to the tenets of any of the regular, not to speak of the feminist, women's organizations, and very skeptical of such organizations' ability to accomplish much. Many of the interviewees expressed the view that to be successful women must work directly through existing political parties. "Any other road is unrealistic," commented a West Berlin psychologist; "What good does it do to offer women a wailing wall," said the chairwoman of the Social-Democratic Women of Bavaria, "to succeed, we must grow through regular party work"; "Feminists are too far removed from reality: refusal to participate in regular party work — why that is utter nonsense," opined sociologist Helge Pross. However, those women who are active in political parties and in their parties' women's organizations complain of discrimination there and find their effectiveness still minimal.

THE GDR'S "DEMOCRATIC WOMEN'S LEAGUE OF GERMANY"

In the GDR, there is no women's movement as such; there is only one women's organization, the Democratic Women's League of Germany (DFD), started in 1947. In the mid-1970s it had 1.3 million members in 16,800 branches and was represented by 35 delegates in the GDR parliament.(17) Its members come from all strata of the population, "irrespective of party membership or political orientation"; however, the overwhelming majority of all administrative posts are in the hands of SED members.(18) Its self-declared functions include: political-ideological work among women; drawing women from all strata of the population into active participation in social life; winning women over to productive work; and easing the burden of working women and particularly of working mothers. More specifically, the DFD has engaged in numerous economic, social, and educational activities. It has, for instance, participated in discussions concerning the national economic plan; it has worked actively toward the extension and improvement of child care facilities; and it has published educational booklets relevant to women's interests, for example, one aimed at promoting equal division of household chores among children, irrespective of sex.(19) However, since the mid-1960s, and more even since its 10th Federal Congress in 1975, the DFD has focused its attention primarily on nonworking (and to a lesser extent on part-time working) women. It is today primarily a social club for such women, providing a place where they can get together, make new contacts, and take courses in cooking, sewing, and child care.(20) It was this service function to nonworking women, almost exclusively, that GDR women emphasized when this author inquired about the purposes of this women's organization. "At the outset," explained an East Berlin editor, "the DFD was needed as an information agency for women. Consciousness-raising and motivating women toward productive work were among its primary functions. But all this is no longer necessary. This is why today the DFD caters primarily to nonworking women, and especially to older women who have retired." "Since the introduction of the 'baby year'," added GDR sociologist Herta Kuhrig, "we have had more young women join us also, especially those who are worried about their ability to handle simultaneously marriage, a child, and a career." "Our working women," explained ethics professor and GDR representative to the UN Commission on the Status of Women, Helga Hoerz, "are now fully taken care of by the party, the labor union, and other socio-economic organizations in the GDR. We do not need a special women's organization to represent their interests."

In West Germany, then, women's organizations as a whole appear to have played a very limited role in recent years in awakening women's (and to some extent men's) consciousness; but they have been providing a discussion forum for women's problems. However, as far as actually influencing the shaping and implementation of policies aimed at furthering women's emancipation in West Germany is concerned, women's organizations are just at the beginning stages.(21)

And in the GDR, there is no women's movement as such anywhere. There is only one national women's organization which has become primarily a social organization for nonworking GDR housewives. The functions incumbent on Western women's organizations of raising women's consciousness, altering social attitudes, and leading the struggle for equal rights for women under the law, in the economy, in political life, and in society at large have, in the GDR, been taken over from the very outset by the Party, the legislature, and the executive branch of government.

7 Summary and Conclusions

The two Germanies that emerged from the ashes of the Third Reich inherited from their mutual past virtually identical legacies of sex prejudices, sex stereotyping, sex discrimination in education and on the job market, and a sex-based division of roles in the home and in society at large. There have been considerable changes over the years, and especially during the past few decades; yet, neither West nor East Germany has been able to rid itself completely of such traditional age-old views and patterns. But there are very significant differences between the two Germanies in regard to both the de jure and the de facto "emancipation" of women.

Since the end of the 1940s, a basic, broad, general, equal rights provision has been embodied in the constitutions of both the FRG and the GDR. But in specific legislative areas, from extensive maternity leaves at full pay (including the "baby year" off for working mothers) to laws stipulating equal pay for equal work, the GDR has been pathbreaking; while legislatures and courts in the Federal Republic have merely begun in recent years to follow haltingly, grudgingly, and reluctantly into her footsteps.(1) The difference is most pronounced in the area of "women's furtherance." The GDR has legislated what in practice amounts not merely to affirmative action but to extensive reverse discrimination, referred to in the GDR itself as "differentiation" and described in one West German book as "discrimination in favor of women so that discrimination against women can be eliminated."(2) Under her present constitution (and virtually from the very outset),(3) state and enterprises have been under obligation to create special facilities for, and extend special privileges to, working women and mothers; and educational institutions, similarly, are under orders to grant special concessions to female students in general and to mothers enrolled as part-time or full-time students in particular. Without such special privileges and concessions, one West German study on women in the GDR explained, "any guarantee of equal rights by itself would have been inadequate."(4)

West Germany, on the other hand, has no laws of any kind providing specifically for the furtherance of women (with the sole exception of a provision facilitating the retraining of mothers who want to rejoin the labor force after a prolonged period at home). But in recent years, "liberal" West German voices have been calling increasingly for women's furtherance legislation, similar to that already on the books in the GDR. Annemarie Renger, for four years (1972-1976) president and thereafter vice-president of the West German parliament, presents the case openly and succinctly: "If the constitution ... wants to lay claim to altering the life of future generations," she says "women must be purposefully furthered, <u>even if this includes a redistribution at the expense of men</u>. . . ."(5)

Whatever laws there may be on the books, they can be no more than a beginning, no more than the basic foundation upon which true equality can be built. And although there are considerable differences in the status of women in the two Germanies and in the progress toward equality they have made over the years, <u>complete</u> equality of the sexes is surely still wanting in both.

In West Germany, after more than three decades of law reforms, equal rights still exist to a considerable extent on paper only. Official West German government publications readily admit that "equality under the law is one side of the coin, reality the other. Women are still suffering under deep-rooted prejudices which prevent them from taking full advantage of the equal opportunities guaranteed them."(6) In fact, as the Investigative Commission on Women and Society found, West German politics is still predominantly a male preserve, West German industry is run almost completely by male business executives. Women are still less well educated than men, they do not have equal opportunity to embark on the career of their choice, they constitute one third of the labor force and one half of the unemployed, they earn, on the average, one third less than male workers and employees, and their social standing is still well below that of men.(7) Talking about the "many disadvantages women in our society are still exposed to," Federal Chancellor Helmut Schmidt said in December 1976 that in the job market in particular, the lack of equality for the nearly 10 million working women was "apparent."(8) And, says a publication of the Federal Ministry for Education and Science, the concept of a division of labor in which "the woman belongs in the home and the man in the hostile world is still deeply rooted in the consciousness of both [West German] men and women."(9) (This "housewife consciousness" of girls, a recent book on women in the Federal Republic charges, is still all too frequently instilled in them in their home and is further promoted in school.)(10) But, to some extent, sex discrimination — in this case, in part legal in nature — is perhaps most drastically illustrated in the case of West Germans who marry non-Germans. A West German woman who marries a foreigner is exposed to de facto and de jure discrimination, and the more southern, the more exotic, the more alien her husband, the greater the de facto discrimination. She becomes a "semiforeigner" herself and not until the law was changed in 1975 could her children automatically become German citizens.(11) The wife of a German man, on the other hand, becomes a quasi-German; she needs no residence or work permit (as does the foreign husband of a German woman) and her children have always had German citizenship automatically.(12)

At a December 1979 meeting of the German Council of Women in Mainz, male representatives of all major political parties fielded questions of some 500 women-delegates. They had a tough time finding convincing answers, but they were all in agreement on one point: equality as stipulated in the Constitution has not been achieved and there is no sign of true emancipation, freedom, and independence of women.(13) Little wonder that representatives of West German women's organizations, at a 1979 conference in Koenigswinter near Bonn, resentfully charged that "we live in a partiarchy, a male-dominated society that has been repressing women for thousands of years."(14) And West German sociologist and specialist on FRG women's affairs Helge Pross concurs. In her 1979 address to the International Political Science Association, Dr. Pross conceded that "Political opinion today demands that the executive committees of political and politically orientated organizations should include a few women"; but she concluded that West Germany is still "a state dominated by men. Men make the laws, men form the executive, men administer the law, men lead the political parties.... It is not only the political system ... but also other social areas of national relevance that are controlled by men ... power and control are a male monopoly."(15) And elsewhere she commented: "We don't need an equal rights amendment; we have to change a whole cultural tradition."(16)

In the GDR, the education of the present generation of young women is already at par with that of young men; curricula are essentially the same for all; and attempts to instill concepts of sex equality start at the nursery school level and are continued through the university. Virtually all working-age women who are not sick or temporarily tied down by small children hold jobs or are full-time students. Under strong social pressure to "take her place in society," the full-time housewife, so common in West Germany, is an almost nonexistent phenomenon in the GDR. Deeming at least some aspects of the status of East German women worthy of imitation, a booklet on "Marriage and Family in the Two German States," published by the West German Friedrich-Ebert Foundation, comments: "The possibility of combining marriage and motherhood with professional life, such as has become a reality in the GDR, can also provide a series of examples for our society...."(17)

Yet, official and semi-official GDR sources do not deny that, even in their country, age-old prejudices are still not completely wiped out and everyday reality does not yet fully correspond to the model so strongly advocated and coveted by the authorities. "It cannot be disputed that some remnants of traditional views on the role of women still linger on," writes an East German author;(18) "overcoming inhibitive traditions and backward ways of thinking and acting is a long process," acknowledges another.(19) And the Party Central Committee, while proclaiming proudly that "women have taken up their places everywhere in our society," admits that "problems remain which also in the future will demand our special attention."(20)

Although in all areas of life GDR women have achieved a much higher degree of equality with men than have their counterparts in West Germany, full de facto equality is still eluding them. True, earning differences between the sexes are considerably greater in West than in East Germany,(21) but GDR women are still overrepresented in lower paying "typical female" lines of endeavor. Conscious attempts to prepare women for leading positions date back to the very outset,(22) and a much higher percentage of East German than of West German women have actually reached high positions in the economy and on the political stage, but GDR women are still grossly underrepresented in positions of real power. Although GDR law stipulates that husbands may not merely "help out" but must do their fair share in the education and care of children and the conduct of the household,(23) and although, in fact, more men can be seen pushing baby carriages or carrying groceries in East Berlin, Leipzig, or Dresden than in West Berlin, Munich, or Cologne, East German women (and mostly working women at that) still do over 75 percent of all the chores connected with taking care of the home and the children (see table 5.2).

Lenin always promised that once capitalism had been overthrown, "legal equality of men and women would prevail." But even he hastened to admonish: "This, however, is not enough. Equality before the law is not equality in life."(24) Representing the official GDR position, Inge Lange, member of East Germany's Party Central Committee, expresses similar views and shows awareness of lingering problems: "We have achieved equal rights for women. But to these equal rights must correspond equal conditions for their implementation. . . . It is a laborious struggle between progress and backwardness."(25) GDR sources list at least three steps as necessary to enable women to realize the equality promised them by law.

(1) In accordance with prevailing economic realities, such material conditions must be created and steadily perfected as are essential for women to make full use of their equal rights, especially in the areas of politics, work, and education.

(2) By use of political-ideological persuasion, there must be promoted among men and women the correct views on the role of the woman in society and in the family that corresponds to the nature of socialist humanism. What matters here above all is to make word and deed correspond to each other and to subject backward views and behavior patterns . . . to courageous but helpful and sympathetic criticism.

(3) . . . Through women's furtherance measures, the consequences of century-old discrimination must be eliminated step by step.

SUMMARY AND CONCLUSIONS   165

Work loads must be divided with due consideration to the extra burden women bear as mothers.

All this involves a complicated and protracted process. . . .(26)

No such planned concentrated efforts are being effectively promoted, nor could they be expected to be promoted, in a decentralized pluralistic society such as the Federal Republic.

In conclusion, then, complete de facto sex equality cannot be found in either the Federal Republic or the GDR. But any researcher or even casual observer will find that East German women are far ahead of their West German counterparts in educational and professional opportunities; in their participation in the work force, in government, and in society; and, in general, in the way in which they find their "equal rights" implemented. From all available evidence, it seems apparent that the lion's share of the credit or blame for such significant dissimilarities must go to the respective social systems, each with its very different ideology, social fabric, economic framework, political structure, and with resulting differences in society's approach to the "emancipation of women." Although GDR women are still somewhat underprivileged, it is this difference in approach, above all, that does not allow for the conclusion that in the GDR all is as it is in the Federal Republic, merely a little better. It goes much deeper than this, for the difference in society's approach strongly affects the entire outlook of the citizenry; it affects the attitudes of authors, editors, teachers, managers, courts, and even the attitudes of husbands and parents; it affects the material and psychological independence, the very self-image of the women themselves. It is the difference between a society steeped in the Judeo-Christian heritage of male dominance and one ideologically committed to Marxist-Leninist ideology which has always prescribed equality of the sexes; it is the difference between a society in which powerful interests are still emotionally linked to much of the sex role division of yesteryear and one in which sex equality has become one of the country's primary aims; between a pluralistic society in which conservative newspapers and speakers freely oppose the entire concept of working mothers, referring to them as "bad mothers" and "neglecters and destroyers of families,"(27) and a uniformly guided society in which all means of information and communication encourage women, including mothers, to seek the economic independence that comes from gainful employment. It is also the difference between a society in which women have to fight for their rights (and are so hesitant to stand up and be counted that it took a Federal minister years to find a single female employee willing to bring suit for equal wages), and one in which each plant has a special commission for the protection of women's rights and a shop-steward committee under obligation to expose and rectify wrongs perpetrated consciously or unconsciously against women (and in which women freely appeal their cases to court if they feel that plant bodies have not given them proper satisfaction).(28) The FRG is a society in which women find major obstacles in their way if they attempt to prepare themselves for previously all-male occupations (in 1974, for instance, a 22-year-old licensed female pilot shocked the all-male board of Lufthansa and much of West German society when she brought suit to compel the airline to hire her as its first female flying officer trainee),(29) while the GDR is one in which women are consciously "furthered" to study for and take up "typically male" jobs and professions. The FRG is a society in which it is deemed basically a private matter for mothers of young children who want to work to find a place where they can leave their youngsters, while the GDR considers the provision of proper child care facilities as a social problem and a social responsibility to be attended to by the state, by local political units, and by economic enterprises. In all, it is the difference between a society in which women still have a very low self-image in comparison with men – a self-image that has hardly changed at all in recent years(30) – and one in which it is apparent even to the casual observer that women have considerable self-esteem and self-respect (surely to a great extent because of the economic independence that emanates from guaranteed gainful employment opportunities).

Under the circumstances, whatever progress has been achieved in the "emancipation of women" in West Germany has come about very slowly and very gradually against the opposition of powerful interests bent on maintaining the status quo, and against the opposition also of the many who found and still find it difficult to change age-old traditional attitudes and practices. Moreover, as has been shown throughout this book, most of the limited headway made has been of very recent origin. In a 1976 publication, the Federal Ministry for Youth, Family and Health points out that even West Germany's liberal coalition (the ruling SPD, supported by the liberal FDP) has given priority to the abolition of the existing legal discrimination against women only since 1969.(31) The women's organization of the conservative CDU released a statement that it "had started as early as 1973 an extensive discussion on the position of women in our society."(32) Only in very recent years, really only since the 1970s, the Federal Ministry attests, have more female candidates been running for enterprise councils, have women begun to form more groups to represent their own interests, have women established counselling centers, and have women increasingly participated in proposing new laws. This has all taken place, so says the ministry, under the slogan "if women want to be helped, they must help themselves." Only in very recent years have the efforts of those West German women and women's groups who have been working to overcome past sex discrimination shown any noticeable effect. "There is not much well-documented evidence as yet," comments the ministry, but it is, nevertheless, observable that women have started to make themselves noticed as a power group among politicians and among leading organizations." Only in very recent years have the political programs of the major parties even begun to be supplemented by women-oriented goals; only very recently has the elimination of discrimination against women been incorporated into work shop

SUMMARY AND CONCLUSIONS 167

programs of labor unions and other organizations. But all these steps, all these discussions, all these statements of what ought to be are only a beginning, a "strategy of transition," as the ministry calls it, which can lead to "full integration of women into society only if and when men and women together stand up for a comparable participation of both sexes in all areas of life." So far, the enhanced activity of women has found support among some men but "examples are still infrequent."(33) Since men can be won over but gradually, the responsibility for carrying on the laborious strife for the emancipation of women in the Federal Republic rests with West German women themselves, and they simply have not been doing and are not doing enough. This, at least, is the opinion of many observers, exemplified by Helge Pross's remarks to the August 1979 meeting of the International Political Science Association.(34)

> The crucial prerequisite for [West German] women achieving a greater share of power lies in their own hands: they need to become active by forming new alliances, they need to become active in citizens' action groups and similar initiatives. In order to achieve this, further changes in the female psychological make-up will be necessary: more self-assurance, self-confidence and courage to become active in public; they will have to become more politically orientated, better qualified — in short, they will have to become less self-discriminating. Here, I think, an observation is applicable which at least in Germany can be made time and time again: people are defeated not so much by their opponents as by themselves.

Thus, the struggle for equal rights for women in West Germany has been, and still is, an uphill struggle all the way.

In the GDR, on the other hand, the ideological commitment to the cause was there long before the new society was formed. In Marxist-Leninist tradition, the GDR has always considered the emancipation of women not merely vastly important to the women themselves, to their own development, well-being and personality, but also absolutely essential to society at large in its effort to "build socialism." As early as the mid-1950s, the SED central committee stated in this vein that, without the active participation of women in all areas of social life, the GDR as a state power would be "unthinkable."(35) Today, East German authorities will be the first to admit that much still needs to be done; but there is no denying that the Party, the government, and all public organizations have gone out of their way to promote sex equality in education, on the job market, in society at large, and even in home and family life. Contrary to West Germany, all the progress made in that area in East Germany has been presented to GDR women on a silver platter. And also contrary to West Germany, all-out efforts are continuing in the GDR to remedy lingering inadequacies and to raise women to a status of essential equality with men.

One final note: It is sometimes argued that substantial unemployment in the Federal Republic as compared with a labor shortage in the GDR is a contributory and perhaps a major factor accounting for differences in the status of women in the two Germanies. There is certainly some truth to such contention. While gainful employment is not equivalent to emancipation, it is, nevertheless, true that women's emancipation can hardly be attained without the economic independence that emanates primarily from participation in the labor force. But, on the other hand, there is overwhelming evidence that at least up to now the centrally planned economies (where employment is usually a right, guaranteed in the constitution) have been the ones that have achieved and have been able to maintain relatively full employment, while market economies (where joblessness is considered a private matter and overall employment hinges largely on the vicissitudes of the market) have usually been plagued by unemployment problems. Hence, even if West Germany's unemployment problem were shown to be a causal factor, this would in no way negate the thesis that differences in the status of women in the two Germanies are primarily attributable to the respective social system and to resulting differences in society's approach to "sex equality."

Notes

Chapter 1

(1) This, of course, does not apply to all German lands under Hitler's control. Apart from the areas annexed by the Nazis and returned after the war (such as Austria), some pre-Nazi German territories east of the Oder-Neisse line were incorporated into Poland and the USSR, making post-Potsdam Germany about 138,000 square miles in area, as compared with the 1919 post-Versailles German territory of 181,000 square miles.

(2) In the 1949 and the 1968 Constitutions of the GDR, there were still many references to a unified Germany. Article 8 of the 1968 Constitution, for instance, speaks of "overcoming the division of Germany imposed on the German nation by imperialism," and of "the gradual approachment of the two German states until their unification on the basis of the foundation of democracy and socialism." But the 1974 Law for the Amendment and Alteration of the Constitution of the German Democratic Republic (so extensive and with such decisive alterations that it virtually amounts to a new constitution) practically negates any possibility of unification and openly aims at close ties with the USSR. (For more detail, see Die neue Verfassung der DDR, pp. 9-15.)

(3) Stolper, p. 418; Gleitze, p. 169.

(4) Lieberman, p. 122.

(5) Scholl, Joswig, Huebner, et al., p. 14; also Florath, p. 48.

(6) Leptin, p. 51.

(7) The West Germans, it should be pointed out, have voluntarily made substantial reparation payments, and paid pensions to Jews abroad who

formerly lived on West German territory. The GDR has made no payments to Jews abroad, but pays sizable pensions to "victims of fascism" who live in the GDR, which includes all Jews residing there.

(8) For the FRG in constant 1962 prices from Volkswirtschaftliche Gesamtberechnungen, p. 108; for the GDR in constant 1967 prices from "Das Sozialprodukt der DDR," p. 123.

(9) Between 1960 and 1975, for instance, consumer prices rose by more than 75 percent in the FRG but remained unchanged in the GDR (Handbook of Economic Statistics, 1976, p. 43).

(10) Menschik and Leopold, for instance, say that the GDR is the ninth most industrialized nation in the world (p. 32).

(11) According to statistics published by the U.S. Central Intelligence Agency, Czechoslovakia led the GDR in per capita GNP during the 1960s and until the mid-1970s. Since then, East Germany has pulled slightly ahead. Actually, the Soviet Union's per capita output during the past ten or twelve years has also been very close to that of East Germany (as the table below shows). But living standards in the Soviet Union are not estimated as being as high as those in either Czechoslovakia or East Germany, largely because the Soviet Union spends a much higher percentage of its GNP on investments and military expenditures than either of the other two.

Per capita GNP
(in 1978 U.S. dollars)

Year	Czechoslovakia	GDR	USSR
1960	$2,708	$3,066	$2,559
1965	3,141	3,291	3,078
1970	3,643	3,839	3,801
1973	3,994	4,164	4,230
1974	4,213	4,279	4,363
1975	4,399	4,378	4,431
1976	4,494	4,436	4,556
1977	4,667	4,600	4,657
1978	4,821	4,682	4,799

(Source: Computed from figures for GNP and population in Handbook of Economic Statistics, 1979, pp. 25 and 50.)

(12) Obviously, conditions varied from country to country and from era to era. Even the "industrial revolution" took place earlier in some parts of the Western world than in others. This extremely brief and very general historic commentary, and the attempt to summarize in two paragraphs some relevant developments in pre-1945 Germany, are

intended merely as an introduction to the theme of this book, i.e., a comparison of the status of women in the two, post-World War II, German states.

(13) Gast, p. 19.

(14) For a somewhat more detailed discussion, in German, of women's gainful employment in Germany between 1848 and 1945, see Menschik, pp. 40-55.

(15) Originating from the Latin, the word emancipation is a concept that dates back to the days of slavery and originally meant "setting free" (Menschik, p. 57). In connection with women's rights, it has come to mean "liberation" rather than setting free — liberation from sex discrimination and from subjugation by men, and liberation also from age-old stereotyped views that have long prescribed different roles for the two sexes in virtually all areas of life.

(16) <u>Familienpolitik und Familienplanung in beiden deutschen Staaten</u>, p. 42.

(17) Rosten, p. 198.

(18) At present, the preponderance of women prevails in the above 45 age groups only; in younger age brackets, the number of men and women are approximately even.

(19) Engels, p. 181.

(20) Marx and Engels, Vol. 32, pp. 582-83.

(21) Lenin, <u>On Women's Role in Society</u>, p. 41.

(22) Bebel, p. 14 and 303.

(23) Lenin, <u>The Emancipation of Women</u>, p. 113.

(24) For this and other comparisons of the position of women in the U.S. and the USSR, see Shaffer.

(25) <u>Familienpolitik</u>, pp. 60-61.

(26) <u>Zwischenbericht der Enquete Kommission Frau und Gesellschaft</u>, p. 4.

(27) Ibid., p. 5.

(28) <u>Bulletin</u>, Bonn, No. 3, Jan. 10, 1975, p. 17.

(29) <u>Social Report</u>, Bonn-Bad Godesberg, 1 (1977): 4.

(30) <u>Information FRG: Women</u>, pp. 1-3.

(31) Muench, p. 57.

(32) Tappendorf, p. 6.

(33) On the initiative of East German Communists and of the Soviet occupational forces, the East German Communist and Social-Democratic parties were merged in early 1946 to form the SED. It soon became evident (1) that the SED was to be the ruling party in East Germany (although other parties still exist and run in GDR elections, with the number of seats in the Parliament predetermined for each party), and (2) that the Communists were to constitute the dominant element in the SED. Today, the SED is, in effect if not in name, the Communist Party of the GDR.

(34) Tappendorf, p. 7.

(35) Helwig, <u>Frau '75</u>, p. 11.

(36) Lange, <u>Aktuelle Problem</u>, p. 6.

(37) Ibid., p. 5.

(38) <u>SED Program</u>, pp. 39-40.

Chapter 2

(1) The FRG Constitution states that "all human beings," and the GDR Constitution that "all citizens" are equal under the law. Both contain the statement that "men and women have equal rights." The FRG Constitution contains the additional sentence that "no one is to be discriminated against or given preference to because of sex . . . ," but otherwise mentions women specifically only once, in connection with military service. In the GDR Constitution, women are mentioned numerous times, for instance, in regard to special privileges extended to them, rights to equal pay for equal work, equal rights in marriage and in the family. For the FRG, see <u>Grundgeset, fuer die Bundesrepublik Deutschland</u>, Arts. 3 and 12a, pp. 20 and 25; for the GDR, see "Grundlegende Menschenrechte und ihre garantien," Art. 20, 24, and 38, pp. 33-34, 35 and 39.

(2) <u>Arbeitsrecht</u>, Section 53, p. 1.

(3) The German word "foerdern" will henceforth be translated as "further" and "Foerderung" as "furtherance." The word "foerdern" does

not have an exact English equivalent since its meaning contains elements of "further," "stimulate," "encourage," "promote," and "advance the interest of."

(4) "Grundlegende Menschenrechte," Art. 20, p. 34.

(5) "Die (1949) Verfassung der Deutschen Demokratischen Republik," p. 32.

(6) Menschik and Leopold, p. 24; also, Lieser, pp. 921-922.

(7) <u>Grundgesetz</u>, Art. 117, p. 90.

(8) <u>Entscheidungen des Bundesverfassungsgerichts</u>, Vol. 3, Berlin, 1954, pp. 225 and 259 ff.

(9) For a discussion of this issue see, for instance, Ramm, p. 41.

(10) Maier, p. 124. Other violations of Art 3, can be encountered, such as the frequent case of a government labor office demanding, as condition for payment of unemployment compensation, that an unemployed mother prove that she has someone to take care of her children (a person is "unemployed" only if he or she is <u>able</u> and <u>willing</u> to work), while similar proof is not required of unemployed fathers (ibid., p. 127).

(11) Ibid., p. 125.

(12) Court decision of Jan. 15, 1955, cited in Menschik, p. 124.

(13) This wording in Art. 24 of the GDR Constitution of 1968 was not altered by the extensive 1974 revision. See "Grundlegende Menschenrechte," p. 35.

(14) See, for example, Lieser, p. 929.

(15) <u>FGB</u>, §10.

(16) <u>FGB-K</u>, 1966, p. 55.

(17) Ibid., 2nd ed., 1967, p. 39.

(18) Ibid., 3rd ed., 1970, p. 60.

(19) This statement of the 1936 Constitution of the USSR was omitted in the 1977 Constitution.

(20) Riemann, Heilborn, and Luebchen, p. 28.

174   WOMEN IN THE TWO GERMANIES

(21) For a discussion of this issue, see, for instance, Lieser, p. 927.

(22) The Constitution of Bavaria, for instance, mandates that "Men and Women receive equal pay for equal work." ("Verfassung des Freistaates Bayern," § 168). The Constitution of the city-state Bremen stipulates that "For equal work, youth and women are entitled to the same pay as men." ("Land-verfassung der Freien Hansestadt Bremen," § 53). And there are similar provisions in the constitutions of other Laender (all cited in Arbeitsrecht, pp. 52-1 to 59-2).

(23) DDR Handbuch, p. 329.

(24) Art. 18 in the 1949 Constitution.

(25) Art. 24 in the 1968 and 1974 Constitutions of the GDR (see Constitution/GDR).

(26) DDR Handbuch, p. 329; AGB/GDR, § 2, p. 70.

(27) Frauen, p. 10; AGB/GDR § 244, p. 144. In the GDR, the state underwrites the cost of the program; in the FRG, the state health insurance program pays up to 25 DM per day for prenatal maternity leave; the employer pays the rest. Since July 1, 1979, postnatal maternity was extended to 22 weeks for "women who are dependent on employment for an income". The employer pays the mother's full salary for the first six weeks. For the remaining four months, the state pays DM 750 per month and all compulsory insurance and pension premiums (Christian Science Monitor, Feb. 27, 1980, p. 15). For restriction of income to mothers dependent on job, and for further details, see The Situation of Women in the Federal Republic of Germany, p. 33.

(28) Joint Resolution, May 27, 1976, p. 25.

(29) AGB/GDR, § 246, p. 144-45. Under this paragraph, the paid "baby year" off can also be taken by any worker other than the child's mother, if that worker, rather than the mother, has charge of the child's education and care. But for obvious reasons, this provision is rarely used.

(30) These provisions date back to a Decree of May 29, 1972, on equal conditions for university students and workers (GBl. II, No. 27, p. 320).

(31) Foreign Affairs Bulletin 18, No. 4 (Feb. 3, 1978): 27.

(32) GBl. II, 1961, pp. 533 ff.

(33) GBl. II, 1967, p. 248.

(34) GBl. II, 1972, p. 307.

(35) "Anordnung des Reichsarbeitsminister ueber Arbeitsverkuerzung fuer Frauen, Schwerbeschaedigte, und minderleistungsfaehige Personen," Oct. 22, 1943. Arbeitsrecht, §2, p. 400-2.

(36) Arbeitsrecht, pp. 410-2 and 411-1. Bremen, Hamburg, and West Berlin are "city states."

(37) GBl. 1966, §125; also "Verordnung ueber die durchgaengige Arbeitswoche," May 3, 1967, §8. Cited from GBA, p. 245, in Honeckers neues Arbeitsgesetzbuch, p. 51.

(38) AGB/GDR, §185, p. 129. The broadening of the law to include all full-time working women 40 years or over extended the household day off to an additional 270,000 GDR women (Foreign Affairs Bulletin 18, No. 4 (Feb. 3, 1978): 27).

(39) AGB/GDR, §223, 224, 233 and 234, pp. 139, 141 and 142.

(40) Frauen, p. 13; Dornberg, p. 97.

(41) AFG, §33-51, pp. 20-29; Frauen und Bildung, pp. 92-93; Frauen, pp. 45-48 and 99.

(42) For computation of financial aid under the World Furtherance Laws, a monetary value is placed on housework as the woman's "profession."

(43) Helwig, Frau '75, p. 72; Frauen und Bildung, p. 94. Using official government sources, DGB Geschaeftsbericht, p. 27, gives the percentage for 1973 as only 16.9 percent and for Sept. 1976 as 23.9 percent.

(44) Menschik and Leopold, p. 36.

(45) "Mutterschutzgesetz," p. 1637.

(46) GBl. I, April 12, 1961, §123-133, p. 27, cited in §123.

(47) GBl., 1965, p. 83.

(48) For these and other ordinances, decrees, and laws for the furtherance of women, and for greater details on their contents, see Die Frau in der DDR, pp. 76-79; Allendorf, p. 128; Kuhrig, pp. 87-90, 100-101, and 138-140; and Zur Erfuellung des sozialistischen Programms, pp. 37-61 passim.

(49) AGB/GDR, p. 71.

(50) Ibid., § 30, pp. 80-81.

(51) AGB/GDR, § 240, p. 143.

(52) Ibid., § 241, p. 143.

(53) Ibid., § 251, p. 146.

(54) Ibid.

(55) Helwig, Frau '75, p. 84.

(56) AGB/GDR, § 160, p. 121. Emphasis mine. Pensioners, male or female, are also encouraged in the GDR, and with certain restrictions permitted in the FRG, to work part-time while drawing their retirement pensions.

(57) For the GDR position on this issue, see, for instance, Hein, p. 134.

(58) Helwig, Frau '75, p. 85. For details, see chapter 3.

(59) "Decree on the Introduction of the 40-Hour Work Week and the Increase in Minimum Vacation of Full-Time Working Mothers with Several Children," of May 10, 1972, GBl.II, No. 27, 1972, p. 313. For working mothers who worked on swing shifts, the law was applicable as long as they had two children under 16. [The normal work week had been reduced from 45 to 43 3/4 hours per week, and for workers who work three shifts from 44 to 42 hours per week, in 1967 (GBl.II, 1967, § 1, p. 237)].

(60) Joint Resolution, May 27, 1976, p. 25.

(61) The 1977 Labor Law Code, somewhat more vaguely, refers to "mothers of several children under 16" and decrees for them a "shortened work week as compared to other workers, according to legal directives" (AGB/GDR, § 160, p. 121). Since the GDR has declared her intention of soon reducing the overall work week to 40 hours, this phrasing would provide the basis for a reduction of the work week to less than 40 hours for mothers of two or more children.

(62) Jancar, p. 530.

(63) "Studien zur Geschichte der Lage der Arbeiterinnen in Deutschland von 1700 bis zur gegenwart," p. 153.

(64) Frauen, p. 22.

(65) Arbeitsrecht, pp. 350-59 passim; also Frauen, p. 22.

(66) Arbeitsrecht, § 11, pp. 403-04.

(67) Ibid., § 9, p. 403.

(68) BVerfGe, Berlin, 1953, Vol. 6, p. 389.

(69) AGB/GDR, § 210, pp. 135-36.

(70) Honeckers neues Arbeitsgesetzbuch, p. 50.

(71) Grundgesetz, Art. 12a, pp. 25-26.

(72) Arbeitsrecht, pp. 101-04.

(73) Hamburg Stern, Dec. 14, 1978, pp. 24-26.

(74) "Gesetz zum Schutz der erwerbstaetigen Mutter," Arbeitsrecht, § 2-14, pp. 400-1 to 400-11, passim.

(75) GBl. 1637, 1950.

(76) AGB/GDR, § 240-250. Virtually all of the protective legislation contained in the 1977 Labor Law Code can also be found in the Code of Labor Laws of 1961 that preceded it. For a discussion of it see, for instance, Statkowa, pp. 59-60.

(77) Probleme der Frauen - Probleme der gesellschaft, p. 43. Emphasis added.

(78) Unless otherwise indicated, all comments above were made personally by the individuals mentioned to this author.

(79) Simmat, p. 103.

(80) BGB, 75th ed. (as of May, 1960), § 1356.

(81) Ibid., § 1360.

(82) Pross, Ueber Bildungschancen fuer Maedchen in der Bundesrepublik, p. 36.

(83) Civil Code, § 1627, 1630, 1634, pp. 365-66.

(84) Ibid., § 1589, 1705, 1707 and 1708, pp. 356 and 381-82.

(85) BGB, § 1705, p. 1542; FGB, § 46.

(86) Court decision of July 29, 1959. Neue juristische Wochenschrift, 1959, pp. 1483-1487.

(87) Cited in Juristenzeitung, Jan. 19, 1968, p. 41.

(88) "Bericht der Bundesregierung ueber Mannahumen zur Verbesserung der Lage der Frau," p. 8.

(89) Familienpolitik, p. 5.

(90) Social Report, (Bonn-Bad Godesberg), 7-77, p. 3.

(91) EheRG, 1421/22. The paragraphs of the old Civil Code that were changed by the EheRG are all incorporated in the new BGB, replacing the previous wording. For §1356 and 1360, see BGB, pp. 1264 and 1272.

(92) Vorschlaege zum neuen deutschen Familienrecht, Berlin, GDR, 1949.

(93) "Thesen ueber die Wirkungen der Ehe im allgemeinen," p. 103.

(94) "Mutterschutzgesetz," § 14.

(95) Ibid., § 16.

(96) FGB, p. 43.

(97) FGB-K, p. 60.

(98) For the Kassel decision, see Treffpunkt (a periodical published by the Federal Ministry for Youth, Family and Health in Bonn) No. 9, 1978, p. 3. For the Karlsruhe decisions, see Mundzeck, p. 35.

(99) Treffpunkt, No. 6, 1977, p. 4.

(100) The extent of West Germany's actual adherence to the principle of pluralism is questioned by opponents on the extreme right and the extreme left. The Nazi Party is outlawed; and left-wing "radicals" and especially communists are largely denied state employment, not merely in sensitive positions but also for jobs such as letter carriers. In recent years, such employment denial has been applied, so claim left-wing groups, not only to so-called "radicals" but even to more moderate socialists who advocate gradual and not revolutionary or violent social change. For a recent reference to the so-called Berufsverbot (literally: job prohibition), Gerd Schroeder, then chairman of the governing SPD's youth organization, told in an interview in April 1980 about his group's strong opposition to such politically motivated job restrictions (Vorwaerts, April 24, 1980, p. 6).

(101) FGB, § 5. The new West German Family Law also states that "marriage is to be engaged in for life" (EheRG, §1353, p. 1421; cf. FGB, p. 1258), but contains none of the other moral mandates of the GDR Family Law Code.

(102) Art. 38. See "Verfassung der Deutschen Demokratischen Republik von 6 April, 1968," p. 224 for the 1968 Constitution; Die neue Verfassung der DDR, p. 92 for the 1974 revision.

(103) FGB, § 4, p. 36.

(104) Verfuegungen und Mitteilungen des Ministeriums fuer Gesundheitswesen der DDR, No. 3, 1968.

(105) Beyer and Piater, p. 24.

(106) Civil Code, § 1565-1568, p. 350. A man could, for instance, be found guilty for committing adultery, a woman for failing to keep house or prepare meals properly. Should both have happened, the court would be likely to determine which came first, and then assign guilt correspondingly. Should the husband be able to prove, for instance, that he took a mistress because the wife didn't take proper care of his supper, the court might assign three-fourths of the guilt to her, and one-fourth to him (Dornberg, p. 100). An advanced state of insanity was also reason for divorce (Civil Code, § 1569, pp. 350-51).

(107) Helwig, Frau '75, p. 26.

(108) Frauen, p. 67.

(109) EheRG, § 1565, p. 1423; also BGB, p. 1367.

(110) EheRG, § 1566, p. 1324; also BGB, p. 1374. Spouses can be deemed to live separately, the law explains, even if they occupy the same dwelling.

(111) EheRG, § 1565, p. 1423; also BGB, p. 1367.

(112) EheRG, § 1568, pp. 1423-1424; also BGB, p. 1376.

(113) "Marriage and Divorce Decree," p. 849.

(114) FGB, § 24, p. 55.

(115) Ehe und Familie in beiden deutschen Staaten, p. 28.

(116) DDR Handbuch, p. 273.

(117) FGB-K, p. 125.

(118) Neue Justiz, 1973, Nr. 2, p. 37.

(119) FGB, § 24, p. 55.

(120) Civil Code, p. 304. Specifically exempted are items "intended exclusively for the personal use of the wife, e.g., clothing, ornaments, and working implements" (Ibid., §1366, p. 304.).

(121) Ibid., p. 306.

(122) Ibid.

(123) BGB, § 1363, p. 1287. The law provides for certain exceptions such as a house over which both spouses have joint decision making power, since disposal of it would effect both substantially.

(124) FGB, 13.

(125) For the FRG, see BGB §1363, p. 1287 and 1478, p. 3145 (for 1478, also EheRG, p. 1423); § 1478 also provides that personal presents and inheritances, even if acquired during the marriage, remain the personal property of the recipient. For the GDR, see FGB, § 13 and 40.

(126) FGB, § 40.

(127) EheRG, § 1587 and 1587a-1587p, pp. 1426-1431; also BGB, pp. 403-431.

(128) EheRG, § 1578 h, p. 1430; also BGB, pp. 1390-1391.

(129) Social Report, No. 7, 1977, p. 5.

(130) Frauen, p. 70.

(131) Familienpolitik, p. 50.

(132) Civil Code, § 1578, p. 353.

(133) EheRG, § 1569-1586 passim, pp. 1424-1426; also BGB, pp. 1377-1403.

(134) "Marriage and Divorce Decree," p. 849.

(135) Grandke et al., p. 264.

(136) Helwig, Frau '75, p. 28-29.

(137) Riemann, Heilborn, and Luebchen, p. 31.

(138) DDR Handbuch, p. 274; identical figures are also given in Helwig, Frau '75, pp. 29-30.

(139) Grandke et al., p. 265. Emphasis added.

NOTES   181

(140) Krejci, p. 103.

(141) Civil Code, p. 302.

(142) Helwig, Frau '75, p. 18; Krejci, p. 163.

(143) EheRG, § 1355, p. 1421; also BGB, p. 126; FGB, § 7; FGB-K, p. 53.

(144) Krejci, p. 163.

(145) Statkowa, p. 47; DDR Handbuch, p. 461. In the GDR, one East German mark (M) is exchanged at an official rate of 1:1 for a West German mark (DM); in West German banks, East German marks were traded at approximately 4M = 1 DM in 1978. The DM exchange rate for the US dollar was approximately $1 = 2 DM in 1978, somewhat higher at the beginning, slightly lower at the end of the year; but it has dipped considerably below 2 DM since then.

(146) Frauen, p. 50.

(147) "Verordnung ueber die Erhoehung der staatlichen geburtenhilfe und die Verlangerung des Wochennurlands," p. 314. Before 1973, birth allowances were graduated, 500 M for the first child, 600 for the second, 700 for the third, 850 for the fourth, and 1,000 M for the fifth and all subsequent children (Tappendorf, p. 24).

(148) Familienpolitik, p. 16. In some exceptional cases, tax benefits for children still exist in the FRG; for instance, single mothers are granted a head of household exemption of 3,000 DM per year (Jede werdenede Mutter, p. 27).

(149) Information FRG: Women, section 4; Frauen, p. 53; So schaffe ich es allein, p. 12. The provision on household help is contained in the 1974 "Law for the Improvement of Performance of the Social Health Insurance System." See Treffpunkt, No. 7, 1977, pp. 6-7.

(150) Directives, IX SED Party Congress, pp. 63 and 69; Statkowa, pp. 43 and 46; "Verordnung zur Gewaehrung von Krediten zu verguenstigten Bedingungen au junge Ekelente," § 3 and 4, p. 316; "Anordnung ueber die finanzielle Unterstuetzung von Studentinnen mit Kind au den Hoch - und Fachschillen," § 2 and 2, p. 321.

(151) SED Program, pp. 26-27.

(152) Facts About Germany, p. 327; also Information FRG: Women, section 3.

(153) Unsere Sozialversicherung, pp. 58-59.

(154) Ibid., pp. 60-61.

(155) Ibid., pp. 70-71. Disability, sickness, and accident insurance are not covered in this book, either for West or East Germany, unless of special relevance for the main topic of this comparative study.

(156) Helwig, Frau '75, p. 82.

(157) Reply to inquiry, in letter from managing director of the Verband Deutscher Rentenversicherungstraeger, dated Jan. 31, 1979.

(158) See, for instance, Zwischenbericht, p. 15 and 22; Social Report, No. 1, 1977, p. 6; Frauen, p. 72.

(159) Although a voluntary retirement insurance program exists, it is very expensive and is only rarely subscribed to by individuals without an income of their own, and especially not for amounts that would enable the policy holder to have a reasonable, regular pension in old age. For a wife to have a retirement income equal to that of her husband, he might have to pay premiums equal to one-fifth and more of his gross income (if he not only wanted to keep up with his current accumulation, but also make up for years of pension accumulation prior to marriage).

(160) Zwischenbericht, p. 22.

(161) Rentenverordnung, § 5 and 6.

(162) Ibid., § 7; "Implementation Order" to Ibid., § 11.

(163) Rentenverordnung, § 17.

(164) Ibid.

(165) Ibid., § 4.

(166) Implementation order to Ibid., § 11.

(167) Rentenverordnung, § 7.

(168) Ibid.

(169) Familienpolitik, p. 32. For progress made, see footnote 27 in this chapter.

(170) Unsere Sozialversicherung, pp. 67 and 71. See also, Helwig, Frau '75, p. 83. As of January, 1980, 99.8 percent of such survivors' pensions went to widows. Out of 3.8 million recipients, only 8,000 were widowers. (The Situation of Women, p. 73.) But a widow loses her widow's pension if she remarries.

(171) Zwischenbericht, p. 15.

(172) Rentenverordnung, § 19.

(173) Ibid., § 19 and 50.

(174) DDR Handbuch, p. 938.

(175) Rentenverordnung, § 54. The basic principle of "higher pension plus 25 percent of the lower" applies to most cases where an individual is entitled to two pensions; if an individual is entitled to more than two pensions, the principle becomes "highest plus 25 percent of the second highest." Only "honorary pensions" for fighters against and victims of fascism are paid in addition to any other pensions. [Spouses and children supplements, in any case, are paid only once (ibid, §50)].

(176) Unsere Sozialversicherung, pp. 66-67; Fremdwort Rente, pp. 5-6; see also Frauen, p. 73.

(177) Rentenverordnung, § 3. As compared with the Soviet Union and the other socialist countries of East Europe, the 15-year minimum work requirement in the GDR is the lowest; in most others, it is 25 years for men and 20 for women. But the retirement age, with the only exception of Poland, is lower in the others – as a rule, 60 years for men and 55 for women (Turgeon, p. 49).

(178) Rentenverordnung, § 34 and 37.

(179) Ibid., § 54.

(180) Ibid., # 3.

(181) Ibid., § 16.

(182) Mitteilungen der Landesversicherungsanstalt Berlin 25, No. 12 (Dec. 1976): 335.

(183) See, e.g., Ehe und Familie, p. 31.

(184) "Mutterschutzgesetz," p. 1037.

(185) Familienpolitik, p. 35; Ehe und Familie, p. 32.

(186) "Gesetz ueber die Unterbrechung der Schwangerschaft," p. 89. See also Neues Deutschland, March 10, 1972. The text of the law, and of other laws passed simultaneously that are concerned with the implementation of the statute on abortions, can also be found in Zur Erfuellung, pp. 53-59.

184 WOMEN IN THE TWO GERMANIES

(187) Familienpolitik, pp. 34-35.

(188) Ehe und Familie, p. 34.

(189) "Gesetz ueber die Unterbrechung der Schwangerschaft," p. 89.

(190) For an almost identical statement, see, for example, Statkowa, p. 44.

(191) Allendorf, p. 182.

(192) Menschik and Leopold, pp. 37-8.

(193) Focke, "Rechte und Chaucen der Frau in Staat und Gesellschaft," p. 646.

(194) Helwig, Frau '75, p. 34; also Familienpolitik, pp. 36-37.

(195) GBl. 1/76, Jan. 25, 1976, p. 1213; see also, Social Report, May 1, 1977, pp. 20-22; Familienpolitik, pp. 26-37; So schaffe ich es allein, p. 37.

(196) Informationen des Bundesministeriums fuer Jugend, Familie und Gesundheit, Dec., 1976, p. 2.

(197) Ibid.

(198) Ibid.

(199) Ibid., July 7, 1977, p. 3; Dec. 1976, pp. 6-7.

(200) Ibid., Dec. 1976, p. 6.

Chapter 3

(1) SYB/FRG and GDR, 1977. Note that some of the difference in the percentage of people above retirement age is accounted for by women reaching retirement age at 65 in the FRG but at 60 in the GDR. (As discussed in chap. 2, the general retirement age for men is the same — 65 years — in both German states.)

(2) Note in Table 1.2 above that, in 1976, females constituted 53.5 percent of the GDR's but only 52.4 percent of the FRG's population; and there is virtually no difference in the below 40 age groups.

(3) SYB/FRG, 1977, pp. 29, 59, and 602; SYB/GDR, 1977, p. 388. See also Warum, pp. 15-18. If one included full-time students of working age among the gainfully employed in the GDR (not too unrealistic under

GDR conditions since most students receive fair-sized living allowances and some even regular wages in addition to cost-free education), the percentage would be above 86.5 percent. The percentage was given as 86.5 percent for 1975 (Statkowa, p. 17) and as 86.6 percent for 1976 (Neues Deutschland, March 9, 1977).

(4) The figure, reportedly, passed 50 percent in 1977 (See, for example, Scott, p. 32), and remained above 50 percent in 1978 (see table 3.2).

(5) Frauenfoerderung, p. 82.

(6) Engels, p. 181.

(7) Lenin, Werke, Vol. 30, p. 26.

(8) Neuer Weg, 1962, #8, p. 399; see also Protokoll vom IV Bundes-Kongress des DFD, p. 16.

(9) Helwig, Zwischen Familie und Beruf, p. 24.

(10) Questionnaire survey by Norbert Schmidt-Relenberg, cited from Soziale Welt, Nr. 2, 1965, pp. 133 ff. in Helwig, Zwischen Familie und Beruf, p. 24.

(11) Frau und Oeffentlichkeit, pp. 22 and 48.

(12) Helwig, Zwischen Familie und Beruf, pp. 24-25.

(13) Ibid., pp. 20-21. (For an extensive study along these lines, carried out in 1969, see Jaide.)

(14) For a discussion of this issue, see for instance, Helwig, Zwischen Familie und Beruf, p. 17.

(15) Commandeur and Sterzel, p. 87.

(16) Allendorf, p. 10.

(17) Wander, pp. 135-36 and 140. Emphasis added.

(18) In many cities in East Germany, households are now furnished printed check lists of grocery items which can be left at the state owned and operated grocery stores when the couple goes to work in the morning; the groceries can then be picked up or delivered, when one of the spouses gets back from work.

(19) Berichte und Materialien zur Lage der Nationen, p. 84 ff. For a discussion of the issue, see also Ehe und Familie, pp. 12-13.

(20) Social Report (Bonn-Bad Godesberg), No. 1 (1977), pp. 13-14.

(21) Reported in Whitney, p. 6.

(22) Cited from official FRG and GDR sources in Helwig, Frau '75, pp. 68-69. For the FRG, working age for women is 15-65, for the GDR 15-60. Counted as "children" are those under 18 years of age in the FRG, under 17 in the GDR.

(23) The Soviet Union has had a labor shortage since the first five-year plan, introduced at the end of the 1920s, took full effect in the early 1930s. (The existence of a labor shortage in the USSR has been documented in all Western studies on the subject. As examples of such studies, see Feshbach and Rapawy's 1973 and 1976 papers, submitted to the Joint Economic Committee of the U.S. Congress.) Only in isolated cases did unemployment become a problem in other socialist countries, and then primarily in those which allowed the market to play a major role, such as Yugoslavia.

(24) Hein, p. 123. For a thorough Western study of the full-employment phenomenon in the GDR, see the prestigious West German Friedrich Ebert Foundation's Warum gibt es in der DDR keine Arbeitslosigkeit (Why is there no Unemployment in the GDR?).

(25) On December 31, 1978, for instance, when overall there were 114 women for every 100 men in the GDR, the figures were 145 in the 50 to 60-year bracket, and 180 women for every 100 men among those over 60 years of age. (Computed from SYB/GDR, 1979, p. 349).

(26) SYB/FRG, 1955, pp. 110 and 119; 1962, pp. 148-149.

(27) Official news reports, Berlin, June 2, 1978.

(28) Menschik, p. 45.

(29) Whitney, p. 6.

(30) The overwhelming majority of West German schools are not all-day schools. Children usually go to school every other Saturday and for more months than American children; but for most of them, school is over somewhere between 11:30 and 1:30, at different times on different days.

(31) Discussed in Huefner, p. 39.

(32) Cited from GDR sources in Menschik and Leopold, p. 115.

(33) Schuster, p. 56.

(34) Die Frau, April 1977, p. 1.

(35) Probleme der Frauen, pp. 9 and 137.

(36) See Maria Weber, "Concluding Remarks," ibid., p. 148.

(37) Ibid., p. 137.

(38) Schuster, p. 56.

(39) Schmidt, p. 12.

(40) Warum gibt es in der DDR keine Arbeitslosigkeit?, p. 46.

(41) Probleme der Frauen, p. 137.

(42) Gabert, p. 3.

(43) Allendorf, p. 111.

(44) Cited from FRG and GDR sources in Helwig, Frau '75, Tables 33 and 34, pp. 86 and 89.

(45) Statkowa, pp. 17-18.

(46) Helwig, Frau '75, p. 84.

(47) Handelsblatt, June 30, 1978.

(48) Sozialpolitische Umschau, January 28, 1977, p. 1.

(49) Ibid.; also Helwig, Frau '75, p. 86.

(50) Leipziger Volkszeitung, January 21, 1972.

(51) See, for example, Lange, Aktuelle Probleme, pp. 13-15. Inge Lange was, at the time of the writing, a candidate member of the Party's top ruling body, the Politburo.

(52) Tappendorf, p. 19.

(53) In the GDR, especially, any kind of work can be "learned," and a skilled worker's certificate earned, by intensive training, usually through a combination of on-the-job apprenticeship and vocational schooling. Thus, one can, for instance, train for two years and earn a skilled worker certificate for a position of janitor.

(54) "Situation Arbeitsplatz. 'Das ist doch nichts fuer Maedchen,' " Berlin TV, Channel 3, June 12, 1978.

(55) Social Report, No. 1 (1977), p. 7.

(56) This includes kindergarten teachers; a substantial percentage of West German kindergartens are operated by churches.

(57) Die Welt, Jan. 5, 1977.

(58) Sueddeutsche Zeitung, April 20, 1978.

(59) Focke, "Rechte," p. 643.

(60) Several German women interviewed by this author mentioned the "no ladies' restroom" argument as one of the reasons frequently given by employers to deny women access to hitherto primarily masculine jobs.

(61) Weber, "Forderdrungen im Jahr der Arbeitnehmerinnen," p. 681.

(62) Maier, p. 130.

(63) Einheit, October 1972, p. 1315.

(64) Personal interview with Prof. Dr. Eberhard Reblin, a leading authority in the GDR's musical world and one of its outstanding pianists and directors, and with his wife, Lyn Jaldati, the GDR's leading Jewish folksinger.

(65) Die Welt, January 5, 1977.

(66) BZ am Abend (Berlin Evening Times), April 13, 1978.

(67) Focke, "Rechte," p. 643.

(68) SYB/FRG 1978, p. 347.

(69) This was true, already, in 1972. See DDR Handbuch, p. 331.

(70) Epstein, p. 12. It should be pointed out that in the Soviet Union being a lawyer is not very prestigious; and physicians and dentists, although highly respected, are not well paid in the USSR.

(71) SYB/FRG, 1979, p. 340.

(72) Handelsblatt, July 27-28, 1978.

(73) Zwischenbericht, p. 13.

(74) Helwig, Frau '75, p. 76; Weibliche Vorgestzte in Deutschland, p. 13; Handelsblatt, June 24-25, 1977. Handelsblatt gives the percentage of

women in "really leading positions" for 1974 as 1.8 percent, and for 1975 as 2.1 percent, a decline as compared with 1969, when it reportedly was 2.8 percent.

(75) Handelsblatt, July 24, 1978.

(76) Schiffner, p. 5.

(77) Weibliche Vorgestzte, p. 13 gives the percentage as 12 percent; SYB/FRG, 1977, p. 92 as 20.6 percent; Social Report, Nr. 1, (1977), p. 9 as 25 percent. Among the women who own enterprises that employ 10 or more workers, 59 percent inherited their businesses, 33 percent founded them themselves, and 8 percent bought them. (Social Report, No. 1 (1977), p. 9.)

(78) Das schoene Geschlecht und die gleicherechtigung in der DDR, pp. 50-51.

(79) LPG-Bauer auf neue Art, p. 71.

(80) Die Frau in der DDR, pp. 13 and 55-57.

(81) This was, for instance, strongly emphasized by Helge Pross, West German sociologist and expert on German women, East and West, in a personal interview with this author in Giessen in the summer of 1978.

(82) Menschik and Leopold, inside cover page, and also passim.

(83) Ibid., p. 192.

(84) Ibid.

(85) "Gute Startbedingungen und Freude an der Arbeit," Frankfurter Allgemeine Zeitung, April 14, 1978.

(86) Weibliche Vorgestzte, p. 12.

(87) Ibid., pp. 12 and 14.

(88) Ibid., p. 13.

(89) Reported by Lily Joen, herself chief executive of a company manufacturing thermo-electric measuring instruments. See Dornberg, p. 90.

(90) Menschik and Leopold, p. 94 and 118. For instance, in the case of applicants with children in their households, 71.6 percent of the respondents with vocational school or college degrees, but 78.3 percent of those without such degrees, opted for the male applicant (ibid., p. 118).

190   WOMEN IN THE TWO GERMANIES

(91) Helwig, "Das Jahr der Frau in der DDR," p. 61.

(92) Helwig, Frau '75, p. 68.

(93) Zwischenbericht, p. 14.

(94) Weibliche Vorgestzte, p. 14.

(95) For GDR managers, the legal obligation placed on them to "keep" jobs for women who take off from work temporarily to have a baby poses a real problem. They must find temporary replacements; and in an economy with a perennial labor shortage, this is not easy, especially since they are not allowed to lay off the "temporary" replacements either, but must find new jobs for them.

(96) Gast, p. 15.

(97) Keim, p. 11.

(98) Handelsblatt, July 15-16, 1977. Also Whitney, p. 6.

(99) Keim, p. 6.

(100) Frankfurter Allgemeine Zeitung, July 25, 1975.

(101) See, for instance, Krejci, p. 167.

(102) Dornberg, p. 91.

(103) Gast, pp. 208-209; Menschik and Leopold, p. 81; Helwig, "Das Jahr der Frau in der DDR," p. 61.

(104) Gast, p. 205. Note, though, that by 1974, over 21 percent of GDR mayors were women (table 3.13).

(105) Gast, p. 16. See also Helwig, Frau '75, p. 12.

(106) Gast, pp. 82 and 85.

(107) Zwischenbericht, pp. 28-29.

(108) Focke, "Rechte," p. 644.

(109) Various SYB's/FRG, 1950s-1978.

(110) Tappendorf, p. 22; Allendorf, p. 142.

(111) The percentage was 50.0 percent in 1976 and 50.6 percent in 1977 (SYB/GDR, 1977, p. 437; and 1978, p. 393).

(112) Statkowa, p. 16.

(113) "Aktivitaet der DDR," p. 33; Die Frau in der DDR, p. 22.

(114) Salomon, passim.

(115) Menschik, p. 43. Actually, maximization of the couple's combined income is probably the dominant economic incentive. It is theoretically possible for the lower-paid spouse to be the deciding factor in the choice of the family's domicile. This would be the case if that spouse could locate a job somewhere at a positive wage differential that would more than offset a cut in wage the higher-income earning spouse might have to accept.

(116) Frankfurter Rundschau, Section on "Frau und Gesellschaft," March 13, 1976, p. V. Note slight difference from monthly percentages computed in table 3.18.

(117) Helwig, Frau '75, p. 80 and Weibliche Vorgestzte, p. 13 give it as 20 percent, Zwischenbericht, p. 12 as 30 percent.

(118) Handelsblatt, June 24-25, 1977.

(119) Zwischenbericht, p. 45; Focke, Speech, p. 11.

(120) Note that since pensions are based on lifetime earnings, the average pensions of women are adversely affected by lower hourly wages, fewer hours worked per week, and fewer years worked during a lifetime. And as we have seen in Chap. 2, West German widow pensions are only 60 percent of those of their deceased husbands. The discrepancy would be still larger, were it not for the fact that widows, but not widowers, who had worked themselves are entitled to their own pension plus 60 percent of that of their deceased spouse. In 1974, one out of every three female pensioners but only one out of every four male pensioners received more than one pension – men, for instance, received veterans' pensions, in addition to their regular ones (Zwischenbericht, p. 49).

(121) Ibid., pp. 49-50. For age group 60-65, the percentages were 26 for men and 43 for women.

(122) Winkelraeter, p. 89.

(123) Die Bedeutung des Art. 3, pp. 3 and 39.

(124) Winkelraeter, p. 90.

(125) Rohmert and Rutenfranz, passim.

(126) In 1955, the West German parliament actually adopted Agreement Nr. 100 of the International Labor Conference in Geneva about "equality of pay for male and female workers for equivalent work" (Menschik, p. 124). But apart from the abolition of the women wage categories, it has had little practical impact on West Germany's remaining inequality of pay scales.

(127) Discussed in Informationen fuer die Frau, p. 15.

(128) Dornberg, p. 88.

(129) Ibid.

(130) Probleme der Frauen, p. 141.

(131) Menschik, p. 157.

(132) Social Report, 6-77, p. 4. That not one woman willing to bring suit could be found for years was also reported in numerous other West German newspapers and magazines and told to this author by several interviewees.

(133) Ibid., pp. 1 and 6.

(134) NRZ-Nachrichtendienst (a press agency). Most newspapers, June 24, 1978.

(135) June 24, 1978, for instance in Die Welt.

(136) Winkelraeter, p. 94.

(137) Menschik and Leopold, p. 107. See also Helwig, Frau '75, p. 80 and Krejci, p. 165.

(138) "Die Frau," p. 684.

(139) This was the finding also of Dornberg, p. 87.

(140) Helwig, Frau '75, p. 79 gives the wage differential as 23 percent for 1972, but it has narrowed somewhat since then. For percentages of women employed in various branches see table 3.7.

(141) Menschik and Leopold, p. 108.

(142) Ibid., pp. 108 and 110.

(143) Ibid., p. 110.

(144) So schaffe ich es allein, p. 32.

NOTES 193

(145) DGB Geschaeftsbericht 1974-1976, p. 85.

(146) Familienpolitik, p. 23. The survey mentioned covered the entire FRG territory.

(147) So schaffe ich es allein, p. 32.

(148) Dornberg, pp. 97-98.

(149) Probleme der Frauen, p. 76.

(150) Computed from SYB/GDR, 1978, p. 334. The number of places in these facilities decreased greatly not only in percentage of totals, but in absolute numbers also. In 1960, there were 10,913 places in sleep-over homes for prekindergartners; in 1970, 7,519; and in 1977, 5,237. The enrollment drop in seasonal prekindergarten care centers was even more drastic, from 12,373 in 1960 to 9,193 in 1970, and to a mere 897 in 1977.

(151) Computed from SYB/GDR, 1978, pp. 35 and 284. The number of places in seasonal kindergartens dropped from 58,328 in 1960 to 34,500 in 1970, and to a mere 3,424 in 1977.

(152) Menschik and Leopold, pp. 50 and 99.

(153) The "baby boom" in the GDR, discussed in chap. 2, is in part the result of suddenly increasing birthrates, from a low of 179,127 in 1974 to 223,102 in 1977 (Was und Wie, Feb. 1978) and in part of decreasing infant mortality rates, down from 18.5 per 1,000 live births in 1970 to 13.0 in 1977, Ibid., January 1977).

(154) Statkowa, p. 37; Allendorf, p. 186; Report, CC/SED, 1976, pp. 47-48; Socialist Life and its Value, p. 80.

(155) Lange, Aktuelle Probleme, pp. 10-11.

(156) Statkowa, p. 37. A virtually identical statement can be found in Kuhrig, p. 152.

(157) Ibid., pp. 37-38; Tappendorf, p. 10. State subsidies in 1974 amounted to 170 M monthly per child in nurseries and 50 M per kindergarten child (Die Frau in der DDR, p. 67).

(158) Ehe und Familie, p. 22. Apart from Berlin, school-preparatory kindergartens can be found in West Germany in any numbers only in Bremen and Hamburg.

(159) TV program "Frauen im Beruf," shown on West German television on Oct. 3, 1977, and repeated on Feb. 27, 1978.

(160) The Situation of Women, p. 41.

(161) Dornberg, p. 97.

(162) Overall, there were 26 children per teacher in day care centers in the GDR in 1963, and 21 in 1974 (Die Frau in der DDR, p. 68). In kindergartens, the number of children per teacher had been 16.5 in 1963 and had dropped to 11.9 in 1977. In seasonal kindergartens where children stay during the farmers' busy season only, the number of children per teacher was much smaller yet – 6.9 in 1977 as compared to 13.7 in 1963 (SYB/GDR, 1978, p. 284) – perhaps because these institutions and the number of places in them are being phased out rapidly, while teachers cannot readily be shifted to new types of assignments at the same rate (because workers no longer needed in their old jobs are not simply laid off or discharged in the GDR, without new jobs being provided for them).

(163) Katzenstein, p. 253.

Chapter 4

(1) Der Spiegel, January 25, 1979.

(2) Beauvoir, p. 8. Emphasis added. The work was originally published in French in 1949 under the title Le Deuxieme Sex, and in English four years later as The Second Sex. In an interview in 1975, Simone de Beauvoir reiterated her view that women will remain oppressed as long as "the myth of motherhood and the motherly instinct in general are not successfully destroyed." (Der Spiegel, June 30, 1975, p. 32.)

(3) Menschik and Leopold, p. 47.

(4) Zwischenbericht, p. 6. The 70 percent figure is for 1971, but has hardly changed since.

(5) Frauen und Bildung, p. 8.

(6) Zwischenbericht, pp. 6-7.

(7) Frauen und Bildung, pp. 10-11.

(8) Henkelmann, p. 30.

(9) Whitney, p. 6.

(10) For a brief discussion of this issue, see Kuhrig, p. 26.

(11) See, for example, relevant passages in the FGB, discussed in Chapter 2, and in Jugendgesetz der DDR (GDR Youth Law), passim, not discussed in the chapter on "German Women under the Law," since it simply assumes educational equality for boys and girls and therefore does not go into this issue in detail.

(12) Menschik and Leopold, p. 148.

(13) Dannhauer, p. 106.

(14) Ibid., p. 109.

(15) Ibid., p. 188.

(16) See, for example, Kossakowski and Otto.

(17) Allendorf, p. 99.

(18) Reported in Helwig, Frau '75, pp. 47-48.

(19) For a description of the approach of school books, and for examples such as the ones given, see Huefner, p. 138 and also "Die Frau in der BRD" (the woman in the FRG) in Moeller and Liedloff (a recent book used in elementary German classes in the United States), p. 245.

(20) For details on the AEM study, see Nordwest Zeitung, Oct. 27, 1979; and The German Tribune, Nov. 11, 1979, p. 16.

(21) Frauen und Bildung, p. 11.

(22) Zwischenbericht, pp. 7-8.

(23) Ibid., p. 8.

(24) Reported on in Helwig, Frau '75, pp. 47 and 49.

(25) Zwischenbericht, p. 8.

(26) Note, as pointed out in chap. 3, in West Germany, enrollment of 1 to 3 year olds in nurseries is minimal, but the percentage of preschoolers over 3, enrolled in kindergartens, has been rising rapidly in recent years.

(27) Familienpolitik, p. 24.

(28) Kuhrig, p. 21; Tappendorf, p. 17.

(29) Allendorf, p. 106.

(30) As in West Germany and much of the rest of Europe, the big, hot meal is eaten at noon.

(31) See, for example, Wander, p. 60.

(32) Helwig, Frau '75, p. 44. See also Familienpolitik, pp. 27-28.

(33) See, for example, Helwig, Frau '75, p. 46.

(34) Sozial Report, No. 4 (1977), pp. 10-11. See also Helwig, Frau '75, p. 50.

(35) There are very few exceptions; but English, for instance, is an elective in some schools. And there are obviously special schools for special types of students, such as individuals with certain handicaps.

(36) Berufsausbildung, p. 48.

(37) Zukunftssichere Berufsausbildung, p. 8.

(38) Berufsausbildung, p. 22. In 1973, for instance, first year trainees in North Rhine-Westphalia and in Rhineland-Pfalz attended vocational schools on the average for only seven 45-minute periods per week.

(39) Ibid., pp. 11-12.

(40) Sozial Report, No. 1 (1977), p. 10.

(41) "Grundlegende Menschenrechte," p. 36. Emphasis added.

(42) Neues Deutschland, July 24 and July 31, 1978.

(43) Menschik and Leopold, p. 66.

(44) Deppe-Wolfinger and Freiberg, p. 410.

(45) Sources vary slightly as to maximum stipend paid under this special program. Deppte-Wolfinger and Freiberg, p. 410, gives it as "80 percent of net wage"; Tappendorf, p. 21, as "up to 80 percent of average net wage, in addition to the basic stipend"; and Menschik and Leopold, p. 66, as "up to 90 percent of average net wage."

(46) Menschik and Leopold, p. 66., Berufsausbildung, pp. 21 and 34.

(47) Deppe-Wolfinger and Freiberg, p. 410.

(48) Berufsausbildung und Berufslerkimp in Beiden deutscher Staaten, p. 11.

(49) Klein und Reischock, p. 58.

(50) Focke, "Rechte," May 27, 1975. Former Minister Katherina Focke also pointed out that even the same training curriculum does not lead to the same kinds of jobs. If, for instance, male and female banking trainees take the same courses and graduate with the same diploma, young women are subsequently likely to find themselves behind the "small loan windows," while young men soon advance to positions such as "investment adviser."

(51) Sozial Report, No. 1 (1977), p. 11.

(52) Helwig, Frau '75, p. 51.

(53) To educate women costs time, money, and effort. Hence, there are occasional reports of enterprises that procrastinate and do not "further" women as they are supposed to, according to law — especially if they fear that such furtherance might, in the short run, interfere with the fulfillment of their plan. (For examples cited from Einheit and from Neues Deutschland, see Menschik and Leopold, p. 95.)

(54) Lange, Aktuelle Probleme, pp. 19-20.

(55) Die Frau in der DDR, p. 43.

(56) SYB/GDR, 1979, p. 297.

(57) Anger, p. 471.

(58) Ibid., p. 476.

(59) Dornberg, p. 88.

(60) Ibid., p. 89.

(61) Helwig, Frau '75, p. 45.

(62) Ibid., p. 46.

(63) Even in 1969, estimated costs ran from DM 16,300 for a degree as assistant medical technician (6 semesters) and DM 19,200 for a social worker's degree (8 semesters) to DM 36,900 for an MD (15 semesters, total) and DM 38,800 for a degree in education, qualifying the recipient to teach at a Gymnasium (16 semesters) (Menschik, pp. 109-110).

(64) West German author, editor, publisher, and specialist on women in both Germanies wrote, for instance: "In the case of a son, father and mother usually put education in the center of their interest [in West Germany], while they see the daughter first and foremost as a future housewife and mother" (Helwig, Zwischen Familie und Beruf, p. 20).

(65) Helwig, Frau '75, p. 62.

(66) Katzenstein, p. 247; Helwig, Frau '75, p. 65.

(67) Katzenstein, p. 247.

(68) GB1, Part II, No. 27, p. 321, May 29, 1972.

(69) Same as for attending vocational schools. For slight discrepancies in reports of maximum stipends available, see footnote 45 in this chapter.

(70) Tappendorf, p. 21.

(71) Ibid.

(72) Helwig, Frau '75, p. 63.

(73) Frauen und Bildung, p. 84.

(74) Proposals by the Federal Ministry for Education and Science include, for instance, requests for the establishment of adequate child care centers for the young children of students, ibid., p. 85.

(75) Die Frau in der DDR, p. 43.

(76) Tobias, p. 3.

(77) Volks-, Berufs-, Wohnraum-, und Gebaeudezaehlung am 1. Januar 1971.

Chapter 5

(1) Information FRG: Women, Section 6.

(2) Myrdal and Klein, p. 36.

(3) Social Report, 2-75, pp. 4-6. "Household chores" or "housework," referred to by Dr. Pross here, and by the author throughout this chapter, does not include such "typically male" jobs as changing light switches, painting the garage, or mowing the lawn.

(4) "Die Rolle des Mannes und ihr Eiufluss auf die Wahlsuseglichkeit der Frau," pp. 2-14.

(5) When former Minister for Youth, Family and Health Katherina Focke, aware of the situation, presented her and the SPD's case for a shorter workday and workweek, she emphasized that the extra free

time must not mean more leisure time for men and more time for women to do their housework; that to the contrary, it must go hand in hand with a division of household chores between husband and wife (Focke, "Rechte," p. 645) – a suggestion more easily made than implemented.

(6) Helwig, Frau '75, p. 92.

(7) Myrdal and Klein, p. 36.

(8) Treffpunkt, No. 6, 1977, p. 4.

(9) Mitmachen macht Mut, p. 3. The Federal Ministry for Youth, Family and Health suggests to them that they use their spare time to further their education and to help with volunteer charity work.

(10) Social Report 2-75, p. 6.

(11) Information FRG: Women, Section 6.

(12) Reported in Hertz-Eichenrode, p. 3.

(13) Sozial Report, No. 1, 1977, pp. 24-25.

(14) Hertz-Eichenrode, p. 3.

(15) Ibid.

(16) A recent study stated: "In the GDR, they also sleep together before and outside of marriage. The problem of premarital sex occupies primarily sex education experts, the problem of extra-marital sex primarily divorce courts" (Menschik and Leopold, p. 152).

(17) Neue Justiz, 1952, p. 136.

(18) Ibid., p. 377. Emphasis added. For more details on the treatment of the family under the law in the FRG and the GDR, see chap. 2.

(19) Menschik and Leopold, p. 28.

(20) Katzenstein, p. 251.

(21) Ibid., pp. 251 and 253.

(22) Kuhrig, p. 12.

(23) Lange, Aktuelle Probleme, pp. 23-25.

(24) Lipold et al., p. 113.

(25) Dornberg, p. 91.

(26) Channel 2, Berlin, March 25, 1978.

(27) Helwig, "Das Jahr der Frau in der DDR," p. 63.

(28) Deine Gesundheit, No. 3, 1975.

(29) Grandke et al., p. 198.

(30) Allendorf, p. 92.

(31) Menschik and Leopold, p. 193.

(32) Grandke et al., p. 197.

(33) Lange, Aktuelle Probleme, pp. 24-25; also Menschik and Leopold, p. 184.

(34) Report, CC/SED, 1976, p. 115-116.

(35) Ibid., p. 215.

(36) Lange, Aktuelle Probleme, p. 29.

(37) Ibid., pp. 26-27.

(38) Die Wirtschaft, 1974, No. 22, p. 13.

(39) Information FRG: Women, section 3.

(40) Sender Freies Berlin, June 8, 1978.

(41) Runge, p. 273.

(42) Plat, p. 101.

(43) Statkowa, p. 45.

(44) Menschik and Leopold, p. 29.

(45) Katzenstein, p. 252.

(46) Lange, Aktuelle Probleme, p. 42.

(47) Report on West German TV, Channel 2, Berlin, March 25, 1978. The GDR's Statistical Yearbook does not show which of the spouses sues for divorce.

(48) Dornberg, p. 91.

NOTES   201

Chapter 6

(1) Whitney, p. 6.

(2) Dokumente zum Internationalen Jahr der Frau, p. 20.

(3) Ibid., p. 41. Also The Situation of Women, p. 60.

(4) Hamburger Abendblatt, April 25, 1980.

(5) Dokumente, pp. 22, 42, 45, and 48.

(6) Ibid., p. 42.

(7) Ibid., pp. 25, 26, 100, and 101.

(8) Ibid., 91.

(9) Ibid., pp. 37, 39, 86, and 96-99.

(10) This does not include West Germany's new, ecology oriented, political party, the "Greens." As this book goes to press, this new party is still essentially in its formative stage, its future as yet very uncertain.

(11) Dokumente, p. 53.

(12) Ibid., pp. 29 and 31.

(13) Ibid., pp. 93 and 95.

(14) Muench, p. 57.

(15) The summary discussion and analysis of the three types of feminist organizations presented here is based largely on Muench's analysis; but see also Sozial-Report, Frauenfragen, 8-77, pp. 8-9.

(16) Muench, p. 57.

(17) Die Frau in der DDR, p. 26.

(18) DDR Handbuch, p. 188.

(19) Scharnhorst.

(20) DDR Handbuch, p. 188; Die Frau in der DDR, p. 26; Statkowa, p. 52. Occasionally, men also enroll in such homemaking courses; but the great majority of students are women.

(21) In a personal communication, West German sociologist and specialist on FRG women's affairs Helge Pross replied to an inquiry by this author as follows: "Your inquiry made me aware how little I know about the effectiveness of independent West German women's organizations. This is probably a symptom of their relatively minimal political significance. Women's divisions in the large organizations, primarily in the political parties ... are probably of somewhat greater consequence. But even here, I cannot readily find relevant information" (personal letter, dated June 30, 1980). In another personal communication, Hannelore Mabry, founder and head of West Germany's feminist FFP, expressed similar views. She wrote to this author not only that her own organization is still "politically insignificant," but that even the "influence of women's organizations in parties, labor unions, and enterprises is minimal" (personal letter, dated July 9, 1980).

Chapter 7

(1) There are several paragraphs in the GDR Constitution specifically referring to women's equal rights ("irrespective of sex") to vote, work, hold public office, receive an education at public expense, etc. ... The FRG Constitution, on the other hand, refers to women only twice, once in the general equal rights provision (Art. 3) and once in a paragraph that allows for women 18 to 55, to be called up for hospital service (but not to bear arms) in cases of national emergency (Art. 12a).

(2) Menschik and Leopold, pp. 24 and 36.

(3) The first special women's furtherance plans were incorporated into the "Law on Protection of Mothers and Children and the Rights of Women" in 1950 (GB1 1637, Sept. 27, 1950).

(4) Menschik and Leopold, p. 24.

(5) <u>Sozial Report 6-77</u>, p. 5. Emphasis added.

(6) <u>Frauen</u>, p. 5.

(7) <u>Zwischenbericht</u>, passim.

(8) <u>Frauen und Bildung</u>, p. 12.

(9) Ibid., p. 10.

(10) Menschik, p. 131.

(11) The reform of the citizenship law took effect on January 1, 1975 (<u>Dokumente</u>, p. 4).

(12) Dornberg, p. 152.

(13) The German Tribune, Dec. 2, 1979, p. 14.

(14) Koelner Stadt Anzeiger, March 6, 1979.

(15) Pross, "Prerequisites," pp. 3 and 4.

(16) Cited in Whitney, p. 6.

(17) Ehe und Familie, p. 60.

(18) Statkowa, p. 13.

(19) Allendorf, p. 110.

(20) Report, CC/SED, 1976, p. 115.

(21) Dornberg, p. 87.

(22) The Second Party Congress in 1947 stated that it was "an urgent matter for the party to entrust ever more political functions to women . . . and to train women for such tasks" (Entschliessungen I, p. 216). And since 1967, especially, the party has given much consideration to the underrepresentation of women in positions of political leadership. Since then, the party has issued several decrees and introduced several measures to prepare more women for leading positions (Menschik and Leopold, pp. 81-82).

(23) FGB-K, p. 60.

(24) Lenin, Werke, Vol. 30, p. 364.

(25) Inge Lange, reporting as chairperson of the Berlin Commission for Women to the CC of the SED on Feb. 24, 1973. Cited in Menschik and Leopold, p. 38.

(26) Kuhrig, p. 10-11.

(27) Inge Gabert referred to conservative Bavarian newspapers which headlined speeches given by CDU and CSU speakers with such expressions during the 1976 election campaign. See Gabert, p. 2.

(28) Katzenstein, p. 255.

(29) Dornberg, p. 95.

(30) Richter, p. 49.

(31) Dokumente, p. 3.

(32) Statement by the Women's organization of the Christian Democratic Union of Germany, in ibid., p. 93. Emphasis added.

(33) Ibid., pp. 21-22.

(34) Pross, "Prerequisites," p. 11.

(35) Cited from 1956 SED documents in Gast, p. 253.

Glossary

Abitur. (FRG and GDR) Examination on completion of college-preparatory school program (in West Germany, for instance on completion of Gymnasium), qualifying student for admission to university.

AFG. (FRG) Arbeitsfoerderungsgesetz. Work furthering law. 1969.

AGB. (GDR) Arbeitsgesetzbuch. Labor Law Code. 1977. Replaces GBA.

ASF. (FRG) Arbeitsgemeinschaft Sozialdemokratischer Frauen. Working team of SPD women.

BAfoG. (FRG) Bundesausbildungsfoerderungsgesetz. Federal Law for the furtherance of education. 1971.

Berufsaufbauschule. (FRG) Type of non-college level vocational school. (See Table 4.1.)

Berufsfachschule (FRG) Type of non-college level vocational school. (See Table 4.1.)

Berufsschule (FRG) Type of non-college level vocational school. (See Table 4.1.)

Bezirk (pl. Bezirke). District. In the GDR, one of 14 large GDR administrative units.

Bezirkstag (pl. Bezirkstage). (GDR) Bezirk parliament.

BGB. Buergerliches Gesetzbuch. Civil Code. Predates turn of twentieth century; still fully in force in 1949 when separate constitutions for the two Germanies were drawn up.

BGL. (FRG and GDR) Betriebsgewerkschaftsleitung. Labor union executive board, enterprise level.

BRD. Bundesrepublik Deutschland. Federal Republic of Germany; FRG.

Bundesgezetzblatt. (FRG) Federal Gesetzblatt. (See GBl)

Bundesrat. Although classified as the "upper" house of the FRG parliament, it has no major legislative functions and is primarily consultative in nature. (See also Bundestag).

Bundesrepublik. See BRD.

Bundestag. Lower but yet primary house of FRG parliament. It exercises all major legislative functions. (See also Bundesrat).

Bundesverfassungsgericht. See BVerfGe.

BVerfGe. (FRG) Bundesverfassungsgericht. Federal Constitutional Court.

CC. Central Committee. See Zentralkommittee.

CDU. (FRG) Christlich-Demokratische Union. Christian Democratic Union. A conservative party. One of West Germany's major parties. Actually exists also in the GDR, but as a powerless minority party.

CSU. (FRG) Christlich-Soziale Union. CDU sister party in Bavaria. Very conservative party.

DDR. Deutsche Demokratische Republik. German Democratic Republic; GDR.

DFD. (GDR) Demokratischer Frauenbund Deutschlands. Democratic Women's League of Germany.

DGB. (FRG) Deutscher Gewerkschaftsbund. German Labor Union Federation.

DM. (FRG) Deutsche Mark. German mark. Currency of the FRG. 1 DM = 100 Pfennige.

EheRG. (FRG) Ehe-Reformgesetz. Marriage Reform Law (MRL). Official title: "Erstes Gesetz zur Reform des Ehe und Familienrechts" - First Law for the Reform of Marriage and Family Law. 1976.

Erweiterte Oberschule. (GDR) Advanced high school, leading to the Abitur.

GLOSSARY 207

Enquete Kommission: Frau und Gesellschaft. (FRG) Investigative Commission on Woman and Society, set up by the FRG Parliament in November 1976.

Fachgymnasium. (FRG) Vocationally oriented upper-level Gymnasium. (See Table 4.1.)

Fachhochschule. (FRG) Vocational College. (See Table 4.1.)

Fachoberschule. (FRG) Type of non-college level vocational school. (See Table 4.1.)

Fachschule. (FRG and GDR) Type of non-college level vocational school. (See Table 4.1.)

FDGB. (GDR) Freier Deutscher Gewerkschaftsbund. Free German Labor Union Federation.

FDP. (GDR) Freie Demokratische Partei. Free Democratic Party. A liberal party, considerably smaller in size than the CDU or the SPD.

FFP. (FRG) Foerderungskreis zum Aufbau der Feministischen Partei. Furtherance Circle for the Formation of a Feminist Party. Munich-based West German feminist organization, headed by Hannelore Mabry.

FGB. (GDR) Familiengesetzbuch. Family Law Code. 1965.

FGB-K. (GDR) Familiengesetzbuch-Kommentar. Commentary on Family Law Code, published in 1966 under auspices of GDR Ministry of Justice.

FRG. See BRD.

Frauenlohngruppen. (FRG) Women wage categories which provided for discriminatorily low wages for women. See also Leichtlohngruppen.

GBA. (GDR) Gesetzbuch der Arbeit. Code of Labor Laws. 1961. See also AGB.

GBl. (FRG and GDR) Gesetzblatt. Official legal gazette; publishes new laws.

GDR. See DDR.

Gemeinde. (pl. Gemeinden) Municipality.

Gesamthochschule. (FRG) Combination institution of higher learning. (See Table 4.1.)

Gesamtschule. (FRG) Combination high school. (See Table 4.1.)

Gesellschaft mbH. See GmbH.

Gesetzblatt. See GBl.

GmbH. (FRG) Gesellschaft mit beschraenkter Haftung. Company with limited liability (similar to our corporation).

Gymnasium. (FRG) College preparatory high school. (See Table 4.1.)

Hauptschule. (FRG) Regular high school. (See Table 4.1.)

Hoehere Berufsfachschule. (FRG) More advanced type of Berufsfachschule.

INFAS. Institut fuer angewandte Sozialwissenschaft. Institute for Applied Social Sciences.

Kreis. (pl. Kreise) County.

Kunsthochschule. (FRG and GDR) College level school of fine arts.

Laender. Plural of Land.

Land (pl. Laender). (FRG) Political unit, comparable to a state in the U.S.

Landtag (pl. Landtage). (FRG) Land parliament.

Leichtlohngruppen. (FRG) Light wage categories. Still the lowest paying wage categories, with virtually all workers in it female, the Leichtlohngruppen have replaced the Frauenlohngruppen since the mid-1950s, when courts held that the equal rights clause in the constitution means also equal pay for equal work for all.

M. (GDR) Mark. Currency of the GDR. 1 M = 100 Pfennige.

MRL. (FRG) See EheRG.

Paedagogische Hochschule. (FRG and GDR). College level school of education.

Polytechnische Oberschule. (GDR) Polytechnical high school. Uniform, general-education high school.

Realschule. (FRG) Type of high school. (See Table 4.1.)

GLOSSARY 209

SED. (GDR) Sozialistische Einheitspartei Deutschlands. Socialist Unity Party of Germany. See chapter 1, footnote 33.

Sonderschule. Special school.

SPD. (FRG) Sozialdemokratische Partei Deutschlands. Social Democratic Party of Germany. A moderately socialist party. One of West Germany's major parties.

SYB. (FRG and GDR) Statistical Year Book.

VeB. (GDR) Volkseigener Betrieb. People-owned (state) enterprise.

Verlag. Publishing House.

Volkskammer. (GDR) "People's Chamber", GDR parliament.

ZK. Zentralkomitee. Central Committee, usually referring to the CC of the Communist Party or, in the case of the GDR, of the SED.

Zerruettungsprinzip. (FRG and GDR) Irreparable break-down principle. Principle accepted as reason for granting divorce, i.e., whenever marriage has irreparably broken down.

Zwischenbericht. Interim report.

References

AFG. See Arbeitsfoerderungsgesetz.
AGB/GDR. See Das Arbeitsgesetzbuch der DDR.
"Aktivitaet der DDR im internationalen Jahr der Frau." DDR-Komitee fuer Menschenrechte, Schriften und Informationen, No. 1 (1975), pp. 29-38.
Allendorf, Marlis. Women in Socialist Society. New York: International Publishers, 1976.
Anger, Hans. Probleme der deutschen Universitaet: Bericht ueber eine Umfrage unter Professoren und Dozenten. Tuebingen: J.C.B. Mohr, 1960.
"Anordnung ueber die finanzielle Unterstuetzung von Studentinnen mit Kind an den Hoch- und Fachschulen." Gesetzblatt II, No. 27 (1972): 321.
Arbeitsfoerderungsgesetz. Bonn-Bad Godesberg: Federal Ministry for Labor and Social Regulations, 1977.
Arbeitsrecht, Sammlung aller Wichtigen in der Bundesrepublik und in ihren Laendern einschliesslich Berlins geltenden arbeitsrechtlichen Vorschriften. Munich: C.H. Beck'sche Verlagsbuchhandlung. January 1977.
de Beauvoir, Simone. Das andere Geschlecht. Hamburg: Rowohlt, 1963.
Bebel, August. Die Frau und der Sozialismus. Stuttgart: Dietz, 1895.
Benjamin, Hilde. Vorschlaege zum neuen deutschen Familienrecht. Berlin, GDR: Deutscher Frauen Verlag, 1949.
"Bericht der Bundesregierung ueber Massnahmen zur Verbesserung der Lage der Frau." Bundestagsdrucksache, Bonn-Bad Godesberg, Aug. 1, 1972.
Bericht des Zentralkomitees der Sozialistischen Einheitspartei Deutschlands an den IX Parteitag der SED, Berichterstatter: Genosse Erich Honecker. Berlin, GDR: Dietz Verlag, 1976.
Berichte und Materialien zur Lage der Nation, 1971. Bonn-Bad Godesberg: Federal Ministry for Intra-German Matters, 1971.

Berufsausbildung und Berufslenkung in beiden deutschen Staaten. Bonn-Bad Godesberg: Friedrich-Ebert-Stiftung, 1975.

Beyer, Karl Heinz; and Piater, Lilli. Die Familie in der DDR. Berlin, GDR: State Secretariat for West German Questions, 1969.

BGB. See Buergerliches Gesetzbuch for up to date version. (See The German Civil Code for the original, 1896, version.)

Bildungsgesetz. See "Gesetz ueber das einheitliche sozialistische Bildungssystem-Bildungsgesetz."

Bildungs- und Weiterbildungsbereitschaft von Frauen bis zu 45 Jahren. Bonn-Bad Godesberg: Federal Ministry for Youth, Family and Health, 1976.

Buergerliches Gesetzbuch. Munich: C.H. Beck'sche Verlagsbuchhandlung, 1977.

Civil Code. See The German Civil Code.

Commandeur, Werner; and Sterzel, Alfred. Das Wunder drueben sind die Frauen. Bergisch Gladbach: Gustav Luebbe Verlag, 1965.

Constitution/FRG. See Grundgesetz fuer die Bundesrepublik Deutschland.

Constitution/GDR. For the original Constitution, 1949, see "Die (1949) Verfassung der Deutschen Demokratischen Republik"; for the 1968 Constitution, see "Verfassung der Deutschen Demokratischen Republik;" for relevant sections of the 1968 Constitution in the form of the "Law for the Supplementation and Alteration of the Constitution of the GDR" of Oct. 7, 1974, see "Grundlegende Menschenrechte." For the complete text of the GDR Constitution, as revised in 1974, see Die Neue Verfassung der DDR.

Dannhauer, Heinz. Geschlecht und Persoenlichkeit. Eine Untersuchung zur physischen Geschlechtsdifferenzierung in der Ontogenese. Berlin, GDR: Deutscher Verlag der Wissenschaften, 1973.

Das Arbeitsgesetzbuch der DDR. Berlin, DDR: Sekretariat der Volkskammer der Deutschen Demokratischen Republik, 1977. (First published in Gesetzblatt, Part I, No. 18, June 22, 1977.)

Das Familienrecht der DDR-Kommentar. Berlin, GDR: Ministerium der Justiz, 1970.

Das Gesundheitswesen der Bundesrepublik Deutschland. Stuttgart-Mainz: Federal Ministry for Youth, Family, and Health, 1975.

Das schoene Geschlecht und die Gleichberechtigung in der DDR. Berlin, GDR: State Secretariat for West German Questions, 1970.

"Das Sozialprodukt der DDR." Wochenbericht (Deutsches Institut fuer Wirtschaftsforschung), no. 16, 1975.

DDR Handbuch. Bonn-Bad Godesberg: Federal Ministry for Intra-German Matters, 1975.

"Deklaration zur Beseitigung der Diskriminierung der Frauen." (a resolution of the UN General Assembly of Nov. 7, 1967) DDR-Komitee fuer Menschenrechte, Schriften und Informationen, No. 1 (1975): pp. 47-52.

Deppe-Wolfinger, Helga; and Freyberg, Jutta V. "Zur sozialen Lage der Frauen in der BRD und in der DDR." Blaetter fuer deutsche und internationale Politik. No. 4 (1971), pp. 406-18.

DGB Geschaeftsbericht, 1974-1976: Frauenarbeit (women's work) 1974 to 1976. Duesseldorf: Deutscher Gewerkschaftsbund (German Trade Union Federation) No date.
Die Bedeutung des Art. 3 des Bonner Grundgesetzes fuer die Lohn-und Arbeitsbedingungen der Frauen. Cologne: Rechtsgutachten erstattet von Alfred Hueck, fuer die Bundesvereinigung der Deutschen Arbeitsverbaende, 1951.
"Die Frau." Kleine Enzyklopaedie. Leipzig: Leipziger Verlag Encyclopaedie, 1968).
Die Frau in der DDR - Fakten und Zahlen. Berlin, GDR: Staatliche Zentralverwaltung fuer Statistik, 1975.
Die neue Verfassung der DDR. Cologne: Verlag Wissenschaft und Politik, 1974.
"Die (1949) Verfassung der Deutschen Demokratischen Republik." Handbuch der Volkskammer der Deutschen Demokratischen Republik. 2nd ed. Berlin, GDR: Volkskammer der DDR, 1957.
"Die Rolle des Mannes und ihr Einfluss auf the Wahlmoeglichkeit der Frau." (Empirische Untersuchung des INFAS, Institute fuer angewandte Sozialwissenschaft, Bonn-Bad Godesberg.) Dokumentation des Bundesministeriums fuer Jugend, Familie und Gesundheit, Bonn-Bad Godesberg: Federal Ministry for Youth, Family and Health, February, 1976.
Direktive des IX Parteitages der SED zum Fuenfjahrplan fuer die Entwicklung der Volkswirtschaft der DDR in den Jahren 1976-1980. Berlin, GDR: Dietz Verlag, 1975.
Directives, IX SED Party Congress. See Direktive des IX Parteitages.
Dokumente zum Internationalen Jahr der Frau. Bonn-Bad Godesberg: Federal Ministry for Youth, Family and Health, 1976.
Dornberg, John. The New Germans. New York: Macmillan, 1976.
Ehe und Familie in beiden deutschen Staaten. Bonn-Bad Godesberg: Friedrich-Ebert-Stiftung, 1972.
EheRG. See "Erstes Gesetz."
Effective Facharbeiterausbildung von Arbeiterinnen. Berlin, GDR: Verlag Tribuene, 1976.
Engels, Friedrich. Der Ursprung der Familie, des Privateigentums, und des Staates. Berlin, GDR: Dietz, 1964.
Enquete Kommission. See Zwischenbericht.
"Entschliessungen des II Parteitages zur politischen Lage." Dokumente der SED. Berlin, GDR, 1948.
Epstein, Cynthia F. Woman's Place. Berkeley and Los Angeles: University of California Press, 1970.
"Erstes Gesetz zur Reform der Ehe und Familienrechts (1. EheRG) vom 14. Juni 1976." Bundesgesetzblatt, Part 1 Z, 1977 A, Bonn June 15, 1976, pp. 1421-1464. (This publication contains all paragraphs of the Fourth Book of the BGB that were changed by the EheRG. For a complete version of the revised, 1977, BGB, with very extensive comments and explanations, see Buergerliches Gesetzbuch.
Facts About Germany. Bonn-Bad Godesberg: Press and Information Office of the Government of the Federal Republic of Germany, 1975.

Familiengesetzbuch der Deutschen Demokratischen Republik mit wichtigen Nebengesetzen. Berlin, GDR: Ministerium der Justiz, 1970. (Original version adopted on Dec. 20, 1965 and published in Gesetzblatt der Deutschen Demokratischen Republik, No. 1, 1966.)

Familienpolitik und Familienplanung in beiden deutschen Staaten. Bonn-Bad Godesberg: Friedrich-Ebert-Stiftung, 1977.

"Familienrecht" (as amended by the First Law for the Reform of Marriage and Family Law – Erstes Gesetz zur Reform des Ehe-und Familienrechts – of June 14, 1976) Buergerliches Gesetzbuch 20, Fourth Vol., June 15, 1976. (The original verison of the BGB Civil Code was published on August 18, 1896.)

Feshbach, Murray; and Rapawy, Stephen. "Labor Constraints in the Five-Year Plan." Soviet Economic Prospects for the Seventies (Papers submitted to the Joint Economic Committee, Congress of the United States). Washington: U.S. Government Printing Office, 1973, pp. 485-563.

Feshbach, Murray; and Rapawy, Stephen. "Soviet Population and Manpower Trends and Policies." Soviet Economy in a New Perspective (Papers submitted to the Joint Economic Committee, Congress of the United States). Washington: U.S. Government Printing Office, 1976, pp. 113-54.

FGB. See Familiengesetzbuch der Deutschen Demokratischen Republik.

FGB-K. See Das Familienrecht der DDR-Kommentar.

Florath, Walter. "Die sozialistische Planwirtschaft in der DDR." Entwicklung, Probleme, Perspektiven. Frankfurt am Main, 1972.

Focke, Katherina. "Rechte und Chancen der Frau in Staat und Gesellschaft." Bulletin No. 69, June 2, 1975, pp. 643-47.

Focke, Katherina. Speech delivered in Dortmund, Aug. 11, 1976. Mailed to the author by the German Information Center, New York, in February, 1977.

Frau und Oeffentlichkeit. Bad Godesberg: Institut fuer angewandte Sozialwissenschaft, 1965.

Frauen. Bonn-bad Godesberg: Press and Information Center of the Federal Government, February 1978.

Frauen und Bildung. Bonn-Bad Godesberg: Federal Ministry for Education and Science, 1977.

Frauenfoerderung-BGL-Frauenausschuesse. Berlin, GDR: Sekretariat des Bundesvorstandes der FDGB, 1966.

Fremdwort Rente. Frankfurt am Main: Verband Deutscher Rentenversicherungstraeger, no year.

"Fundamental Human Rights." See "Grundlegende Menschenrechte."

Gabert, Inge. Talk given at the state conference of the ASF (Arbeitsgemenschaft Sozialdemokratischer Frauen – Working Team of Social-Democratic Women) in Munich on March 5, 1977. ASF Mitteilungen, Sonder-Beilage (special insert), Munich: ASF Landesverband Bayern, no date.

Gardiner-Sirtl, A. "Ein Lob fuer berufstaetige Frauen." Schoene Welt, Jan. 1978, p. 35.

Gast, Gabriele. <u>Die politische Rolle der Frau in der DDR</u>. Duesseldorf: Bertelsmann Universitaetsverlag, 1973.
<u>GDR. 100 Questions and Answers</u>. Berlin, GDR: Panorama DDR-Auslandspressagentur, 1978.
"Gemeinsamer Beschluss des ZK der SED, des Bundesvorstandes des FDGB und des Ministerrates der DDR vom 27. Mai, 1976." <u>DDR-Komitee fuer Menschenrechte, Schriften, und Informationen</u>, No. 3, 1976, pp. 19-26.
<u>The German Civil Code</u>. Translated and annotated by Chung Hui Wang. London: Stevens and Sons, 1907.
"Gesetz ueber das einheitliche sozialistische Bildungssystem-Bildungs-gesetz." <u>Gesetzblatt</u>, Part I, No. 6, 1965. Published also in <u>Staatliche Dokumente zur sozialistischen Jugendpolitik in der DDR</u>, Berlin, GDR, 1970.
"Gesetz ueber den Mutter – und Kinderschutz und die Rechte der Frau." (Mutter Schutzgesetz) <u>Gesetzblatt</u>, Part I, Sept. 27, 1950, p. 1037.
"Gesetz ueber die Unterbrechung der Schwangerschaft." <u>Gesetzblatt</u>, Part I, No. 5, 1972, p. 89.
Gleitze, Bruno. <u>Die Wirtschaftsstruktur der Sowjetzone und ihre gegen-waertigen sozial - und wirtschaftlichen Tendenzen</u>. Bonn-Bad Godesberg: Federal Ministry for Intra-German Matters, 1951.
Grandke, Anita; Gysi, Jutta; Orth, Klauspeter; Rieger, Wolfgang; and Schreiter, Thomas. "Die Wirksamkeit der Bestimmungen des FGB ueber Familienaufwand und Unterhalt." <u>Neue Justiz</u>, No. 7, 1977, pp. 196-203 and No. 9, 1977, pp. 263-68.
Gregory, Paul and Gert Leptin. "Other Things Equal: Diverse Economies in Similar Societies," Paper presented in Sept., 1976 at the combined annual meeting of the American Economic Association and the Association for Comparative Economic Studies in Atlantic City (Preliminary draft).
<u>Grundgesetz fuer die Bundesrepublik Deutschland</u>. Bonn-Bad Godesberg: Bundeszentrale fuer politische Bildung, Stand, June 1974.
"Grundgesetz fuer die Bundesrepublik Deutschland,"[(original version, adopted on May 23, 1949) with all amendments and alterations in 34 separate revisions] in <u>Arbeitsrecht, Sammlung aller Wichtigen in der Bundesrepublik und in ihren Laendern einschliesslich Berlins geltenden arbeitsrechtlichen Vorschriften</u>, Munich: C.H. Beck'sche Verlagsbuchhandlung, January 1977.
"Grundlegende Menschenrechte und ihre Garantien: Grundrechte und Grundpflichten der Buerger." From the Constitution of the GDR of April 6, 1968, in the form of the Law for the Supplementation and Alteration of the Constitution of the GDR of Oct. 7, 1974. (Gesetz-blatt, Part I, 1974, p. 432). Reprinted in <u>DDR-Komitee fuer Menschenrechte, Schriften und Informationen</u>, No. 3 (1976), pp. 33-45.
<u>Handbook of Economic Statistics</u>. Washington, D.C.: CIA, various years.
Hauff, Ingrid. "Gedanken zum internationalen Jahr der Frau." <u>DDR-Komitee fuer Menschenrechte, Schriften und Informationen</u>, Nr. 1, 1975, pp. 42-46.

Hein, Eva. "Das Arbeitsgesetzbuch sichert die Foerderung und den Schutz der Frauen." Arbeit und Arbeitsrecht, No. 3 (1978), pp. 133-36.

Helwig, Gisela. "Das Jahr der Frau in der DDR: Ein Resuemee," Deutschland Archiv 9 (Jan. 1976): 59-63.

Helwig, Gisela. "Frauen erobern Technik und Wissenschaft." Deutschland Archiv 10, No. 7, July, 1977, pp. 680-81.

Helwig, Gisela. "Frauenfoerderung und Familienpolitik in der DDR." Deutschland Archiv 8, 1975, Sonderheft, (special issue), pp. 46-57.

Helwig, Gisela. Frau '75 (Bundesrepublik Deutschland - DDR.) Cologne: Verlag Wissenschaft und Politik, 1975.

Helwig, Gisela. Zwischen Familie und Beruf: Die Stellung der Frau in beiden deutschen Staaten. Cologne: Verlag Wissenschaft und Politik, 1974.

Henkelmann, Walter. "Beschaeftigungspolitische Perspektiven zur Foerderung der Frauen." Probleme der Frauen - Probleme der Gesellschaft. Arbeitschancen, Lohngleichheit, Vorurteile. Protokoll der Arbeitstagung des DGB, (a symposium). Nov. 6-7, 1975. Cologne: Europaeische Verlagsanstalt, 1976.

Hertz-Eichenrode, W. "Die Deutsche Frau - befreit durch Mann und Maschine." Die Welt, August 5, 1975.

Hoerz, Helga E. "Die Rolle von Leitbildern im Kampf um die Gleichberechtigung der Frau im Kapitalismus." Deutsche Zeitschrift fuer Philosophie, Berlin, GDR, Vol. 24, No. 6, 1976, pp. 645-658.

Honeckers neues Arbeitsgesetzbuch. Bonn-Bad Godesberg: Friedrich-Ebert-Stiftung, 1977.

Huefner, A. "Das neue Familienleitbild." In Fuer die Befreiung der Frau. Frankfurt am Main: Rowohlt, 1972.

Information Federal Republic of Germany: Women. Bonn-Bad Godesberg: Press and Information Office of The Federal Republic of Germany, 1975.

Information FRG: Women. See Information Federal Republic of Germany: Women.

Informationen fuer die Frau. Bonn-Bad Godesberg: Informationsdienst des deutschen Bundesrates, Bundesvereignigung deutscher Frauenverbaende, Feb. 1, 1978.

Jaide, Walter. Junge Arbeiterinnen. Munich: Juventa Verlag, 1969.

Jancar, Barbara. "Zur Rolle der Frau in der kommunistischen Gesellschaft." Osteuropa, July 1976, pp. 528-48.

Jede werdende Mutter hat ein Recht auf Hilfen. Bonn-Bad Godesberg: Federal Ministry for Youth, Family and Health, 1975.

Joint Resolution, May 27, 1976. See, "Gemeinsamer Beschluss."

Jugendgesetz der DDR. Bonn: Bundesanstalt fuer gesamtdeutsche Fragen, no date. (Reproduced from the original version in the Gesetzblatt der Deutschen Demokratischen Republik, Berlin, GDR: Office of the GDR Council of Ministers, Jan. 31, 1974, Part I, No. 5, pp. 45-59.)

Katzenstein, Alfred. "Male and Female in the German Democratic Republic." In Sex Roles in Changing Society, edited by George H. Seward and Robert C. Williamson. Random House, 1970, pp. 240-56.

Keim, Walther. "38 Frauen unter 458 Maennern," Sozialreport, August 1976, pp. 10-11.
Klein, Helmut, and Wolfgang Reischock. Bildung fuer heute und morgen. Berlin, GDR: State Secretariat for West German Questions, 1968.
Koritz-Dohrmann, Adelheid. "Die praegende Kraft von Vorurteilen im Recht." Probleme der Frauen - Probleme der Gesellschaft. Arbeitschancen, Lohngleichheit, Vorurteile. Protokoll der Arbeitstagung des DGB, (a symposium). Nov. 6-7, 1975. Cologne: Europaeische Verlagsantalt, 1976.
Kossakowski, Adolf; and Otto Karlheinz. Psychologische Untersuchungen zur Entwicklung sozialistischer Persoenlichkeiten. Berlin, GDR: Verlag Volk und Wissen, 1971.
Krejci, Jaroslave. Social Structure in Divided Germany. New York: St. Martin's Press, 1976.
Kuhrig, Herta. "Die Gleichberechtigung der Frauen in der Deutschen Demokratischen Republik." DDR-Komitee fuer Menschenrechte, Schriften und Informationen, No. 5, 1973.
Lange, Inge. Aktuelle Probleme der Arbeit mit den Frauen bei der weiteren Verwirklichung der Beschluesse des VIII Parteitages der SED. Berlin, GDR: Dietz Verlag, 1974.
Lange, Inge. "Die Frau im gesellschaftlichen Leben der DDR." Einheit, No. 9, 1975, pp. 954-961.
Leben und arbeiten in Berlin. Berlin: Senator fuer Arbeit und Soziales, 1977.
Lenin, V.I. The Emancipation of Women. New York: (no publisher given), 1935.
Lenin, V.I. On Women's Role in Society. Moscow: Novosti Press Agency, 1973.
Lenin, V.I. Werke. Berlin, GDR: (Institut fuer Marxismus/Leninismus), 1961. Dietz Verlag, 1961.
Leptin, Gert. Die deutsche Wirtschaft nach 1945: ein Ost-West Vergleich. Opladen: Leske Verlag, 1971.
Lieberman, S.A. The Growth of European Mixed Economies. Cambridge, Mass.: Schenkman, 1977.
Lieser, Joachim. "Gleichberechtigung im geteilten Deutschland. Betrachtungen zur rechtlichen Entwicklung." Deutschlan-Archiv 2, No. 9, (1969): 919-40.
Lieser-Triebnigg, Erika. "Das neue Arbeitsgesetzbuch der DDR." Deutschland Archiv 10, No. 12, Dec. 1977, pp. 1268-1289.
Lipold, Gerhard, et al., Das Zeitbudget der Bevoelkerung. Berlin (GDR): Verlag die Wirtschaft, 1971.
LPG-Bauer auf neue Art: Die moderne sozialistische Landwirtschaft in der DDR. Berlin, GDR, 1970.
Maier, Irene. "Gleiche Rechte — gleiche Chancen, Konsequenzen aus Art. 3 des Grundgesetzes," Probleme der Frauen - Probleme der Gesellschaft. Arbeitschancen, Lohngleichheit, Vorurteile. Protokoll der Europaeische Verlagsanstalt, 1976.
"Marriage and Divorce Decree." See "Verordnung ueber Eheschliessung und Eheaufloesung."

Marx, Karl; and Engels, Friedrich. Werke. Berlin, GDR: Dietz Verlag, 1965.
Mende, Josef, and Wuensch, Werner. "Probleme der Frauenfoerderung in der Energiewirtschaft." Arbeit und Arbeitsrecht, No. 11, 1969.
Menschik, Jutta. Gleichberechtigung oder Emanzipation? Frankfurt am Main: Fischer Taschenbuch Verlag, 1971.
Menschik, Jutta; and Leopold, Evelyn. Gretchens rote Schwestern: Frauen in der DDR. Frankfurt am Main: Fischer Taschenbuch Verlag, 1974.
Mitmachen macht Mut: Frauen koennen mehr. Bonn-Bad Godesberg: Federal Ministry for Youth, Family and Health, no year.
Moeller, Jack and Leidloff, Helmut. Deutsch Heute: Grundstufe. Boston: Houghton Mifflin, 1974.
Muench, Eva Marie von. "Zwischen Kampf und Krampf." Die Zeit, March 21, 1975, p. 57.
Mundzek, Heike. "Die Partnerschaftliche Ehe." Schoene Welt, January 1978.
"Mutterschutzgesetz." See, "Gesetz ueber den Mutter – und Kinderschutz und die Rechte der Frau."
Myrdal, Alva and Klein, Viola, Die Doppelrolle der Frau in Familie und Beruf. Cologne-Berlin: Kiepenhever & Witsch, 1971 (First ed., 1962).
New Constitution/GDR. See Die neue Verfassung der DDR.
Pifer, Alan. Toward a New Society. New York: Carnegie Foundation of New York, (no date).
Plat, W. Die Familie in der DDR. Frankfurt am Main: S. Fischer, 1972.
Probleme der Frauen - Probleme der Gesellschaft. Arbeitschancen, Lohngleichheit, Vorurteile. Protokoll der Arbeitstagung des DGB, (a symposium), Nov. 6-7, 1975. Cologne: Europaeische Verlagsanstalt, 1976.
Programm der Sozialistischen Einheitspartei Deutschlands. Berlin, GDR: Dietz Verlag, 1976.
Pross, Helge. "Prerequisites for Sharing Power: The German Case." Manuscript prepared for delivery at the Moscow Congress of the International Political Science Association, August 12-18, 1979.
Pross, Helge. Ueber Bildungschancen fuer Maedchen in der Bundesrepublik. Frankfurt am Main: Suhrkamp, 1969.
Protokoll vom IV Bundeskongress des DFD (Minutes of the IV National Congress of the Democratic Women's League of Germany), May 16-19, 1952, Berlin, GDR: Bundessekretariat des DFD.
Ramm, Thilo. "Gleichberechtigung und Hausfrauensache." Juristenzeitung, January 1, 1968.
Rentenverordnung. See "Verordnung ueber die Gewaehrung."
Report, CC/SED, 1976. See, "Bericht des Zentralkommittees."
Richter, Horst Eberhard. "Vorurteile gegenueber Frauen - Ursache und Wirkungen." Probleme der Frauen - Probleme der Gesellschaft. Arbeitschancen, Lohngleichheit, Vorurteile. Protokoll der Arbeitstagung des DGB (a symposium), Nov. 6-7, 1975. Cologne: Europaeische Verlagsanstalt, 1976, pp. 47-58.

Riemann, Tord; Heilborn, Hans; and Luebchen, Gustav-Adolph, Recht und Gesetz im Sozialismus. Berlin, GDR: Auslandspressagentur, 1976.

Roby, Pamela A. "Shared Parenting: Perspectives from Other Nations." School Review, May, 1976, pp. 415-431.

Rohmert, W.; and Rutenfranz, J. Arbeitswissenschaftliche Beurteilung der Belastung und Beanspruchung an unterschiedlichen industriellen Arbeitsplaetzen. Berlin: Federal Ministry for Labor and Social Order, July 1, 1975.

Rosten, Curt. Das ABC des Nationalsozialismus 5th ed. Berlin: Kommissionsverlag Schmidt, 1933.

Runge, Erika. Frauen - Versuche zur Emanzipation. Frankfurt am Main: Suhrkamp, 1974. (first ed., 1969)

Salomon, Alice. Die Begruenderin des sozialen Frauenberufs in Deutschland. Ihr Leben und ihr Werk. Cologne and Berlin: Hans Muthesius, 1958.

Scharnhorst, Erna. Sueppchen kochen, Zeitung lesen, Erziehung zur Gleichberechtigung. Berlin, GDR: Demokratischer Frauenbund Deutschlands, 1970.

Schiffner, Andrea. "Um die Dreissig alleinstehend." Frankfurter Rundschau, Section "Frau und Gemeinschaft," March 1976.

Schmidt, Helmut. Regierungserklaerung 1976 fuer die 9. Legislaturperiode. Bonn-Bad Godesberg, 1976.

Scholl, Gerhard; Joswig, Heinz; Huebner, Heinz-Werner et al., The Planned Socialist Economy of the German Democratic Republic. Berlin, GDR: Auslandspressagentur GmbH., 1977.

Schuster, Verenate. "Auf 'Fussangeln' nicht vorbereitet." Der Tagespiegel, November 13, 1977, p. 56.

Scott, Hilda. "Women's Place in Socialist Society: The Case of Eastern Europe." Social Policy, April 1977, pp. 32-35.

SED Program. See, Programm der Sozialistischen Einheitspartei Deutschlands.

Shaffer, Harry G. "How Emancipated is the Soviet Woman as Compared with her Sister in the United States?" Oesterreichische Osthefte 19 (Winter 1977): 245-64. (Also published, in slightly abridged form, in Kansas Business Review, No. 3, Nov. 1977, pp. 1-9.)

Simmat, William. "Die praegende Kraft von Vorurteilen in der Arbeitswelt." Probleme der Frauen - Probleme der Gesellschaft, Arbeitschancen, Lohngleichheit, Vorurteile. Protokoll der Arbeitstagung des DGB, (a symposium), Nov. 6-7, 1975. Cologne: Europaeische Verlagsanstalt, 1976, pp. 102-11.

The Situation of Women in the Federal Republic of Germany. Bonn-Bad Godesberg: Federal Ministry for Youth, Family and Health, 1980.

So schaffe ich es allein. Frankfrut am Main: Verband alleinstehender Muetter und Vaeter, 1977.

Socialist Life and its Values: Aspects of Advanced Socialist Society in the GDR. Berlin, GDR: Panorama DDR, Auslandspressagentur, 1978.

Somerville, Rose M. "China and Sex Role Changes." Adult Leadership, Dec. 1975, pp. 137-141.

Statistisches Jahrbuch der Deutschen Demokratischen Republik. Berlin, GDR: Staatsverlag der DDR, various years.
Statistisches Jahrbuch fuer die Bundesrepublik Deutschland. Wiesbaden: Statistisches Bundesamt, various years.
Statistical Yearbook, FRG. See Statistisches Jahrbuch fuer die Bundesrepublik Deutschland.
Statistical Yearbook, GDR. See Statistisches Jahrbuch der Deutschen Demokratischen Republik.
Statkowa, Susanne. Die Frau im Sozialismus. Berlin, GDR: Auslandspressagentur, 1976.
Stolper, Wolfgang. The Structure of the East German Economy. Cambridge: Harvard University Press, 1960.
"Studien zur Geschichte der Lage der Arbeiterinnen in Deutschland von 1700 bis zur Gegenwart." in Die Geschichte der Arbeiter unter dem Kapitalismus 18, Berlin, 1963.
SYB/FRG = Statistical Yearbook, FRG. See Statistisches Jahrbuch fuer die Bundesrepublik Deutschland.
SYB/GDR = Statistical Yearbook, GDR. See Statistisches Jahrbuch der Deutschen Demokratischen Republik.
Szalai, Alexander, ed. The Use of Time: Daily Activities of Urban and Suburban Populations in Twelve Countries. The Hague: Mouton, 1973.
Tappendorf, Lilo. "Gleichberechtigung und Foerderung der Frauen in der DDR," DDR-Komitee fuer Menschenrechte, Schriften, und Informationen, No. 1, 1975, pp. 6-25.
"Thesen ueber die Wirkungen der Ehe im allgemeinen." Neue Justiz, 1949.
Tobias, Petra. "Emanzipation der Frau bei uns keine Phrase." Universitaetszeitung. Leipzig: Karl Marx University, 1978.
Turgeon, Lynn. "Income Maintenance in the Soviet Union — in Eastern and Western Perspective." Manuscript, received by author September 1977.
"UN Declaration on the Elimination of Discrimination Against Women." See, "Deklaration zur Beseitigung der Diskriminierung der Frauen."
USSR: People's Well-being. Moscow: Novosti, 1975.
USSR: Some Implications of Demographic Trends for Economic Policies. Washington, D.C.: CIA, January 1977.
Unsere Sozialversicherung. 5th rev. ed. Berlin: Bundesversicherungsanstalt fuer Angestellte, August 1977.
"Verfassung der Deutschen Demokratischen Republik vom 6. April, 1968." In Herwigg Roggermann, Die Verfassung der DDR, Opladen: Leske Verlag, 1970, pp. 211-239.
"Verordnung ueber die Erhoehung der staatlichen Geburtenhilfe und die Verlaengerung des Wochenurlaubs." Gesetzblatt, Part II, No. 27, 1972, p. 314.
"Verordnung ueber die Gewaehrung und Berechnung von Renten der Sozialversicherung — Rentenverordnung" Gesetzblatt, Part I, No. 22, April 4, 1974, pp. 201 and 215.

"Verordnung ueber Eheschliessung und Eheaufloesung." Gesetzblatt, Part I, November 24, 1955, p. 849.

"Verordnung zur Gewaehrung von Krediten zu verguenstigten Bedingungen an junge Eheleute." Gesetzblatt, Part II, No. 27, 1972, p. 316.

Volks-, Berufs-, Wohnraum, und Gebaeudezaehlung am 1. Januar 1971. Berlin, GDR: State Central Statistical Administration, 1972, Vol. 5.

Volkswirtschaftliche Gesamtberechnungen. Stuttgart und Mainz: Statistisches Bundesamt, 1975.

Vorschlaege zum neuen deutschen Familienrecht. See Benjamin, Hilde.

Wahner, R., "Frauen in der DDR und in der BRD." Probleme des Friedens und des Sozialismus, No. 6, 1978.

Wander, Maxie. Guten Morgen Du Schoene: Frauen in der DDR. Darmstadt und Neuwied: Hermann Luchterhand Verlag, 1978.

Warum gibt es in der DDR keine Arbeitslosigkeit? Bonn-Bad Godesberg: Friedrich-Ebert-Stiftung, 1977.

Weber, Maria. "Concluding Remarks." Probleme der Frauen, - Probleme der Gesellschaft, Arbeitschancen, Lohngleicheit, Vorurteile. Protokoll der Arbeitstagung des DGB (a symposium). Cologne: Europaeische Verlagsanstalt, 1976.

Weber, Maria. "Forderungen im Jahr der Arbeitnehmerinnen." Gewerkschaftliche Monatsschrift, No. 11, 1972.

"Weibliche Vorgesetzte in Deutschland. Geliebt, Gehasst: Die Chefin." Wirtschaftswoche, August 8, 1975, pp. 12-15.

Whitney, Craig R. "West German Women: Few Gains in Equality Since the War." The New York Times, January 18, 1977.

Winkelraeter, Liesel. "Entlohnung weiblicher Arbeitsnehmer – Standortanalyse." Probleme der Frauen - Problem der Gesellschaft, Arbeitschancen, Lohngleichheit, Vorurteile. Protokoll des Arbeitstagung des DGB (a symposium) Nov. 6-7, 1975. Cologne: Europaeische Verlagsanstalt, 1976.

Winter, Kurt. Das Gesundheitswesen in der Deutschen Demokratischen Republik. Berlin, GDR: Verlag Volk und Gesundheit, 1974.

Wissenwertes ueber Berlin. Berlin: Senator fuer Arbeit und Soziales, 1977.

Zukunftssichere Berufsausbildung. Bonn: Federal Ministry for Education and Science, 1975.

Zur Erfuellung des sozialistischen Programms. Berlin, GDR: Staatsverlag der Deutschen Demokratischen Republik, 1975.

Zwischenbericht der Enquete Kommission. Frau und Gesellschaft (gemaess Beschluss des deutschen Bundestages.) Drucksache 7/5866, Bonn-Bad Godesberg: Verlag Dr. Hans Heger, November 11, 1976.

List of Periodicals

(Included are only periodic publications actually used and cited in the text.)

Adult Leadership. (US) Washington, D.C.: Education Association of the US. Monthly (Sept.-June).
Arbeit und Arbeitsrecht. (GDR) Berlin, GDR: Verlag Die Wirtschaft. Twice monthly.
ASF Mitteilungen. (FRG) Munich: ASF Landesverband Bayer. Irregularly.
Blaetter fuer deutsche und internationale Politik. (FRG) Cologne: Pahl Rugenstein-Verlag. Monthly.
Bulletin. (FRG) Bonn-Bad Godesberg: Press and Information Service of the Federal Government. Every two weeks.
BZ (Berliner Zeitung) am Abend. (GDR) Berlin, GDR. Daily newspaper.
Christian Science Monitor. (US) Boston. Daily newspaper.
Current Sweden. (Sweden) Stockholm: Svenska Institutet (Distributed by the Swedish Information Service, N.Y.). Irregularly.
DDR Komitee fuer Menschenrechte: Schriften und Informationen. (GDR) Berlin, GDR: GDR Committee for Human Rights. Quarterly.
Deine Gesundheit. (GDR) Berlin, GDR: National Committee for Health Education. Monthly.
Der Spiegel. (FRG) Hamburg: Spiegel Verlag. Weekly.
Der Tagesspiegel. (FRG) Berlin, West. Daily newspaper.
Deutsche Zeitschrift fuer Philosophy. (GDR) Deutscher Verlag der Wissenschaften. Monthly.
Deutsches Institut fuer Wirtschaftsforschung: Wochenbericht. See Wochenbericht.
Deutschland Archiv. (FRG) Cologne: Verlag Wissenschaft und Politik Berend von Nottbeck. Monthly.
Die Frau. (FRG) Frankfurt am Main: Evangelische Frauenarbeit in Deutschland. Monthly.
Die Welt. (FRG) Bonn. Daily newspaper.
Die Wirtschaft. (GDR) Berlin, GDR: Verlag Die Wirtschaft. Weekly.
Die Zeit. (FRG) Hamburg: Verlag Gerd Bucerius. Weekly.

Einneit. (GDR) Berlin, GDR: (SED Central Committee) Dietz Verlag. Monthly.
Entscheidungen des Bundesverfussungsgericht (Decisions of the Federal Constitutional Court) (FRG) Karlsruhe: Verlag G. Siebeck. (Formerly published in Berlin, West) Irregularly.
Foreign Affairs Bulletin. (GDR) Berlin, GDR: Press Department of the Ministry of Foreign Affairs. Every ten days.
Frankfurter Allgemeine Zeitung. (FRG) Frankfurt am Main. Daily newspaper.
Frankfurter Rundschau. (FRG) Frankfurt am Main. Daily newspaper.
Frau. See Die Frau.
GBl. (Gesetzblatt). (FRG and GDR) Bonn-Bad Godesberg for the FRG; Berlin, GDR for the GDR: Released by the respective ministries of justice. Irregularly.
The German Tribune. (FRG) Hamburg: Reinecke-Verlag. Weekly.
Gesetzblatt. See GBl.
Gewerkschaftliche Monatshefte (FRG) Cologne: Deutscher Gewerkschaftsbund. Quarterly.
Hamburg Stern. See Stern.
Hamburger Abendblatt. (FRG) Hamburg. Daily newspaper.
Handelsblatt. (FRG) Duesseldorf: Handelsblatt GmbH. 5 times weekly.
Informationen des Bundesministeriums fuer Jugend, Familie und Gesundheit. (FRG) Bonn-Bad Godesberg: Federal Ministry for Youth, Family and Health. Irregularly.
Informationen fuer die Frau. (FRG) Bonn-Bad Godesberg: Informationsdienst des deutschen Bundesrates, Bundesvereinigung deutscher Frauenverbaende. Monthly.
Juristenzeitung. (FRG) Tuebingen: J.C.B. Mohr. Twice monthly.
Kansas Business Review. (US) Lawrence, Kansas: The University of Kansas Press. Monthly.
Koelner Stadt Anzeiger. (FRG) Cologne. Daily newspaper.
Leipziger Volkszeitung. (GDR) Leipzig. Daily newspaper.
Mitteilungen der Landesversicherungsanstalt Berlin. (FRG) Berlin-Charlottenburg: Amtliches Veroeffentlichungsblatt. Monthly.
Neue juristische Wochenschrift. Munich: Beck'sche Verlagsbuchhandlung. Weekly.
Neue Justiz. (GDR) Berlin, GDR: (Ministry of Justice) Staatsverlag der DDR. Twice monthly.
Neuer Weg. (GDR) Berlin, GDR: (SED Central Committee) Dietz Verlag. Twice monthly.
Neues Deutschland. (GDR) Berlin, GDR, Daily newspaper.
The New York Times. (US) New York. Daily newspaper.
Nordwest Zeitung. (FRG) Oldenburg. Daily newspaper.
Oesterreichische Osthefte. (Austria) Vienna: Oesterreichisches Ost-und Suedosteuropa Institut. Quarterly.
Probleme des Frieden und des sozialismus. (GDR) Berlin, GDR: Dietz Verlag. Monthly.
Schoene Welt. (FRG) Munich: Sueddeutscher Verlag. Irregularly.
School Review. (US) Chicago: University of Chicago Press. Quarterly.

Social Policy. (US) New York: Social Policy Corp. 5 times yearly.
Social Report. English version of Sozial-Report.
Sozial-Report. (FRG) Bonn-Bad Godesberg: Federal Government of the FRG (no further information on publisher given). Irregularly.
Soziale Welt. (FRG) Goettingen: Verlag Otto Schwartz und Co. Quarterly.
Sozialistische Arbeitswissenschaft. (GDR) Berlin, GDR: (Staatssekretariat fuer Arbeit und Loehne, Zentrales Forschungsinstitut fuer Arbeit) Verlag Die Wirtschaft. 8 times yearly.
Sozialpolitische Umsdhau. (FRG) Bonn-Bad Godesberg: Press and Information Service of the Federal Government. Irregularly.
Spiegel. See Der Spiegel.
Sueddeutsche Zeitung. (FRG) Munich. Daily newspaper (combined Saturday-Sunday edition).
Stern. (FRG) Hamburg: Gruner and Jahr. Weekly.
Tagesspiegel. See Der Tagesspiegel.
Trefrpunkt. (FRG) Bonn-Bad Godesberg: Federal Ministry for Youth, Family, and Health. Irregularly.
Universitaetszeitung. (GDR) Leipzig: Karl Marx University. Monthly.
Verfuegungen und Mitteilungen des Ministeriums fuer Gesundheitswesen der DDR. (GDR) Berlin, GDR: Ministry for Health. Irregularly.
Vorwaerts. (FRG) Bonn-Bad Godesberg: Neuer Vorwaerts-Verlag Nau und Co. Weekly.
Was und Wie. (GDR) Berlin, GDR: (SED Central Committee) Volksverlag fuer Agitation und Anschauungsmittel. Irregularly.
Welt. See Die Welt.
Wirtschaft. See Die Wirtschaft.
Wirtschattswoche. (FRG) Duesseldorf: Gesellschaft fuer Wirtschaftspublizistik. 6 times weekly.
Wochenbericht. (FRG) Berlin, West: (Deutsches Institut fuer Wirtschaftsforschung) Duncker und Humblot. Weekly.
Working Life in Sweden. (US) New York: Swedish Information Service, Swedish Consulate General General. Irregularly.
Zeit. See Die Zeit.

Index

Abortion
  FRG, 49, 52-53
  GDR, 50-52
Adenauer, Konrad, 88
Advancement opportunities
  FRG, 77
  GDR, 78, 82
Agricultural Workers
  education, GDR, 125
Alimony, FRG and GDR, 39-40
  in old Civil Code, 38-39
Assembly line jobs, FRG, 74, 100-01
Association of German Female Academicians, FRG, 155
Automechanics, trainees, FRG and GDR, 73

Baby year, GDR, 16-17, 26, 46, 83, 105, 159, 161
Baehre, Inge-Lohre, 88
Bartels, Hildegard, 88
Bauman, Edith, 89
Beauvoir, Simone de, 110
Bebel, August, 8
Benjamin, Hilde, 30
Books, children's
  FRG, 115-17
  GDR, 116-17
  in Weimar Republic, 5
Bundestag, FRG, 84-85

Bundestag, FRG (Cont.)
  See also government officials, elected
Business schools, FRG, 127

Career women
  FRG, 80
  GDR, 80
Carstens, Karl, 88
Central Committee (SED), GDR, 89, 167
Chemical industry, FRG and GDR
  jobs in, 73
  students of chemistry, GDR, 134
Child support, state, FRG and GDR, 40-42
Childcare facilities
  FRG, 19, 59-60, 82, 103-05
  GDR, 11, 19, 59-60, 69, 80, 103, 105-07, 167
  quality of, FRG and GDR, 107-09
Childbearing
  FRG, 37, 111-13, 138, 140-41
  GDR, 11, 30-33, 113-14, 144-47, 163-64
  and employment of mothers, FRG and GDR, 28-30
  See also Role identity, Books, Childcare, Child support

Children born out of wedlock, FRG and GDR, 143
Civil Code (BGB), 12-13, 15, 28-30, 33-39
Clergy. See Ministers
Cohabitation, FRG and GDR, 143
Commentary of Family Law, GDR, 14
Commerce, jobs in,
　FRG, 72
　GDR, 72, 102
Communal living, FRG and GDR, 143
Communication
　jobs in, FRG and GDR, 72
　journalists
　　FRG, 74
　　GDR, 75
Conference, women's first, early history, 5
Constitution(al law)
　FRG, 6, 10, 12-13, 16, 25, 29, 47, 100, 110, 125, 162-63
　GDR, 6, 12-16, 20, 30-32, 125, 161
　U.S.A., 8
　USSR, 9
Constitutional Court, FRG, 13-14, 24, 29, 31, 52
Construction
　jobs in FRG and GDR, 72
　wages for, GDR, 102
Curricula
　historical perspective, 5
　in grade school
　　FRG, 118
　　GDR, 118
　in higher education
　　FRG, 133
　　GDR, 122-24, 134
　in secondary education, FRG, 119-23
　See also Education, Vocational Training

Dannhauer, Heinz, 114
Data Processing, trainees for, FRG and GDR, 73
Day Mothers, FRG, 19

Democratic Women's League of Germany (DFD), GDR, 30, 158-59
Discrimination
　FRG, 10, 36, 47, 74-75, 81-82, 93, 99-102, 117, 129-30, 158, 162, 166
　GDR, 74-75, 82, 94, 102, 161
　in protective legislation, 26-28
　prohibited by constitution, FRG and GDR, 12
　See also Equal remuneration, Wage categories
Divorce
　and child custody, FRG and GDR, 39
　and pension rights
　　FRG, 31, 36-38
　　GDR, 38
　counseling for, 154
　division of property in, FRG and GDR, 35-36
　increase of, FRG and GDR, 148-52
　laws regarding, FRG and GDR, 33-36
　See also Alimony
Domestic employees
　FRG, 127
　Pre World War I, 5
Drop-outs
　in college
　　FRG, 130
　　GDR, 131
　in secondary schools, FRG, 122

Economic recovery and progress, FRG and GDR, 2
Education, FRG and GDR, 110-34
　FRG, 10, 19-20, 83
　GDR, 11, 20-21, 83, 102, 144
　and financial assistance, 19-22, 125-27, 131-33
　See also Books; Curricula; Education, early

INDEX 229

Education (Cont.)
    childhood; Education, grade school; Education, higher; Education, secondary; Vocational training
Education, early childhood
  home, FRG and GDR, 111-17
  preschool
    FRG, 19, 113, 117-18
    GDR, 19, 52, 113, 118, 163
  See also Childcare facilities
Education, grade school
  FRG, 117
  GDR, 113, 118
Education, higher
  FRG and GDR, 17, 110, 128-34
  FRG, 20
  GDR, 20-21
  Paying for, 131-33
  Pre World War II, 4-5
  See also Curricula, Vocational training
Education, secondary
  FRG, 20, 119-23
  GDR, 122-23
Education, trade schools. See Vocational training
Einemann, Irene, 101
Emancipation. See Women's liberation
Emma, FRG, 157
Employment
  and attitudes towards, FRG and GDR, 58-61
  FRG, 62, 138
  guaranteed
    FRG, 15
    GDR, 14-16
  historical perspective, 4-6, 56-58
  kinds of jobs, FRG and GDR, 71-77
  labor shortage, GDR, 61-62
  part-time, FRG and GDR, 23, 68-71
  participation rates, FRG and GDR, 55-56
  reasons for women working, FRG and GDR, 67-68

Employment (Cont.)
  unemployment, FRG, 61-66
  See also Equal remuneration; Labor force, participation in; Labor laws; Labor shortage; Labor Unions; Leadership, positions in; Unemployment
Engineers
  FRG, 74
  GDR, 21, 125, 134
  as students, FRG, 133
Engels, Friedrich, 8, 58
Enterprises, ownership of. See Ownership of enterprises
Equal pay. See Equal remuneration
Equal remuneration
  FRG, 9-10, 16, 95-103, 164
  GDR, 16, 95, 102, 161, 164
  early movement, 5-6, 96
Equal rights
  FRG, 6, 9-10, 12-13, 29, 71-77, 98-102, 110, 161-63
  GDR, 6-9, 11-12, 71-78, 82, 102-03, 159, 161, 163-65
  amendment to U.S. Constitution, 8
  See also Education, Equal remuneration, Household chores, Legal rights, Marriage

Family unit, FRG and GDR, 143
FDP, 93
Family and Marriage Laws, FRG and GDR, 27-53, 136
  FRG, 15-16
  GDR, 12-14
  See also Abortion, Child rearing, Child support, Divorce, Marriage, Retirement, Social Security
Federal Constitutional Court. See Constitutional Court, FRG
Federal Ministry for Education and Science (FRG), 112, 115, 162

Federal Ministry for Youth, Family
    and Health (FRG), xiv, 19,
    53, 132, 137, 153-54, 166
Feminist organizations, FRG,
    157-58
Focke, Katherina, 52, 88, 110
Food processing, employees
    FRG, 100
    GDR, 102
Franchise
    pre-war history, 5
    U.S.A., 9
    USSR, 9
Friedrich-Ebert Foundation, 9,
    124, 151, 163
Funke, Liselotte, xv, 27, 64-65,
    69, 88, 93, 102, 156
Furtherance Circle for the Forma-
    tion of a Feminist Party
    (FFP), FRG, 157
Furtherance (laws)
    FRG, 19-20, 60, 162
    GDR, 20-22, 76, 80-81, 94, 102,
        110, 125, 132, 161, 164

Gabert, Inge, xv, 53, 67, 118
GDR Committee for Human
    Rights, GDR, xiv
German Council of Women, FRG,
    153-54
German Female Physician's Assoc.,
    FRG, 155
German Housewives' Assoc., FRG,
    155
German Women's Ring, FRG, 154
Government employees, FRG
    early history, 4-5
Government officials, elected,
    FRG and GDR, 84-89
    See also Bundestag, Volks-
        kammer
Gross National Product, real
    average annual growth
    rates, FRG and GDR, 2

Hassenstein, Bernhard, 105
Helwig, Gisela, xv, 11, 82, 108,
    118, 122, 146
Hempe-Wankerl, Christel, xv, 47

Hesse, Beate, xv, 27, 65
Hitler era. See Nazi era
Hoehborn, Liselotte, 88
Hoerz, Helga, xv, 82, 114, 159
Honecker, Erich, 11, 88, 148
Honecker, Margot, 88
Honors bestowed, GDR, 79
Hotel industry, "bosses" in, FRG,
    77
Household chores
    FRG, 28, 31, 37, 42, 117,
        136-43
    GDR, 11, 31, 70, 116, 136,
        144-48, 163-64
    historical perspective, 3-4
Household day
    FRG, 17-18
    GDR, 17-19
Household employees. See
    domestic employees
Huber, Antje, 27, 65, 88
Humanities, students of FRG, 133

Income
    per capita, pre World War
        II, 1
    See also Equal remuneration
Industrial workers
    early days, 4
    education, GDR, 125
    wages
        FRG, 96-102
        GDR, 102-03
Industries, industrial output,
    eastern and western parts
    of Germany, pre war,
    compared, 1-2
Industry
    heavy, jobs in, FRG and GDR,
        71-72
    wages for, GDR, 102
    light, wages in, GDR, 102-03
International Federation of Women
    Lawyers, FRG, 155
Interruption of pregnancies. See
    Abortion
Investigative Commission on
    Women and Society, FRG,
    9-10, 77, 82, 91,
    112, 115, 117, 162

Jaldati, Lyn, 146
Jewish Women's Association in Germany, FRG, 154
Journalists. See Communication

Katzenstein, Ursula, 68, 146
Kindergarten. See Education, early childhood, preschool; Childcare facilities
Klenner, Anneliese, 27, 60, 146
Koenig, Herta, 88
Koritz-Dohrmann, Adelheid, 28, 53
Koutzfri, Lina, 86
Kuhrig, Herta, xv, 27, 145, 159

Labor. See Employment; Equal remuneration; Unemployment
Labor, division of (in home)
  FRG, 116, 136-43
  GDR, 116, 143-48
  historical perspective, 3-4
Labor force, participation in, FRG and GDR, 55
  ideological differences and differences in attitudes towards, FRG and GDR, 55-61
  reason for, FRG and GDR, 67-68
  what jobs in, FRG and GDR, 71-77
  See also Employment, Labor shortage, Leadership positions, Unemployment; Specific vocations and professions
Labor laws
  FRG, 13-14, 23-26
  GDR, 14, 16-19, 20-23, 24-26
  See also Furtherance (laws)
Labor shortage
  FRG, 62-64
  GDR, 9, 23, 28, 61-62, 102, 127
  as factor in women's emancipation, 168
  during World War II, 6
Labor unions
  FRG, 46, 65-66, 94, 99-100, 103
  GDR, 19, 22, 27, 95

Laender, laws (FRG) 16-18, 53, 111, 117, 125
Lange, Inge, 11, 89, 107, 145, 148, 164
Leadership, positions of and attitudes about, FRG and GDR, 80-94
  and who the leading women in the economy are
  FRG, 80
  GDR, 80
  causes for low numbers
  FRG, 82-83
  GDR, 82-83
  development of, GDR, 20-21
  education for, GDR, 20-21
  in economy, FRG and GDR, 94-95
  in legislative assemblies and appointed government offices, FRG and GDR, 84-89
  in political parties, 89-94
  remuneration for
  FRG, 96-97
  GDR, 102-03
  women, percentage of, FRG and GDR, 77-78
League of Female Jurists, FRG, 155
Legal rights
  FRG, 9, 29
  GDR, 12, 161, 164-65
  historical perspective, 2-3, 5
  See also Constitution, Civil Code, Education, Family and Marriage laws, Furtherance (Laws)
Lenin, 8, 58, 164
  See also Marxism-Leninism and Marxist-Leninist ideology
Lieberwirth, Erika, 88
Light wage categories. See Wage categories
Living standards, FRG and GDR, 2, 67, 147-48

Maier, Irene, 75
Management positions (business), FRG, 77
Manufacturing, jobs in
    FRG and GDR, 71
    pre-World War, 71
Marriage
    and family law. See Family and marriage laws
    and society at large, GDR, 143
    choice of family name, FRG, GDR, and pre-World War II, 40
    minimum age for, FRG and GDR, 40
    roles in
        FRG, 136-43
        GDR, 143-48
    to a foreigner, FRG, 162
    See also Children, Cohabitation, Divorce, Household chores
Marx, Karl, 8
Marxism-Leninism and participation in the work force, 56-58
Marxist-Leninist ideology, 8
    and employment of women, 71
    and emancipation of women, 167
    and equality of the sexes, 165
Maternity leave
    FRG, 16-17, 26
    GDR, 16-17, 26, 161
    figured in retirement income computations
        FRG, 44
        GDR, 45
Mathematics, GDR, 134
Medicine, GDR, 134
    See also Nurses
Menschik, Jutta, xv, 66
Metallurgy, employment in, GDR, 102
Military service
    FRG, 25
    GDR, 25
Ministers
    FRG, 75
    GDR, 75
Mothers, pregnant and nursing
    and army service, FRG and GDR, 25
    special protection of, FRG and GDR, 25-28
    university students
        FRG, 17
        GDR, 17, 21
    See also Abortion, Children born out of wedlock, Maternal death rates, Maternity leave
Mueller, Margarete, 89

Natural sciences, students of GDR, at Karl Marx University in Leipzig, 134
Nazi era, 6, 83, 161
Nehritz, Suse, 146
Noelle-Neumann, Elisabeth, 141
Nurses
    FRG, 24
    GDR, 134
    pre World War II, 5

Old age benefits. See Retirement income
Ownership of enterprises, FRG, 77-78

Parliaments. See Bundestag, Volkskammer
Pawlowski, Tatjana, 101
Pension. See Retirement Income
Performing arts, jobs in GDR, 75
Periodicals, women's
    first, pre World War II, 5
    FRG, 10, 64, 157
    GDR, 113
Politburo, GDR, 89
    See also Political Parties and SED
Political parties
    FRG, 89-94, 156, 166
    GDR, 89-94
    membership, pre World War I, 5
    women's groups in, FRG, 155-56

Political Parties (Cont.)
See also SED
Political power
FRG, 162
GDR, 11
Political rights, equal
FRG, 10
GDR, 12
historical perspective, 5-6
Professional Women's Associations,
FRG, 155
Property, division of. See Divorce
Pross, Helge, xv, 27-28, 47, 61,
64, 80, 100, 137, 140-41,
158, 163, 167
Prostitution, pre-World War II, 4
Protective legislation, FRG and
GDR, 23-28
FRG, 72, 99, 127
or discrimination, 26-28
pre World War II, 4-6, 23
Protestant Women's Work, FRG,
154

Religious Women's Organizations,
FRG, 154-55
Renger, Annemarie, 88, 101, 162
Reparation payments
FRG to Western nations (none
exacted), 2
GDR to USSR, 2
Resources, pre-World War II, 1-2
See also Industries, industrial
output
Retirement Income
Age of, FRG and GDR, 48-49
Additional earnings allowed,
FRG and GDR, 49
and public assistance, necessary, FRG, 97-98
computation of
FRG, 42-45, 97-98
GDR, 42, 45-48
in case of divorce
FRG, 36-38
GDR, 38
pension supplements, FRG and
GDR, 48

Retirement Income (Cont.)
survivors benefits
FRG, 46-47
GDR, 47-48
Rhode, Helmut, 124
Runge, Erika, xv, 151

Schaefer-Sasse, Margaret, 65
Scharnhorst, Erna, 116
Scheel, Walter, 10
Schlaegel, Juergen, 141
Schlei, Marie, 88
Schmalohr, Emil, 105
Schmidt, Helmut, 10, 66, 88, 162
Schmidt-Kohner, 114
Schoenrath, Traute, xv, 146
Schoof-Tams, 141
Schwarzer, Alice, 157
Schwarzhaupt, Elizabeth, 88
SED (GDR), xiv, 10-11, 89, 167
See also Central Committee,
Politburo, and Political
parties
Sell, Barbara von, 27
Service industries, jobs in,
FRG, 71, 76
Simmat, William, 27
Social Sciences, students of,
GDR, 134
Social security legislation,
family law and, FRG and
GDR, 28-53
Socialist-Feminist Action, FRG,
157
Soden, Karin, 86
Solms, Otto Graf zu, 156
Soviet occupied zone of Germany,
territory of, 2
Sund, Olaf, 65, 74
Survivors benefits. See Retirement income, survivors
benefits

Tappendorf, Lilo, 10, 72
Teachers and educators
FRG, 107, 118
GDR, 108, 118
attitudes of professors, FRG
and GDR, 129-30
historical role, 5, 71

Teachers and educators (Cont.)
  students preparing for teaching careers, FRG and GDR, 133
Technical jobs
  FRG, 74
  students preparing for, GDR, 128-29, 133
Textile workers
  GDR, 102
  trainees for, FRG and GDR, 73
Teuschbein, Petra, 88
Thatcher, Margaret, 86
Third Reich. See Nazi era
Time off
  for educational pursuits, GDR, 20-21
  for household chores, FRG, GDR and World War II, 17-18
  for pregnancy and motherhood, FRG and GDR, 16-17, 26
  for sick child, FRG and GDR, 17
Toedtmann, Anneliese, 88
Transportation, jobs in, FRG and GDR, 72
Trade, jobs in
  FRG, 72
  GDR, 72, 103

Unemployment
  FRG, 4, 9, 23, 61-66, 69, 97, 127, 162, 168
  absent in GDR, 45, 61, 66
  See also Labor shortage
  and labor unions, FRG, 65-66
  and political parties, FRG, 65
  historical, 4
Universities. See Education, higher
Unskilled labor, FRG, 74, 99, 101, 111, 122-24

Veil, Simone, 86
Vocational training
  FRG, 20, 65, 75, 111, 124-28, 162

Vocational training (Cont.)
  GDR, 20-22, 73, 75, 124-28
  early demands, 5
  See also Education, Furtherance laws
Volkskammer, 85
  See also Government officials, elected

Wage categories
  FRG, 99-101
  GDR, 102
Wages, hourly
  FRG, 96-102
  GDR, 102
  See also Equal remuneration, Wage categories
Waiters/Waitresses, FRG, 24
Walczak, Leonhard, 141
Weimar constitution, 5
Weimar republic, 5, 56
Women's Association of the Christian Democratic Union of Germany (CDU's)
  FRG, 153
  GDR, 159
  See also Women's organizations
Women's organizations
  FRG, 166
  GDR, 30
Women's Union of the CSU, FRG, 156
Women wage categories. See Wage categories
Working Team of Social Democratic Women (SPD's), FRG, 156
Workshop of Catholic Women's Organizations, FRG, 154

Year of the Woman, FRG, 10, 153

About the Author

HARRY G. SHAFFER is Professor of Economics and Soviet and East European Studies at the University of Kansas. He has travelled widely and carried on research in the Soviet Union and in all the socialist countries of East Europe, except Albania.

Dr. Shaffer holds a Ph.D. degree from New York University. He has published seven books, has given numerous papers and invitational lectures in the United States, Canada, and the Federal Republic of Germany, and has to his credit over forty articles in the general area of Soviet and East European studies in such journals as the American Economic Review, Journal of Industrial Economics, Journal of Higher Education, Problems of Communism, Russian Review, East Europe, Osteuropa, Osteuropa Wirtschaft, Oesterreichische Osthefte, Revue de l'Est, Antioch Review, Soviet and Eastern European Foreign Trade, Kansas Business Review, and Queen's Quarterly.

HQ1630.5 .S52 1981

WITHDRAWN
From Bertrand Library

AP